KAD Publishing

Education

A pathway to success for black children

Keith Davidson & June Alexis

Education

A pathway to success for black children

First published in 2012 by KAD Publishing,
240 Bounces Road, London N9 8LA, UK

British Library Cataloguing in Publication Data

Davidson, Keith & Alexis, June

Education
A pathway to success for black children

ISBN 978 0 9533262 3 5

Contents

Dedication

This book is dedicated to the grandchildren of the authors, namely: Alexia Jai Amara Nkwor, Shanice Jones-Alexis, Myles Alexis, Sian Alexis and Eric Alexis.

Acknowledgements

Firstly, the authors wish to acknowledge the invaluable inspiration gained from the 2009 Community Education Conference entitled 'Building Pupils' Confidence for Learning' held in London. The conference highlighted many of the issues dealt with in this book and was, therefore, the catalyst for the development of this writing project. Specifically, the authors would like to recognise the following organisers and contributors to the September 2009 conference, which influenced the writing of this book:

Organisers
Mr Martin Luther Rodney
Mr Roy Smith
Mr L McKenzie
Mr George Williams
Mrs Kerrie Williams
Mrs Iona Rodney
Miss Florence Sutherland
Miss Velma Davidson
Mrs Veronica Wilson-Hart
Contributors
The Honourable Diane Abbott MP
Mr Mandla Mbandaka
Dr Dwain Neil
Dr Tony Talburt

Secondly, the authors would like to record appreciation to: (1) Mr Arthur Torrington CBE and Dr Dwain Neil for reading the manuscript and for providing many constructive observations and suggestions; (2) The Honourable Diane Abbott, MP for penning the Foreword and Lord Herman Ouseley for writing the Preface; (3) Natalie Nkwor for technical support on the layout of the book; (4) Chay Alexis, Damian Alexis, Dr Terry Sitole, Donovan Davidson, and Natalie Nkwor, for proof reading the manuscript; and

(5) Mr Arthur Torrington CBE, Dr Dwain Neil and Dr Gillian Klein for their endorsement statements of the book.

Thirdly and foremost, the authors give praise and glory to God for the wisdom and knowledge He provided over the many hours of research, discussions and writing.

Foreword

Dr Keith Davidson is a dedicated educationalist who has given a lifetime to fighting for all of our children to achieve their very best in the British education system. He is a warrior for our children. It has been a pleasure and a privilege to work with him down the years.

Like Dr Davidson and his co-author Dr June Alexis, I feel passionately about black educational underachievement, in particular I strongly support their emphasis on the role of parents. It is no coincidence that the Saturday School movement, which is parent driven and relies on voluntary parental contributions, can achieve such excellent results with children that the mainstream school system has often written off. The centre piece of my education program for black children "London Schools and the Black Child" has been over ten years of conferences and events for black parents and community activists giving them the tools to help their children achieve. And these conferences are always packed out. I know, like Dr Davidson and Dr Alexis that the overwhelming majority of black parents are anxious to know how best to support their children in the British school system. Alongside the conferences, I run the Annual London Schools and the Black Child Awards. These awards are designed to celebrate top achieving inner city children.

The section of this book that deals with school exclusions is particularly valuable. In my time as a Member of Parliament some of the most heartbreaking stories I have heard come from mothers whose children have been permanently excluded from school. Often the children in question will join their mothers at the meeting with me. They may look bashful, ashamed or embarrassed to be there. But more often than not they appear to me to be vulnerable children who are in need of a high level of educational and emotional support. Being excluded from school is a tragedy for these children, their family and the entire community. It means that these children's education is disrupted and it is traumatic for their mothers or parents because they have to make difficult choices about how they can get their children's education back on track.

But being excluded can also have a terrible knock-on effect for children's future life. Disrupting children's education can make them less likely to gain qualifications that are so important for a future career. Not being able to secure employment can lead to criminal activity and all the downfalls associated with that. In 2001 the then Director General of the Prison Service, Martin Narey said: "The 13,000 young people excluded from school each year might as well be given a date by which to join the prison service some time later down the line." A decade later these words are just as poignant and just as true. A third of the people caught up in the urban disturbances of 2011 had been excluded from school and the majority had educational difficulties.

Over the years Dr Davidson has touched many lives. And I personally have relied on his knowledge and wisdom. He has supported me in my work on black children from the very beginning. In this book he, and his colleague, have distilled a lifetime of work and learning. It is a treasure house of knowledge which will be of interest to anyone concerned about education. I am proud to call Dr Davidson a friend and urge you to read this book.

Diane Abbott MP

Preface

In throwing down a challenge to all those who have a stake in the education of children, this book offers encouragement and suggestions on how the English education system can be improved for the benefit of all children. Although its focus is on channelling a pathway to provide success for Black children who have been let down collectively by schools, parents, professional experts, education authorities and wider society, the challenge is to ensure that the best quality education is available and accessible to all children.

For the best part of the past two centuries attempts have been made repeatedly to find a way of ending educational under-achievement and improving access to opportunities for education among less well off communities. Both the landmark 1944 Education Act and the 1988 Education Reform Act promised better and fairer outcomes, with radical reforms and 'cradle to grave' opportunities for life-long learning. Tony Blair's mantra of 'education, education, education' in 1997 again raised hopes of universal access to high quality education for all, but it proved to be more a case of rearranging the deck chairs on the Titanic rather than substantive systemic change.

Since 2010, Michael Gove, the Secretary of State for Education, has driven forward the provision of Academies and Free Schools as the flagships for educational excellence for all. The jury is still out about their success but at least he has been demonstrating urgency in addressing the deep-seated fault-lines in the English education system. Gove has also been very bold in pointing out in a speech in May 2012 to independent school head-teachers that the sheer scale of the privately-educated men in positions of power in business, politics, media, comedy, music and sport was proof of a deep problem in British society that is 'morally indefensible'. "More than almost any developed nation, ours is a country in which your parentage dictates your progress", he said.

Elitism in education is not new and it is not unique to England or Britain as a whole. To change the education system and make it work better for all, or for most, requires an understanding of the fundamental flaws and a fierce determination to use power, politics, influence and resources to change the status quo. That is not about some notion of lowering standards or about the politics of envy, nor about holding back specialty gifted and talented children. It is about ensuring that more of what is available for the elites, such as high quality teaching, parental support, learning resources, empathetic and inspirational leadership, community and social support networks and influential role models and mentors are also available in proportionate levels to all children in our society, and particularly in their early years.

'A pathway to success for Black children' brings together a collection of route maps to help all stakeholders to understand the system and its shortcomings and to share in a vision for a renaissance movement that would bring schools, teachers, parents, children, community and social groups together to understand better and fulfil their individual and collective responsibilities to inspire every child to be motivated positively and to realise their intellectual potential.

When it comes to the under-achievement of Black children in the English education system there are many contributory factors. The bias in the class-ridden education system, the schools, the negative stereotyping and the low expectation held by some teachers have been endlessly documented, with substantive back-up, irrefutable evidence. Unless these failings are addressed there is little or no hope for most Black children, especially Black boys – and for other children from 'working' class social backgrounds.

'Every Child Matters' is the central theme of education and children's welfare policies and should be a force to liberate and support greater parental engagement, involvement and empowerment. The role of general, social and formal education begins in the home from birth and is influenced by family, friends and other community and media-type contacts. Parents and families have a vital role to play in challenging the education system. Challenges to the status quo, bias, prejudice and individual professional incompetence are essential in the interest of all children. The local state and local social and community organisations must be enabled to provide the support to facilitate parental empowerment to take up such challenges effectively.

This book examines the systemic fault-lines and provides insights into what works, what requires change and gives examples and suggestions for change. If education is underpinned by the principle that all children have educational potential and that the education system will enable every child to realise their potential, then the doctrine of elitism will have to be challenged and eliminated. To continue sustaining the 'morally indefensible' elitism in education means that those who are well off will always be so and those who are poor and deprived need look no further – their place in society is scripted before birth according to their circumstances, parenthood and social status.

'A pathway to success for Black children' offers a pathway to success for all children who are not a part of the 'elites' but who are equally very special children with intellectual potential who deserve and are entitled to better and fair access to the best possible education that is always available to a well off ruling minority.

Lord Herman Ouseley Kt

Chapter 1

Parents as first teachers

The key principles behind partnership in education

In this chapter, the authors seek to establish a persuasive argument for reigniting the unsurpassed and unrivalled influence that parents can exert on their children's education for life. A renaissance is proposed to restore parents rightly to the frontline of the education process, as authentic 'first teachers' in the life of their children. For many years, the prevailing thinking in the education milieu is that effectiveness can only be achieved through partnership with stake-holding groups, namely: students, parents and teachers. However, genuine and sustainable partnership must be founded on the essential truism that children's education is ultimately the responsibility of the community to which the children belong. This echoes the African proverb that: *'It takes a village to raise a child'.*

Therefore, community, for the purpose of this chapter, is defined broadly, embracing the following:

- Immediate family groups such as parents, grandparents, aunties, uncles and carers.
- Cultural and religious sub-sets or affiliations.
- The local community, that is, the institutions and organisations (nursery groups, supplementary schools, clubs, etc) around which the children's lives are rooted.

Hence, the community, as described above, is the keeper of the children's education and schools merely subcontracted in to support parents in this process. This is a radical redefining of who is accountable for the education of our children.

Parents at the frontline of the education process: the child's first teachers

> *'What the mother sings to the cradle goes all the way down to the coffin.'*
>
> Henry Ward Beecher, *Proverbs from Plymouth Pulpit* (1887)

A community is held together by its language, values, beliefs, traditions and aspirations; all of these ultimately lead to the shaping of an identity that at times we refer to as group character and heritage. Thus, the transmission of the values, heritage and identity of a community is the first and essential step in any comprehensive educational process.

However, these distinctive community identifying traits, as it were, the community's DNA, are central to the education of its children. These qualities can only be effectively taught by (but more correctly caught from) those who are nearest and dearest to the children, namely parents and the community to which the parents and the children belong.

Children go to school (including nursery) already with the ability to speak basic words from the language of their parents. These words are learnt from the early interaction with parents and significant others – siblings, grandparents, aunties and uncles. However, this is the first of many things about the environment that children will learn from their parents. Hence, from the onset of birth (and some may argue from conception and pregnancy) parents take the lead in the education of their children and thereafter remain active at the frontline of the education process.

Parents fulfil the role of being first teachers mainly by concrete demonstrations and the modelling of standards for their children. At this point in children's formative years, learning takes place from observations and practice, by copying their parents' behaviour and actions. For example, drawing on our earlier reference to language, parents have been responsible for children's early use of words such as 'mum', 'dad', 'yes', 'no', the sounds of which are imitations that children reproduce from their parents. Parents are also at the forefront of children's social and motor skills development. They guide their children's progress in basic, but essentials skills, such as the use of a spoon for eating and by guiding children's progression from crawling on the floor to their ability to stand unaided and then advanced to the motion of walking. However, the role of parents remains a dynamic one. It moves beyond the mere teaching and equipping of children with these vital skills, imperative to the early exploration of their environment, to the bestowal of cultural values and standards. This principle of parental leadership in children's education is endorsed by Bruner (1996) in the following statement:

> *'Education does not only occur in classrooms, but around the dinner table when family members try to make joint sense of what happened that day, or when kids try to help each other make sense of the world.'*
>
> (Bruner, 1996, p. XI)

Furthermore, in ancient societies children's education was the sole responsibility of their parents. For example, Moses the great Jewish iconic leader, administrator and law-maker instructed the Israelites thus:

> *'These words, which I command you today, shall be in your heart. You shall teach them diligently to your children, and shall talk to them when you sit in your house, when you walk by the way . . .'*
>
> (Deuteronomy 6: 6, 7).

Therefore, contrary to the assumed model today that defines parents' role as one that is supportive to formal schooling in the education process, the reverse should be the case. Parents are to lead in character building, attitude formation and the setting of values (standards). On the other hand, schools impart knowledge and skills, and should reinforce the spiritual, moral, social and cultural heritages of the communities they serve. However, too often, schools struggle to resonate with the cultural ways and practices of the community.

The attempt to blame black children and their parents

The principle of parental leadership, in the education of children, has been damaged, distorted and undermined. Functionalist education commentators – in other words those who see the problem of underachievement in education as the result of underlying social structures – blame one parent, and what is labelled dysfunctional families, for the under-performance of black and working class children in the education system. In a patronising way functionalists argue that although it is no fault of the children, given their deprived social background, they come to school with negative attitudes, which prevent them taking advantage of the good learning experiences provided by schools (Raffo et al, 2007).

Furthermore, and controversially, some functionalists point to inherited capabilities as causes for underachievement. This is despite the fact that this deplorable view has been discredited methodologically, theoretically and morally. Professor David Gillborn of the Institute of Education (IOE) comments on this lingering, but offensive and insane, revisionist doctrine when he writes:

> *'Perhaps even more dangerous . . . is the position that could be characterised as the new IQism. That is, a situation where the old-style language of 'race', 'intelligence' and 'subnormality' has passed from common use, but essentially similar assumptions are implicit in a belief in ability as relatively fixed and differentially distributed.'*
>
> (Gillborn, 2002, p. 11)

In effect, functionalists and their revisionist ideology seek to make the individual the focus and reason for the underachievement problem in education today.

Progressives or modernists and many black and white educators with an unswerving commitment to social justice will, however, reason otherwise. In their view, it is the reverse that takes place. In other words it is the negative attitude of teachers towards black and working class children that accounts for the underachievement of these children in the education system. In truth and in fact, it is the education system that is underperforming and not the children.

The educational damage inflicted on black children by schools has been well documented for the past 40 years. Bernard Coard and his groundbreaking seminal work exposed and brought to the black community, and the education world in general, a disturbing awareness of the grave damage that was being meted out to black children in the education system. The title of his work, *'How the West Indian child is made educationally subnormal in the British school system: the scandal of the Black child in schools in Britain'*, graphically summarised the way in which many black children were being psychologically and emotionally destroyed in a system that should have been living up to its noble calling. For true education is about building and developing potential and should not undermine or destroy children's self esteem and confidence. In his own words, Coard (1971) says:

> *'The Black child labours under three crucial handicaps: (1) Low expectations on his part about his likely performance in a white-controlled system of education; (2) low motivation to succeed academically because he feels the cards are stacked against him; and, finally, (3) low teacher expectations, which affect the amount of effort expended on his behalf by the teacher, and also affect his own image of himself and his abilities. If the system is rigged against you and if everyone expects you to fail, the chances are you will expect to fail too. If you expect to fail, the chances are you will.'*
>
> (Coard, 1971, p. 25)

Therefore, the functionalists and their attempt to blame black children and their background for the educational underachievement in the school system are at best misguided and at worst cynical in their perpetuation of a culture that seeks to stigmatise black children as inferior. Nevertheless, the present authors will now explore the apparent fracture to the role of parents as their children's first and most important teachers.

The importance of parents' role in children's education is also underscored by Coard who concurs with the view that parents are able to do the most for their children's education. He argues that his booklet was written especially with parents, black teachers and community leaders in mind. And so, without in any way negating the above brief critique of the education system, a 21st century renaissance is needed to re-establish parental and community influence and authority as crucial to children's formative learning experiences. This, the impact of parental and community training of children, echoes a strategic survival principle that Professor Heidi Safia Mirza, formerly of the IOE, termed the process for subverting racist expectations (Mirza, 2008, p. 8).

Voices in support of parental and community renaissance

Today, there are a number of leading community educators and commentators, some of whom may be considered controversial and off-message, who are raising concerns about the influence of street life on the attitude of some black children to schools and to education in general. They contend that there can be an over-emphasis on the causal factors of racism in education to the neglect of parental and community responsibility for leading black children, and in particular black boys, away from the anti school culture of the street and into a greater commitment and love for learning. One such voice leading this view is Dr Tony Sewell. He says:

> *'Many black head teachers and black students are clear that underachievement can* [also] *be due to the individual student, parents, community, peers and, of course, school . . . A Black male today faces anti-school peer pressure that dominates our schools . . . The gospel I preach is a simple one. It asks black young men to look beyond the street and beyond immediate gratification. It asks some hard questions about their own responsibilities: homework, bedtime, respect for peers and adults, good manners, self-control and how to succeed in the system . . . I have no doubt that teacher racism is alive in our schools, but it can't explain the depth and breadth of this underachievement.'*
>
> (Sewell, 2003)

Nevertheless, Mirza (2008) reminds us of the dangers of stereotyping and Gillborn (1990) also challenges the *'Myth of the Afro Caribbean Macho'* with the consequence that these typecasts ultimately work negatively against black boys and their relationship with teachers in the classroom, leading to exclusions from school.

The statement above by Dr Sewell rightly raises the issues of positive attitude and self-discipline that appear to be lacking amongst some children in the education system today, including black children. This attitude is compromising their academic progress and the realization of their potential. Furthermore, Sewell's observation on the impact of street culture draws our attention to the important matter of how we inculcate positive values to our children. This burden clearly falls within the domain of parents and the community, who are first and leading teachers in the education of their children.

This principle also applies, in general, to all children in the education system, irrespective of ethnicity. Other leading experts in the field of race and education, such as Professor Gus John of the IOE and Diane Abbott MP are also giving attention to this issue of parental and community responsibility in many of their pronouncements on the topic. Professor John has this to say on the theme:

> *'The child's best teachers are its parents . . . Education is first and foremost about children's spiritual, moral, cultural and academic development . . . I cannot participate in my child's spiritual, moral, social, cultural and academic development if I am not engaging with where I am, spiritually, morally, socially, culturally and academically . . . If I am kind, loving, patient, encouraging with praise and make the child feel secure, I would have already laid the foundations for the child's positive self image and self esteem.'*
>
> (John, 2006, p. 169, 171)

Diane Abbott MP also comments on this issue, when writing in the Voice newspaper in September 2009:

> *'There is no question that boundaries are important for children, particular boys. And like many mothers I have always been anxious to check boisterous behaviour that might be forgiven in a child of another ethnicity but puts black boys in danger of at best stereotyping or at worst exclusion from school . . . although I adore my son and we are very close I am clear that I am a parent and not a friend. I will*

> *coax, I will persuade but in the end I am the parent and my word goes.'*
>
> (Abbott, 2009)

Thus, there are strong voices in support of a much needed and urgent parental and community renaissance movement to truly restore parents to the frontline of the education process. There are encouraging signs of unanimity and a common desire among race and education practitioners to re-connect parents and the community to the vital task of equipping black children with the necessary spiritual, moral and psychological tools to build their confidence for learning. It is this (confidence in learning) that will bring about a paradigm shift in the relative academic attainment position of black children in the education system.

Despite these concerns regarding the strong negative impact that street and peer culture potentially can exert on black students' performance, it must be acknowledged that research by the Centre for Market and Public Organisation (CMPO) has found that the educational aspirations amongst ethnic minorities have remained comparatively encouraging (CMPO, 2008). This survey established that among girls, 85% of white, 94% of ethnic Pakistani and Bangladeshi, 95% of ethnic Indian and black Caribbean, and 99% of black African pupils want to stay on at school after age 16. Undoubtedly, black girls aged 16 years are highly motivated to pursue the educational route, post secondary schooling. In contrast to girls, the comparative figures for boys are 73% for white boys, 81% for black Caribbean boys and 90% among South Asian and black African boys. Although the figures for black Caribbean boys are lower than those of South Asian and black African boys, a higher proportion of black boys do want to stay on in education post 16 when compared with white boys. However, this does not diminish the concerns raised by the figure for black Caribbean boys relative to that of other non-white ethnic boys. Such data provide currency to the disquiet raised with respect to the negative effects that the anti-school culture of the street and peer groups are having on black Caribbean boys in the education system. The survey also found that black students have long-term hopes of going on to university. Young people's aspiration to achieve educationally was not restricted exclusively to participation in education at the Further Education (FE) stage only. Almost all of the Asian or black African pupils have intentions to apply to university following sixth form or FE studies: 85% for Bangladeshi, Pakistani and black Caribbean and 70% for white pupils. Again, similar to the earlier figures for 16 – 19 FE education, we are detecting a consistent higher aspirational participation rate for black African boys in contrast to black Caribbean boys. Nevertheless, the vast majority of black boys do want to achieve education success, but do they possess the confidence to complement their aspiration?

It is about confidence

Irrespective of the fact that black Caribbean children are generally eager to succeed as demonstrated in their keenness to stay in education beyond age 16, nonetheless, there is a divergence between their aspirations and national examination performances. For example, the national GCSE data for 2010 show that black Caribbean pupils remain the lowest achievers amongst ethnic groups, with a rate of 43% for 5 or more A* – C GCSE grades, including English and mathematics. This represents a 10% attainment gap when compared with the national average for all pupils attaining 5 A* – C GCSE grades, including English and Mathematics. Thus, while the actual GCSE examination results for all categories of pupils have improved over time, the relative position of black Caribbean children to other groups has remained unchanged. To further illustrate this point; in 1991 approximately 26% of white and 31% of Asian pupils gained 5 or more A – C GCSE grades, compared with 13% of black Caribbean children. In 2009 (although a precise like-for-like comparison might not be possible), the respective rates for achieving 5 or more A* – C GCSEs were 70% for whites, 73% for Asians and 63% for black Caribbean. These results highlight the observation that the comparative position for black Caribbean children has remained the same for almost two decades.

However, invariably children who are successful academically at school display a common trait, and that is, they are confident learners! This confidence can be traced back to three key factors, namely: (1) the impact of positive role modelling by parents – parents being first teachers set high standards; (2) additional or supplementary academic support to augment the work carried out by teachers and schools; and (3) the children's involvement in wider and enriching non-academic interests, both at schools and within the wider community to which they belong.

The doctrine that confidence is the defining factor for 'subverting racist expectations' in schools (Mirza, 2008, p. 8) is best illustrated by the annual London School and the Black Child (LSBC) Academic Achievement Awards event initiated and hosted by Diane Abbott MP over the last few years. The purpose behind this event is best stated by Diane Abbott herself, who at one of the LSBC's Award events said: *'The LSBC Awards are part of a broader initiative to raise educational standards and encourage young Black people to achieve their full potential. Success is often conditional on having the help and support of passionate parents, teachers or mentors. The LSBC initiative aims to improve the way young Black people are taught and encouraged in their studies.'*

What stood out from amongst the nominees and recipients of these awards consistently (apart from the fact they all gained outstandingly high examinations grades – A*s in abundance) is that they are models of the confident learner, engaged in a range of school and community pursuits and leadership experiences. Clearly, these educationally enhancing activities, invaluable to the development of self-confidence for learning, were experienced by these young people mainly because parents went out of their way to build these aspects into the holistic educational training for their children. The outcome is that these outstanding students emerged with the great asset of being acknowledged as self-confident learners. This is the vital ingredient for success in education – confidence!

Each child is special

Wittingly or unwittingly, the parents of the young people recognised in Diane Abbott's LSBC academic achievement events are following a model for parental leadership in the education process that can deliver success for black children and all children in the education system for that matter. This model has yet to find its way into current education literature, which focuses traditionally on the school being the key factor to children's success in education. Nevertheless, an understanding of this paradigm of parental leadership in children's education can be a useful conceptual tool for supporting the education of parents into their primary role as first teachers to their children. The first stage of the model starts with the parents recognising that their children are indeed special and unique. It follows, as a general rule that if parents do not themselves see the potential in their children, the probability is that others will not identify the children's capability. It is parents who usually discover and expose to others (that is, family members and relatives in the children's cultural group) the latent talents and interests of the children. Parental recognition of the psychological power of treating their children as special to them cannot be overestimated. The belief that children are precious and unique will be demonstrated by the care and attention children are given. As a consequence, children being the recipient of a 'Joseph type interest and devotion' – Biblical Joseph was given a coat of many colours – will also begin to feel special. Thus, the parents are beginning to build that vital sense of esteem and self-worth will ultimately transform children into confident learners.

The second stage of this conceptual framework makes it an imperative for parents to invest in the holistic growth and advancement of their children. This ultimately means leading and modelling the children's spiritual, moral, physical, social and intellectual development. While schools are tasked with the children's spiritual, moral, social, and cultural development, usually referred to as SMSC, the schools' effectiveness to provide for these crucial aspects of their education is limited. This is due to the reality that teachers and staff are many times at dissonance with the children's spiritual and cultural heritage and cannot impart what they do not possess or what might be opaque to them. Schools are, however, more equipped to guide the children's intellectual and academic advancement than to cater for their unique spiritual and cultural needs. Thus, it brings us back to the duty that rests upon parents, that they should take the lead in the development of the crucial spiritual domain of their children, by utilising their own experiences in teaching their children ways of spiritual discernment and cultural practices and identities. In other words, parents should be assisting their children to learn how to use their cultural toolkit (that is, religious, social and artistic traditions). In essence, we are dealing with spiritual intelligence. This is effectively facilitated through cultural expressions in art, music and other symbolic maps such as reflection, prayer and devotional exercises. Thus, parents are more qualified to address and lead in these areas of their children's growth and development.

At the third stage of the model, parents will intentionally and patiently work with their children to cultivate certain essential values for life (see below). These values will be crucial in guiding the children's every day application of the knowledge, skills and understanding they are expected to gain from the formal education process. Such essential values can be seen as a collection of virtues more accurately summarised as wisdom, which is the moral and ethical compass for guiding our actions in life. It is sometimes said that experience teaches wisdom and in a way this is profoundly true. The practice and internalisation of high values such as hope, justice, respect, fairness, service to others, being a voice for the oppressed and so forth, when displayed by parents in the presence of their children become very important life-shaping lessons for the children. Invariably, they will emulate these values; resulting in the acquisition of that most powerful virtue we call wisdom.

In the penultimate fourth stage of the model, parents will diligently fulfil their partnership role with the schools in the pursuit of their children's academic development (that is, the acquisition of knowledge, skills and understanding). Here, parents can be engaged in a range of supportive activities: following a daily reading and numeracy plan while their children are at primary school level; supervising the children's homework tasks; providing additional private tutoring for the children, complementary to that received in schools; building a stimulating learning environment at home, kitted out with appropriate books and Information Technology (IT) resources; supplementary extra-curricula activities (e.g. visits to museums, libraries, the theatres); and by the inspiration that comes from the parents' own personal involvement in study and professional growth. In so doing, the parents' spirits of aspiration and ambition are transferred to the children, who see their parents as examples and role models to follow.

In the fifth and final stage of this model of parental leadership, parents are rewarded for the fulfilment of their role as first teachers. With satisfaction, they will witness their children's realisation of expertise status in the field of their vocation and mission in life. In developing professional mastery the young persons are able to elevate their employment condition and opportunities from one of market dependency to a sought after specialists in their fields of excellence. In other words, although the mediocre or satisfactory professionals must entice employers, the professionals who are experts in their areas of work will more likely be headhunted by those who need their skills. This brings to mind the perceptive observation made by the well-known black educator, Booker T. Washington in his book entitled '*Up From Slavery*', that the most effective way to counter racial discrimination is to be in possession of the skills and expertise that people want. If you do possess the asset of expertise status others will want to know you, irrespective of the colour of your skin. (Washington, 1901)

In summary, parents lead in education by:

1. Recognising that their children are SPECIAL.
2. Taking responsibility for the children's SPIRITUAL, MORAL and CULTURAL development.
3. Modelling VALUES and exhibiting WISDOM before the children.
4. Working in partnership with schools for their children's ACADEMIC success.
5. Motivating their children to rise to an EXPERT professional or chef d'oeuvre status in life.

However, underpinning this process of parental leadership in education is the uncompromising and compelling message that true education will lead the student into a life of service to humanity and his community.

Meeting the challenge of unsupported parents

There is a cloud of pessimism engulfing some functionalists (that is, back-to-basics politicians and educators) who are suggesting that there is a social and educational parental underclass creating a cycle of deprivation in society today (Raffo et al, 2007). These parents are often times described as heading dysfunctional families. However, community and education leaders, motivated by optimism and hope, must reject this defeatist notion and spearhead a renaissance movement that will lead parents back to the frontline of the education process.

It is important to uphold the above positive and confident assertive response to the functionalist 'put down' of many struggling parents. Nevertheless, the question is still being asked, especially by realists and sometimes by black school leaders and teachers at the chalk-face of bad behaviour in schools by pupils, sometimes glaringly condoned by parents: what do you do in the situation where you have parents who do not have the capacity to be effective first teachers to their children? Walking away from this real challenge is not an option. Concerted support and systematic training must be offered to these parents to transform them into becoming first teachers to their precious gifts, that is, the children, who will ultimately be the future assets of our community and the nation. The present authors use the term 'concerted' in the sense that the recognised institutions in the community such as churches, supplementary schools and mainline schools, community clubs and centres, businesses (including barber shops and hair salons) must get engaged and contribute to the training and resourcing of parents to be better fitted to discharge their duty as first teachers, in keeping with the dynamic model discussed above.

This vision is definitely possible given that, from a motivational point, most parents do want to be good parents to their children. Their misplaced priority in lavishing on their children expensive designer and brand-name clothes and technological gadgets, things that do not really contribute to self-discipline and learning should not mislead us to think that they do not care as parents. Yes, you will always have a hard core of worthless and self-centred parents in the community, destroying young lives through the misuse of drugs and other antisocial activities, but the vast majority of parents who may be very defensive and protective when disciplinary problems do develop in schools are really crying out for help. Their argumentative stance is no more than embarrassment, thinking that they are perceived to be bad parents. They need the support and practical tools to achieve their dream of becoming respectable and good parents. With hard work, the community's institutions mentioned above can help to empower and turn around many parents. It is an adage that there is always a reward for those who sincerely commit themselves to doing good deeds. In this case, the reward is the satisfaction of seeing changed lives, in other words, boys and girls flourishing as confident learners.

The Ben Carson Story

A great example of what parents (or a parent) can do, is to be seen in the life of world-renowned neurosurgeon, Professor Benjamin Carson. Professor Carson is the Director of the Division of Pediatric Neurosurgery at Johns Hopkins Hospital, USA. He is also committed to supporting initiatives and programmes for assisting children to maximize their intellectual potential. As a world-renowned physician, Professor Carson has authored over 100 neurosurgical publications, along with three best-selling books, and has been awarded 38 honorary doctorate degrees and dozens of national merit citations. Amongst his best sellers is the book 'Think Big'. In this particular book he related the story of how a woman who read his first classic, 'Gifted Hands', commented that: '*It's a book about a mother and her influence.*' (Carson,

1992, p. 31) Indeed Sonya Carson was intensely at the frontline of Ben's educational development.

In his early years Ben, like many boys, experienced difficulty at school, falling to the bottom of his class. He became the target for name calling and subsequently displayed an uncontrollable temper and a negative attitude to school. However, his mother was determined that her son would be successful with his studies. She limited his television watching and refused to let him go outside to play until he had finished his homework each day. In addition, she required of him that he should read two library books each week and submit to her written reports on his readings. This is regardless of the fact that she herself could barely read what he (Ben) had written. The outcome of this assertive but loving discipline on Ben was amazing to his teachers and classmates. He began to dazzle his classmates with his new-found thirst for knowledge and within a year he climbed to the top of his class. Tasting academic success became the catalyst for Ben's later outstanding achievements as a great neurosurgeon (Carson, 1992, p. 31–51). Indeed, his mother very profoundly demonstrated one of the messages being advanced in this chapter, which is that parents, as first teachers, are best able to infuse in children that much needed confidence for learning. While Sonya Carson's determination is an inspiration to all parents, for it to remain a unique experience would be a failure to learn its true lesson.

Kenneth Layne, a former London councillor, also related the story of another mother who epitomizes parents who exercise their responsibility as first teachers. Her son is the famous former West Indian fast bowler Wesley Hall, who terrorized leading English and Australian batsmen in the 1960s with his fiery pace bowling. Kenneth Layne and Wesley Hall attended the same secondary school in Barbados and he (Layne) recalled how Hall's mother would diligently supervise Hall's homework by insisting that he should read his completed homework assignment to her before it was submitted to the teacher. Her simple, but effective, strategy was to listen to what was written by Hall in response to his homework task, and then to assess intuitively whether it sounded right to her. This method of hers worked successfully, for the young Hall not only excelled with the cricket ball, but also academically. Today, his post-cricketing career has seen him elevated to national prominence in Barbados.

Another example of the impact of positive parental influence is that of Professor Geoff Palmer. Professor Palmer is considered to be one of Britain's outstanding African Caribbean scientists today and has gained international fame as a leading and renowned cereal grain science expert. Amongst his achievements are being the first European to receive the distinguished American Society of Brewing Chemists Award for distinction in research and good citizenship in science in 1998. In addition to this and other academic accolades, Professor Palmer received the honour of an OBE award from the Queen for his contribution to grain science. He was also voted Black Enterprise UK champion in 2004. However, his educational journey, like in the cases of many other academically successful black professionals, was not an easy one. Palmer could easily have been part of the countless numbers of black teenagers during the period of the 1950s and 1960s that were permanently damaged educationally by an education system that cruelly labelled them as intellectually incapable. This situation was most tellingly described by Coard (1971) in his seminal work (*'How the West Indian child is made educationally subnormal in the British school system: the scandal of the Black child in schools in Britain'*) and discussed earlier in this work. In fact, Palmer himself was classed as educationally subnormal and placed in a secondary modern school in North London. However, his talent as a cricketer was spotted by the local grammar school (Highbury Grammar) and resulted in him being given a place at this school. Although placed in the low stream at Highbury Grammar, Palmer gained six 'O' levels and two 'A' levels when he left school in 1958. He went on to complete an Honours degree in Botany at the University of Leicester in 1964 and later his PhD in Grain Science (Penicuik Community Development Trust Great Exhibitions, 2005–2009). Palmer pointed out that he surmounted the many hurdles before him as a result of his family background. This is what he says:

> *'I had a strong, traditional, black, religious, Jamaican, family-orientated background. I was outside the new young black British culture of cultural isolation, drugs, music and the dole . . . My mother and my aunts were my role models. They gave me my values.'*
>
> (Kemp, 2010)

Indeed, wise parents are the catalyst for their children growing up to be confident and assured persons. Thus, being confident black learners is the only effective immunization (as it were) against the chronic epidemic of institutionalized racism that has afflicted so many black children in the education system for decades. As Professor David Gillborn reminds us:

> *'. . . racism (in its numerous, changing and sometimes hidden forms) pervades the very assumptions that shape our education system. It is present in our forms of assessment; in Whitehall; in the staff room; and in the classroom.'*
>
> (Gillborn, 2002, p. 1)

Conclusion: parents as first teachers is a paradigm shift in the culture of education

For decades since the 1944 Education Act which transformed the education system in the UK and shaped the role of the state in the provision of education, parents have been assigned a periphery involvement in the education process. Schools have been perceived to be the authority for education and learning. Therefore, both metaphorically and literally, parents have been schooled to accept teachers as the experts in the business of education and they, the parents, are but amateurs in the field. In particular, for many years, parents in the black community forthrightly instilled in their children the thought that the teacher knows best. To the child, parents would put it this way: '*If you are not learning and getting on with your work at school, it has to be your fault*'. They too (that is, parents) have been brought up with the understanding that the teacher is always right. This remains the prevailing culture in education today, but in a more subtle way.

In recent years, there has been a plethora of initiatives claiming to give parents more rights and say in education. Examples include: the annual written school report to parents; parents meetings for schools to feedback to parents on their children's progress; the requirement that schools publish a school profile, giving an account of its performance; encouragement to schools to engage parents in the academic target setting programme for monitoring and raising pupils' progress; greater involvement in school governance; parents being consulted on in the formulation and review of school policies; and, most recently, the government's 'free school' policy for parents to become accredited education providers, taking over failing schools or setting up their own schools. However, it is true to say that these developments for bringing parents into more active relationships with schools are precisely what they say, 'more' and not truly 'equal' relationships. A frontline position for parents in education can transform an education system that is underperforming for many children, especially black children, into one where all children will eventually be valued. Only then can we talk about and experience the present elusive dream of 'education for all'.

This vision of a transformation in education that the authors are putting forward cannot be expected to be accomplished overnight. Central to this vision is the goal for communities (and, distinctly so, the black community) to reclaim their pre-eminent and God-given role as owner and shapers of the education process. This is new thinking for parents and the community. It will require a mental U-turn away from a dependency on the state to educate our children, and from protestation where it (the state) fails to deliver on its obligation, to one of taking on the primary duty, as parents, to be the leaders and custodians for our children's education. It is a natural phenomenon for things to be better managed by those who actually own them. Thus, it is more than reasonable and logical to conclude that the education system will perform better under real (and not proxy) parental and community leadership and ownership. To add to this notion of parental and community ownership of education is the principle that ownership requires serious investment of time and resources and unswerving commitment. The good Book (The Bible) says in Ecclesiastes 9:10, '*Whatsoever your hands find to do, do it with all your might.*'

Schools will try to resist this essential change, as their *modus operandi* has long been that they are chieftain in the educational village, where parents, in comparison, are treated as serfs. Hence, adjusting to a reversal of position will not be an easy task. Nevertheless, with sober and reflective thought on the matter (something that teachers should be more experienced with), it can be seen that, paradoxically, the moving of parents and the community into the education driving seat will better serve schools and education in the long term. The schools will gain from the fact that they will more likely have children with higher levels of spiritual, social and emotional intelligence in their population, resulting in positive self-esteem and confidence for learning. As demonstrated in the model for parental engagement and leadership in the education, previously discussed above, schools will then be able to pay attention to the business of building on the work of parents and the community. Its focus will be to ensure that its pupils will experience academic success in the classroom, through high expectations and good-to-excellent standard of teaching within an ethos that uses appropriate cultural resources. Accordingly, schools can fully focus on their role in a broader and integrated education process. Let us work to hasten on this renaissance movement to put parents at the frontline of the education process.

Maud Blair (2007) used the term 'got it' to describe a situation where it dawned upon a headteacher that black pupils possess vast amount of intelligence, talents and leadership potential. This discovery moved the headteacher to devise a new vision for his school, building relationships of mutual recognition and respect between pupils and adults in the school. In her view, Maud Blair likened this dramatic change in the school's attitude to black pupils as: '*. . . equivalent to the sharp focus one gets when one puts on glasses for the first time*'. The present authors borrow the concept 'got it' to suggest that similarly where schools 'get it' that parents are first teachers and the community the ultimate owners of the education process, it will find a clearer vision and a sense of purpose to its work of preparing pupils for academic success and in reinforcing their cultural heritage.

Finally, an example of a school that has found a clearer vision for academic success and also demonstrating commitment to the principle of educating within a cultural context and heritage is Urban Prep, in Chicago, IL, USA. Their transformational story was reported in 'Education Guardian' on 13 October 2009. Urban Prep is a single-sex boys Charter school and part state funded. As a charter school, Urban Prep has similar flexibility to British academies, such as autonomy in the recruitment of staff and curriculum design. Enrolment at the school stands at 450 boys, all of which are African American, with 85% from single parent households. The school's leadership and 90% of the teachers are also African American. In addition to its strategic design of ensuring that the staffing of the school is in synch with the school population, its curriculum is also culturally relevant to the issues confronting urban males. For example, the reading book choices given by teachers to pupils are selected to explore urban writers in order to meet the needs of pupils.

This school appears to have 'got it', in that it is answering the call for schools to be the leaders of change in the community, in contrast to simply being located in the community. In reality, this school is working with the community in taking ownership of the education process. No longer is it the case that pupils must fit into the school's culture, but instead we find the opposite, in that the school's ethos is built around the background of the pupils. Specifically, at Urban Prep, many teachers share the same life experiences as students and, therefore, are able to mentor pupils into ways of coping with the challenges of being an urban male, and more precisely a black urban male. What has been the outcome for this school and its strategy of focusing its curriculum design and staffing to meet the needs of pupils? The Education Guardian report says:

> *'The school has been running for just over three years, but in this time it's had significant successes. When they joined the school, just 7% of students were able to read at the expected grade, yet within a year 79% were able to pass the necessary courses to graduate, compared with 34% for the neighbourhood. Daily attendance is 93%, compared with 75% locally.'*
>
> (Head, 2009)

The message of this chapter calls for a renaissance movement throughout the education system that will recapture the energy and influence of parents taking up their position in the education process as first teachers. This is imperative for the persuasive reason that education must be a community endeavour (a community of learners) and the community starts with parents being the pivotal shapers of community life. It is about reconnecting education back to its lifeblood for it to provide real culturally relevant, vigorous and stimulating experiences for all children. Let the work begin to hasten a great renaissance reconstruct that will put parents at the frontline of the education of their children.

References

Abbott, D (2009) *Your Voice, Your Parenting.* London: The Voice Newspaper , 21 September, 2009.

Beecher, H W. (1887) *Proverbs from Plymouth Pulpit.*

Blair, M. (2007) *How schools and local authorities can make the difference to the education of the Black child* in *Tell it like it is: How our schools fail Black children* Edited by Richardson B. London: Bookmarks Publications and Trentham Books.

Bruner, J (1996) *The Culture of Education.* Harvard University Press.

Carson, B (1992) *Think Big: Unleashing Your Potential for Excellence.* Zondervan Publishing House, Grand Rapids, Michigan, USA.

Coard, B (1971) *How the West Indian child is made educationally subnormal in the British school system: the scandal of the Black child in schools in Britain.* London: New Beacon Books Ltd.

CMPO (2008) *White children's educational aspirations lower than those of most ethnic minorities.* Centre for Market and Public Organisation (CMPO) http://www.bristol.ac.uk/cmpo/news/2008/364.html

Gillborn, D. (1990) *Race, Ethnicity and Education: Teaching and learning in multi-ethnic schools.* London: Unwin /Routledge.

Gillborn, D. (2002) *Education and institutional racism.* London: University of London Institute of Education.

Hall, J (2007) *What can teachers do? What can parents do?* in *Tell it like it is: How our schools fail Black children* Edited by Richardson B. London: Bookmarks Publications and Trentham Books.

Head, J (2009) *Role-model behaviour* Guardian Education*, 13 October 2009.*

John, G (2006) *Taking a Stand: Gus John Speaks on education, race, social action & civil unrest 1980-2005.* Manchester: The Gus John

Partnership Ltd.

Kemp, J (2010) *Cereal academic* Guardian Education, 28 September 2010.

Mirza, H S (2008) *Race, gender and educational desire.* London: University of London Institute of Education.

Penicuik Community Development Trust Great Exhibitions (2005-2009) *Penicuik Greats.* Online: www.kosmoid.net /penicuik/palmer.

Raffo, C; Dyson, A; Gunter, H; Hall, D; Jones, L; and Kalambouka, A (2007) *Education and Poverty* Joseph Rowntree Foundation.

Swell, T (2003) *Look beyond the street.* Online: Guardian.co.uk.

Washington, B T (1901) *Up From Slavery.* Penguin Books.

Chapter 2

Building social capital for learning in the community

In Chapter 1 the authors argued that when children are developed as confident learners they invariably succeed academically. Confidence is mainly encouraged by parents and significant others (extended family members), at that micro community level. This vital work, by parents and others, is in fulfilment of their responsibility as first teachers to their children and also as close range family mentors to the children in their primary and secondary schooling. Thus, this chapter now takes the argument of community ownership of education to what the authors would describe as the macro community level, that is, extending beyond parents and family mentors. It explores the power of the concept of social capital (which includes parents in their role as first teachers) as an important and crucial factor in educational attainment and achievement.

In developing the notion of social capital and successful learning let us begin by noting that social capital in the context of education is about: (1) parental expectations and leadership; (2) the social networks that are available to the children and their family from the community to which they belong; and (3) the range of academic, and extra curricula support that parents, schools and the community provide for building children's confidence and enriching their learning. In essence, social capital is about connections through positive relationships and supportive social structures, which will result in improving the educational attainment and achievement of children.

Socio-economic factors and pupils attainment

It is well recognized in education that children from stronger social and economic backgrounds, or using the social classification label *'middle class'*, succeed in the education system. Educational research studies and commentators credit this outcome to the fact that such children have: (1) the benefit of parents with greater knowledge of how to work the education system to theirs and their children's advantage; (2) higher levels of financial resources deployed to support their educational development; (3) a school system and climate that is more welcoming and compatible to their cultural background and experiences; and (4) higher teacher expectations to aid and build their confidence as learners. In other words, middle class children gain by benefiting from the greater investment their parents make in their educational development. This we describe today as *'social capital'*. And, invariably higher investment produces substantial attainment returns. Therefore, the notion that middle class children's apparent superior school performance is linked to their innate ability or giftedness is without biological foundation. Instead, the comparative differences in performance between middle class children and working class children is attributable more to the considerable degree of investment made in the education of middle class children, at both the micro and macro levels of the social capital dimensions.

The concept of social capital as a tool or arrangement for advancing a person's development educationally, professionally and economically, is not new. Classic examples of social capital would be equivalent to what we generally term the 'old boy network' or professional associations such as freemason groups and other forms of professional support bodies, working for the advancements of those who belong to their fraternities. The concept can also be seen in ordinary life such as where working families extend support to each other by addressing common problems they face or by caring for each other children and relatives.

In particular in the African Caribbean community there has been a tradition of providing financial support and wellbeing through grass root institutions such as the 'partner' which is a basic form of community savings and loans system. Now some of these self help financial institutions have been transformed into regulated credit unions. In addition, the community has, over the past 30 to 40 years, built up a network of supplementary schools to support its children in their educational development and especially in response to the failure of the education system to realise their children's educational potential (see further discussion on supplementary schools below). A number of community pressure groups have also been established over the years. These have been for the purpose of representing and speaking on a range of community matters and influencing changes on issues such as race, education, employment and politics. Examples of some of these groups – some of which are no longer in existence – are the West Indian Standing Conference, the African Caribbean Evangelical Alliance (ACEA), the Caribbean Teachers' Association, the Black

Peoples' Progressive Association in Redbridge, Black Parents Movement, the National Convention of Black Teachers, and others. These organisations with their pioneering work are typical examples of the establishment of social structures (social capital resources), used with successful effect in the development of the community in the decades following the Windrush arrivals in 1948 and the 1960s new settlers from the Caribbean and from Africa.

The principle behind social capital

The present authors' discussion and treatment of the topic here is, therefore, intended to be an acknowledgement of the principle that mutual support and the coming together of people to share resources, information and skills for the furtherance of their common spiritual, intellectual, social, economic and political good have always been a feature of successful communities. Thus, readers are invited to see the notion of social capital as a tool for strengthening cooperation. This can give greater coherence to the business of building the necessary social structures to accelerate the community's ability to discharge its responsibility for the education of its children, within the framework of a national education system that emphasises choice and diversity.

Embracing the concept of social capital must, however, not be for the purpose of riding on the back of a current and fashionable cliché, the latest 'education parlance' or jargon. Neither should it be at the expense of disconnecting from the simplicity of well tried home grown solutions for community education. Rather, the effort of this work, in giving attention to the concept of social capital, can be likened to a good home grown singer, performing without formal musical knowledge, but whose work is now being augmented with the additional skills of appreciating musical notation and sight reading skills for the purpose of lifting and improving his musical performance.

The term social capital is about the value of social networking to a community and its people. It assumes the existence of a close knit community with a high degree of trust and goodwill towards each other, and where there are shared values and aspirations. It requires a culture of dynamic encounters and interactions between members within that community. Social capital is predicated on the belief that cooperation and burden sharing are more effective and efficient ways for advancing both personal and collective development.

Investing in building stronger social capital offers more opportunity for enhancing the quality of life within the community.

> *'There is now a range of evidence that communities with a good 'stock' of such 'social capital' are more likely to benefit from lower crime figures, better health, higher educational achievement, and better economic growth . . .'*
>
> (Smith, 2009, p. 2)

As already stated above, the concept of social capital is not unfamiliar to the black community, but resonates with institutions within the community such as Black Majority Churches (BMC) and supplementary schools. In other words the concept of social capital is not, in reality, a new revelation or discovery. Nevertheless, in the literature on the topic three thinkers have contributed to the current discourse on social capital as an academic tool for understanding and utilizing its power for building social institutions. They are Pierre Bourdieu, James Coleman and Robert Putnam (Smith, 2009).

Leading writers on social capital

Bourdieu distinguished between three forms of capital, namely: economic, cultural and social. The central message behind Bourdieu's work on social capital is that it can produce unequal access to resources and power advantages for an elite class in society, through the cultivation of strong networking relationships, to the detriment of democracy. Thus, privileged individuals seek to maintain their positions using their connections with other groups with similar advantages. In Bourdieu's view, social capital is in synch with both economic and cultural capital. It operates in a social environment that is hierarchically structured. His interpretation of social capital is – from a sociological perspective – viewed through the lenses of a social class frame of reference (Smith, 2009). Thus, Bourdieu focused more on the negative results of social capital and less on how the principle of mutual support and cooperation can become useful in advancing the economic, social and political position of communities.

Coleman in contrast argues that people living in disadvantaged economic backgrounds and working class groups could and should also benefit from the availability of social capital. He is more positive about the potential good that can be derived from communities developing more social structures for their progress and development. Coleman, in contrast to Bourdieu, cannot see why the virtues of social capital should be the exclusive preserve of a privileged few. On the contrary, he is motivated to bestow or to expand the value of connections, trust and relationships to all individuals and groups in society. In essence, Coleman is advocating the power of neighbourhood influence, voluntary associations and social networking organisations to build and provide mutual resources and support to any community for its ongoing development. According to Burnheim (2004):

> *'Coleman identifies three key aspects of social capital:* [1] *obligations and expectations (which depend on the trustworthiness of the social environment,* [2] *the information-flow capacity of the social structure, and* [3] *the presence of norms accompanied by sanctions.'*
>
> (Burnheim, 2004, p. 4)

The first of Coleman's three aspects above is akin to the old code of behaviour that existed between stock exchange dealers and sellers in the City of London, where transactions in stocks and shares were agreed informally on the principle of 'my word is my bond'. Trust was the bedrock of their dealings. Without trust, the community of dealers in shares and bonds would have been weaker and less profitable in their businesses. In transferring the lessons of this example to networking relationships, collaboration and cooperation (that is, actions synonymous to social capital), participating members in this milieu are expected to live up to the principles of contributing and sharing and, therefore, being able to benefit from the synergy or the extra pay off that comes from mutual support. Selfish motives and attitudes (grabbing and running) are incompatible with the culture and spirit of social networking. Thus, in developing a dynamic community, members must learn the virtue and worth of cooperation and sharing. Competition is anathema to social capital. Coleman's second key aspect of social capital is established on the essential need for a free flow of information to support and build an effective networking structure. The dissemination of information is crucial to the capacity for networking groups to function as valuable resource assets to their members and in fostering trust and building dependable relationships between members. The more information (and its quality) that is available to members in networking groups or to a community will greatly assist individuals and the collectives to be better informed in their decision making processes. The third element of Coleman's key aspects of social capital is self evident. All organisations and social groupings will always gradually develop norms and practices to regulate the way members operate and behave towards each other, with the inevitable set of sanctions to curb dissident and anti group behaviour that could undermine the goals, structure and effectiveness of the networking group. These rules and sanctions may never be formalised into written documents. Nonetheless, they are well understood and adhered to by members who are also cognisant of the cost of non compliance to group norms, with its consequential loss of benefits, influence and social support.

A third major contributor to the literature on social capital is Robert Putnam. In many ways it can be said that he made the concept popular through a major piece of study he conducted, and documented in 'Bowling Alone' (Putnam, 2000). According to Putnam, social capital is about connections among individuals, through social networks, the practice of reciprocity and trustworthiness. He placed an emphasis on the spirit of civic commitment and the common good. In articulating the reasons why social capital is important he says:

> '*First, social capital allows citizens to resolve collective problems more easily . . . People often might be better off if they cooperate . . . Second, social capital greases the wheels that allows communities to advance smoothly . . . Where people are trusting and trustworthy . . . A third way in which social capital improves our lot is by widening our awareness of the many ways in which our fates are linked . . . The networks that constitute social capital also serves as conduits for the flow of helpful information that facilitates achieving our goals . . . Community connectedness . . . makes an enormous difference to our lives.*'
>
> (Smith, 2009, p. 5)

In the context of this chapter and its spotlight on the potential for social capital (as a useful conceptual tool) to motivate members and entities within a community to pull together, the above statement by Putnam resonates with this imperative. Pulling together also rings well with the truism that 'unity is strength'. Thus, in unity, a community will be better placed to overcome the obstacles and problems that are impeding its growth. For the black community these obstacles and problems are: (1) the educational attainment of its children; (2) employment and income levels; and (3) political representation and other issues that directly or indirectly affect the well being of the community. Strengthening the community – through networking and other social structures – increases its capacity to advance more securely, through self determination, to finding collective solutions to the three issues above that are challenging the well being of the black community. Applying Putnam's third reason for social capital can be helpful to the black community's effort in self development within the context of a diverse society. Too often its endeavours to overcome barriers and disadvantages in the three areas mentioned above (education, employment and political influence) rely invariably on solo efforts. Far better will be the community's results when more emphasis is placed on groups and organisations systematically engaging in more collaboration and better connectedness in an effort to address these problems. The advantage of better coordinated effort is that organisations and groups can gain from the synergistic outcome of collaboration. By this we mean the collective energy that flows from a sense of unity of purpose and the sharing of resources. This potentially can be achieved without the side effects of participating organisations losing their identities and autonomy. Thus, this much needed working together will be for the betterment of all.

More enlightenment is shed on the notion of social capital by Michael Woodcock (Woodcock, 2001). He identified three types of social capital, namely: (1) bonding social capital; (2) bridging social capital; and (3) linking social capital. Bonding social capital describes ties between people in similar situations, as in the case of immediate family and significant others, such as close friends and neighbours. This form of social capital is at the micro level and brings us back to our discussion in Chapter 1 which stressed the importance of a renaissance movement for re-establishing parents and significant others as children's first and foremost teachers. Bridging social capital, in contrast, is about wider ties within a community, involving friendships and membership of local interest groups or professional bodies. This type of social capital operates more at the macro level within the community. It is about key social structures, institutions and networking groups operating as resources within the community. Thus, our understanding of these aspects to social capital can assist in the task of building and extending the reservoir of support mechanisms needed to effectively develop the community spiritually, educationally, economically and politically.

Linking social capital relates to links and engagements with others outside the immediate community. There is the potential and opportunity to access additional resources beyond the boundary of the community, especially with other ethnic groups who are experiencing similar challenges and barriers to education, economic and political developments. This cross fertilization with other networking groups and bodies beyond one's immediate community can have mutual benefits. For example, the experiences of one group can become a valuable learning tool or case study material for others to document and learn from. But in addition to this, cross cultural and ethnic collaboration on common issues affecting the well being of minority communities can mitigate against: (1) marginalisation and isolation of minority groups by a dominant and powerful group; and (2) the application of a divide and rule policy (setting people and groups against each other).

Social capital has its origin in the community education movement

Interestingly the idea of social capital apparently has its roots in the field of education. According to Putnam (2000) the term was first used by a local American educator by the name of Lyda J. Hanifan in an essay about the development of schools as community centres. However, other commentators credit the concept to John Dewey a renowned 20th century education theorist, who was the inspiration behind the education movement to which Hanifan belonged (Burnheim, 2004). Thus, the term gained recognition within a movement that was about community education and the development of rural community life. The big vision was that schools should become the centre of society for the advancement of community life and active learning. In essence, schools have the potential to be enablers and to provide empowerment to their communities. In the context of this book and its proposition for placing parents and the community on the frontline of the education system, social capital means leadership in community development and self determination. Ultimately, education itself becomes the most effective community intervention plan and strategy for the creation of social capital to secure community development and the removal of social, economic and political barriers and injustices (Burnheim, 2004).

Returning to Robert Putnam, through his work he has been able to identify certain important benefits to be derived from communities building social capital for their future progress and growth. Firstly, he has been able to show that children's development is significantly shaped by the levels of social capital existing in any community. The degree of trust, networks and norms of reciprocity available to the children's family, schools and peer groups will have lasting effects on the children's future choices and educational achievements in life. Secondly, communities with the confidence and capability to intervene with support for educational, social and economic improvements for their members, through the possession of higher rates of social capital, will generally enjoy better educational outcomes and less anti-social behavioural issues such as crime. Thirdly, the gains in higher educational standards, as a result of the positive outworking from social capital resources and support structures can also be beneficial to national prosperity. This can be seen to be a form of '*linking social capital*' as described above, operating at the higher macro level. Finally, the impact of the educational benefits of social capital can be demonstrated not only in instrumental outcomes, as discussed above, but also in higher order gains such as an overall better quality of life and happiness for members in the community.

Poverty and social capital: a third way

Having established that high levels of social capital correlate with academic success for children in the education system, it can also be reasoned that poverty and economic deprivation rob many communities of the capability to secure much needed social capital to support educational achievement and social development in their communities. Nevertheless, the view is gaining ground that we cannot accept the argument that poverty must inevitably result in poor educational attainment for those caught in the poverty trap.

The prevailing orthodoxy from national government today is that 'poverty is no excuse' for low educational attainment. This is also the view of other governments globally. Ministers and others who deny that there is a link between poverty and education are eager to attach that view (that there is a correlation between poverty and educational attainment) either to soft touch lefties, seeking to justify a socialist perspective on education and social class, or to those who simply are offering excuses for ineffective teachers.

Nevertheless, despite this denial from politicians, there is a significant body of research evidence and also the views of many educational experts that children from poor families are likely to fail at school than children whose parents are well off. Surprisingly, the British government's treasury department, in a report, during the tenure of Gordon Brown, concurs with this opinion. It found, in a review of research literature covering a period of over 30 years, that: '*Children from disadvantaged backgrounds are much less likely to succeed in education . . .*' (The Guardian, 14 September 1999)

It is, further, claimed that inspection data from Ofsted will show that the majority of schools in special measures are generally schools with a high proportion of children on free school meals. The level of free school meals is used as a standard indicator for establishing deprivation in education today. On the other hand, the analysis of inspection judgments found that teaching, management and school ethos are consistently judged to be better in secondary schools with students from wealthier backgrounds. The obvious explanation for this is that schools in areas where children are served with higher levels of social capital are more likely to attract better talented school leaders and more effective teachers. A multiplier effect is also added, as the combination of effective school and confident learners result in greater attainment outcomes. Here, we have the situation of a virtuous circle in contrast to the vicious circle of low social capital and ineffective schools that afflict socially and economically deprived communities. This observation is profoundly important as it answers the question as to why in many parts of the world, such as in Africa and the Caribbean, children from poorer backgrounds succeed educationally. In those communities: (1) schools possess committed and dedicated teachers whose expectation of their pupils are not shaped by social factors; and (2) pupils are well supported in cultivating self discipline as an important ingredient to becoming confident learners. Thus, the message in this chapter is that strategies can be developed, by community leaders and others, to build and bring greater social capital resources into ethnic communities in the UK.

A recent scholarly study by a group of researchers based at the School of Education, University of Manchester and supported by the well known Joseph Rowntree Foundation, sought to develop a framework for examining the links between poverty and educational outcomes in the UK (Raffo et al, 2007). In this study the researchers reviewed the literature on poverty and education and concluded that there are two conceptual tools that can explain the reasons for the relationship between poverty and education.

The first they described as the *'Functionalist'* frame of reference, which assumes that education plays an important part in the functioning of society. Thus, the functionalist approach sees the underperformance of students in the education system as the result of dysfunctions at the level of the individual. Students underachieve because of negative family issues, such as broken homes, one parent upbringing and other social related problems. Controversially, other functionalists point to inherited capabilities, although in recent decades this has been discredited in academia. In effect this, the notion that intelligence is hereditary, makes the individual the focus and reason for the problem of underachievement in education today.

The second conceptual perspective identified by the study is termed *'Socially Critical'*. This assumes that education is potentially beneficial and can make a contribution to the economic and social development of the nation. However, the researchers argued that education in its current form reflects unequal distribution of power and resources in society today. Thus, this school of thought implicates the education system for reproducing and sustaining inequality.

The question for readers of this book is where do we go from here with these views on education and poverty as we develop the argument of extending social capital to communities in our society today? It is reasonable to argue that family factors and the distribution of power in society can very well influence educational attainment. The government may even be right that poverty must not be an excuse for educational failures. However, government policies, over time, have yet to produce lasting improvements in educational standards. Therefore, we must identify what has worked in the past and can still work today to aid children in overcoming the poverty barriers.

The anecdotal evidence (both nationally and globally) tells of many children who have defied the notion that poverty and depravation are impediments to educational achievements. The clear reason why many children in poorer communities abroad are doing better in their studies can be linked to the motivation and confidence they (the children) receive, which is generally the result of intentional parental and community support. This has been the drive which has spurred many on, despite their socio-economic background and negative expectations at school.

A third way (that is, the power of motivation and confidence building), in contrast to the 'functionalist' and 'socially critical' perspectives, does not accept being boxed in by negative stereotypes and social class identity. Many black children have been able to scale the achievement barriers by the ingredients of faith and a positive cultural identity. This (faith) is a unique brand among the strands of social capital resources that can be mobilised within a community. Indeed faith works. The Biblical story about Jesus Christ recorded that the Jewish expectation was that nothing good could come out of Nazareth. Nazareth was a very poor area. Nevertheless, the life and work of Jesus Christ defied the myth, as it was written, in the Bible, that Jesus of Nazareth '*. . . grew in wisdom, and in statute, and in favour with God and men.*' (Luke 2: 52) We are also reminded in Philippians 4:13 that '*I can do all things . . .*' Hence, this third way, in conjunction with developing social capital structures and networks, opens the way for real transformation in the attainment, achievement and holistic development of black children and children in other social groups. Let us keep the motivation and confidence building strategy going!

Therefore, can the African Caribbean community construct this third way that the authors are suggesting, and is there a reasonable community infrastructure to advance this vision? The answer is a resounding yes! In the overtly racist and discriminatory periods of the 1960s and 70s, when, as Coard (1971) described, black children were so cruelly abused and placed into those notorious ESN schools, our bold education community leaders fought back and established the supplementary school movement (Simon, 2007). These include pioneering supplementary school institutions and personal initiatives such as:

> '*. . . the Claudia Jones Supplementary Saturday School, the Mandela Supplementary Saturday School, the Queen Mother Moore Supplementary Saturday School, the Malcolm X Supplementary Saturday School . . . Bini Butuakwa, John La Rose and Reverend Wilfred Wood.*'
>
> (Simon, 2007, p. 67 & 68)

These pioneering institutions and community leaders provided us with a well laid platform from which the community can develop a cohesive third way to motivating and building the confidence of black children for learning. Within the African Caribbean community the Black Majority Churches (BMC) as an institution also have a powerful role to play in this respect. Indeed many do operate supplementary schools and were in the vanguard of the early supplementary school movement by making their church rooms available to groups for the purpose of running classes, providing extra lessons in English, mathematics and black history. Therefore, at this point in the chapter, it is fitting to consider the laudable historical role that supplementary schools have played in the building of a significant first layer of social capital in support of the educational needs of the black community and its children.

Black supplementary schools

According to Reay and Mirza (1997) black supplementary schools are to be considered as 'extra schooling' or supplement to mainstream schooling. Historically, these schools have been in existence as far back as the 1950s. They are chiefly self-funding organisations operating mainly on Saturdays and Sundays, but also at times during week days after regular schooling. They can be found situated in church halls, community buildings and sometimes in the homes of black teachers and community activists. While it is difficult to accurately quantify the number of supplementary schools existing in the education system, data by Abdelrazack et al (1999) provide some insight into the scope of this independent support sector to the education system. They reported as many as up to 1,000 such schools identified in London and the Greater London areas.

However, in their small scale study of the black supplementary school movement in 1995, Mirza and Reay (2000) looked at 60 such schools in the London area. In terms of size, these schools on average tended to be in the order of between 30 to 40 pupils. The researchers also found a few schools that were as small as 15 pupils and others with as many as 90 pupils. The age range for pupils in those schools generally varied from between 3 to 18 years, and the average age range being 5 to 16 years. A significant aspect of those schools was that 65% of the teachers were women. This underscores the undeniable leading and pioneering role that black women played in the development of black supplementary schools as an essential educational resource (Social Capital) for the black community. Mirza and Reay (2000) captured this important perspective on the contribution of black women to the black education movement and its struggle to ensure the educational rights of black children, when they commented on the intention of their academic paper, as follows:

> *'. . . to highlight the ways in which Black women's participation as both mothers and educators sheds new light on the traditional conceptualisations of citizenship . . . their active engagement in Black supplementary schools ndemonstrates the paradoxical relationship between individual educational achievement and collective community commitment* [a clear form of Social Capital to the community] *that characterises Black female citizenship . . . the women combine their social capital and emotional capital skills of resourcefulness and networking thus enabling them to become collective transformative agents . . . their radical forms of 'giving back' and their 'education desire' open up a 'third space' of strategic engagement.'*
>
> (Mirza and Reay, 2000, p. 2)

The researchers also, interestingly, placed the development of the black supplementary school movement into a broader historical context. They observed that the schools can be linked to the socialist Sunday schools that existed in the 19th century, which were also, in similar fashion to post Windrush grassroots movements, responding to the community needs of that period. During that time political agitations by groups such as the Chartists, for social reforms, provided the motivation for the working class to aspire to educational development for themselves and their children. Today the black supplementary schools, they argued, have taken up the mantle of such early grassroots leadership movements in the cause of justice and equality, for those who are oppressed and marginalised in the education system. The socialist Sunday schools declined and died away, as the growing middle class of the period increased in influence and were able to use their economic and political muscles to take advantage of the growing grammar school structure to the benefit of their children. The result was that the working class became an under educated group that supplied the manual and semi-skilled labour needed for employment on the land or in the industrialised cities (Musgrave, 1969).

For more than forty years black supplementary schools have provided hope for the black community. A significant body of education leaders in the community are committed to ensuring that black children – despite the challenge of the racism that exists in the education system – will not go the way of 19th and 20th century working class children and become a relatively undereducated group in society. In the judgement of the present authors, black supplementary schools provide an important platform for expanding a network of social capital resources for community building and development, especially in the vital area of educational investment.

In a profound way the greatest function performed by black supplementary schools is that of their unquestioned civic duty role. Today many mainstream schools are either seriously or glibly taking on the fashionable image of being community schools. But black supplementary schools are the genuine article of the concept and practice of community schooling. The teachers staffing black supplementary schools are teachers who are strongly of the belief that it is their duty to use their qualifications and achievements to serve the community to which they belong. As a form of social capital tool, this approach is the opposite – in contrast – to social capital resourcing and support activities to be found amongst contemporary white middle class networking groups, where the main purpose of their existence is to protect the advantages that they managed to build within the education system for their children. In terms of specific outcomes for participating parents, black supplementary schools perform the function of assisting parents with home-school relationships and in motivating and helping children to perform better educationally in mainstream schools.

In addition, these schools act as a city of refuge for many black pupils who are part of the continuing disturbing concern regarding the over-representation of black pupils in school exclusion statistics (see a fuller treatment of this issue in Chapter 4). But in keeping with the name 'supplementary schools', these grassroots institutions indeed have been bridging the gap and compensating for the underperformance of mainstream schools in the delivery of quality education for black children. In so doing, they contribute to the building of a major source of educational resource in the black community, and serve as a demonstration of an emerging collective asset that we can now identify as part of the community's social and cultural capital (Mirza and Reay, 2000). In brief, black supplementary schools fulfil more than a remedial function. They: (1) provide a safe cultural environment that overtly strengthens black children's identity and heritage; (2) support parental engagement, which gives practical endorsement to one of the key messages of this book, which is that parents must be at the frontline of their children's education; (3) emphasise basic skills not as a catching up exercise, but in advancing children's capacity to exploit the curriculum as confident and self assured learners; and (4) seek to complement the children's mainstream educational provision, with the added element of 'tough love', meaning that pampering is eliminated as an inappropriate incentive for cultivating good behaviour and appropriate manners.

The practical education outcomes of the black supplementary school movement, namely raising the attainment level of black children, cannot mask the fact that it also provides a powerful and positive lesson to black children of how not to be overcome by the emotional and psychological crushing force of racism that is endemic in British society, and in particular in the education system. Black supplementary schools liberate black teachers – who are also in many cases teachers in the mainstream sector – and help them to provide invaluable sharp and pointed encouragement and counselling to black children that would otherwise be inappropriate to give black children alongside other racial groups in mainstream schools. For example, supplementary school teachers are able to deploy the necessary specific individual attention that is needed both academically and emotionally in order for the black children to learn how to cope in an environment that overtly and covertly gives off messages that say that black people are inferior to whites. Naturally, the required esteem building cannot be effectively managed, except in the children's home or in an environment such as at a supplementary school, by teachers who have had the experience of combating and enduring racism themselves in education or at the workplace. Too often in the education system black children are made to feel and think that to be black and be academically successful is somewhat abnormal. The extremely damaging message is conveyed to them that academic success is to be associated only with whiteness and Asian-ness. Reay and Mirza (1997) have this to say:

> *'White bias is everywhere in education except in Saturday school . . . Supplementary schools provide a context in which whiteness is displaced as central and blackness can be seen as normative.'*
>
> (Reay and Mirza, 1997, p. 11)

As a movement, black supplementary schools are also a force for generating community solidarity and the building of both social and cultural capital. The spirit of self help and the promotion of individual and family responsibility for education are important features of Black supplementary schools. This can be contrasted with the prevailing middle class self centred use of social networking, professional contacts and personal financial resources to further consolidate their ability to influence the education system for the benefit of their own children. In other words, social capital – middle class style – is focused unashamedly on individualism, with little regard for the educational wellbeing of poorer children in society. Thus, the continuing existence of black supplementary schools give hope to disadvantaged ethnic groups in society, including poor white working class children, that collective self help effort can become a transformative and empowering force for ensuring that their children can experience sustained educational improvement and growth.

For decades black supplementary schools have performed a wonderful recovery job for hundreds of black children written off by schools in the maintained sector as incapable of intellectual attainment. They have turned around children by building and restoring their confidence, enabling them to become academically successful young people, buttressed by the restoration of dignity and belief in who they are and their heritage. This achievement makes black supplementary schools a beacon of light in the quest to formulate reforms that will address the underperformance of the education system. A significant ray that beams out forcefully from the work of these schools is the philosophy of placing the child at the centre of the education process. The ethos of these schools is that black children are well able to learn and will learn in a distinctly child-centred and collaborative learning environment. One supplementary school teacher's comment confirms this practice:

> *'. . . I mean we work in groups there is no sitting in rows but I believe in working in ways which are best for the child so there is a strong focus on the three Rs but also on making the work really interesting for the child, starting from where the child is and integrating things around culture and history. (Verna)'*
>
> (Reay and Mirza, 1997, p. 15)

Thus, black supplementary schools can be a valuable learning centre and a resourceful reservoir for exploring and developing workable strategies for reforming the education system, especially as it relates to the inequality in educational provision for black children and their academic achievement. This problem has been with us for many decades. Therefore, utilising the experience and the pedagogical expertise to be found in this community type educational institution has intellectual authority. It is now a well established principle that self generated solutions to problems have a much greater chance of success than ones handed down externally from armchair or detached experts. This is just one more compelling beaming ray of light from the illuminating black supplementary school movement that should not be wasted or ignored by the education establishment. More importantly, it offers the black community not just a ray of hope, but a blaze of optimism that the community has the capability and capacity to take full responsibility for the education of its children, within the framework of a diverse pluralistic society.

The relationship of black supplementary schools with the education system and more directly with local authorities has been a tortuous and complex one. Many supplementary school teachers have been rightly sensitive to the need to take a pragmatic approach in the development and management of curriculum matters in their own supplementary schools. For example, they try and ensure that the curriculum programme of their institutions would not become an issue of conflict with the children's regular school work. Rather, black supplementary schools emphasise the acquisition of basic skills in literacy and numeracy. But in addition, they provide the opportunity for black children to discover themselves, learn about their history and explore a wider range of experiences for handling the strongly Eurocentric content of the national curriculum. In a way this curriculum innovation by black supplementary schools provides the black children, who attend these schools, with the essential ingredients for their holistic educational development. Thus, black supplementary schools are way ahead in the delivery of an inclusive and differentiated dimension to the national curriculum, for meeting the specific needs of black children. This achievement is not always fully recognised and appreciated. However, it plays a vital role in the successes that black supplementary schools have had in guiding hundreds of black children to academic achievements in GCSE, AS and 'A' level GCEs public examinations.

Despite this pragmatic modus operandi by leaders and teachers in black supplementary schools, the education establishment remains suspicious of these schools and has kept them at a distance. The irrational fear is that these schools are a hot bed for radicalism, and are in danger of creating educational disharmony in the system. There have been stories of how this crazy suspicion of black supplementary schools showed itself in the way some headteachers have treated black teachers on their staff, who they found were also teaching on a voluntary basis in supplementary schools. One incident reported to the present authors, at the 2010 conference of the National Association of Black Supplementary Schools, illustrating this attitude, was the case of a supplementary school teacher who discovered that her handbag was searched by a senior staff member at the school where she was employed as a full time class teacher. In addition to her handbag being searched, she was also questioned by the headteacher about her involvement with the local supplementary school in a manner that suggested that she was engaged in some form of subversive activity. This is just a typical example of the very poor relationship and negative disposition held by some mainstream schools and education leaders towards black supplementary schools. This is at a time when these supplementary schools are acting as educational life support machines for many young black children damaged educationally in mainstream schools. Thus, pioneering black supplementary schools in the past, and existing ones today, have, metaphorically speaking, been restoring countless numbers of black children back from educational and learning unconsciousness to a new found life of love and confidence for learning.

Adding to the observations above, black supplementary schools – as self-sufficient community enterprises – are considered to be 'outsiders' in their relationship with the education system. Nevertheless, this uncomplimentary label, that is, as 'outsiders' need not offend. The danger with integration and assimilation (as social policies and also in terms of general outcomes) is that they can result in compromises on values and principles, leading ultimately to these institutions being at risk of losing their autonomy and even their ownership. Thus, there is wisdom in the black supplementary school movement retaining its autonomy as a community networking and educational resource asset. Furthermore, the 'outsider' position strengthens the argument for the community to construct its own supporting institutions, in order to make real the goal of taking greater ownership and responsibility for the education of its children. Moreover, the community's ownership and responsibility for the education of its children has the additional benefit of it being able to shape the education process to meet the specific spiritual, intellectual, social and cultural needs of black children.

As alluded to in this section, black supplementary schools offer more than just educational support to black children. In addition, they have also been addressing, very successfully, deeper educational issues for black children such as racism, culture and identity and the part these matters play in the education of black children. 'Cultural isolation' a term used by one of Britain's foremost African Caribbean scientist – Professor Geoff Palmer, is a very worrying experience facing many black children in the education system today (Kemp, 2010). But, thankfully black supplementary school teachers have been able to provide opportunities for black children to discover their true selves and to become emotionally and psychologically liberated confident learners, to the relief and joy of many parents. The discourse by these teachers in black supplementary schools invariably will present a more balanced version of world history, in contrast to the traditional Western accounts of history and the negative racial portrayal of black people that black children encounter in mainstream schools (Reay and Mirza, 1997). Furthermore, supplementary schools remain the few bastions and fortifications for preserving the community's distinct cultural heritage, in support of its children's education.

In the past the 1960's concept of 'Black Power' was frowned on by the white establishment and some blacks. However, from a community perspective and logic, the concept of 'Black Power' deals more with blacks purging themselves from the curse of self doubt and inferiority complex to the cultivation of self confidence and self esteem, which, with respect to the matter of education, many black children are greatly in need of today. The 'Black Power' concept of empowerment and identity (although the term Black Power is now silent in current discourses on race issues) is recognised by many schools, which are integrating into their yearly school programme the annual Black History Month (BHM) cultural awareness activities and other cultural enrichment features such as an international day/evening or a Caribbean week. The difference is that, whereas these cultural activities are special events, attempting to deal with the serious issue of the cultural isolation of black children in the education process, they, nevertheless, remain on the periphery of the curriculum of schools rather than serving as an ongoing element in appetizing or stimulating the learning desire of black children. In other words, the impact of the realisation that cultural understanding and bearing (that is, support) are essential to learning will surely have a greater impact when they occupy a sustained and integrated role in curriculum management and pedagogy. Thus, the black supplementary school movement has been consistent in playing an invaluable role in helping black children to find and value their identity and to utilize that understanding in support of their academic advancement. Black children's cultural heritage is actively and intentionally integrated into the work of black supplementary schools. This serves importantly to counterbalance the Eurocentric focus of the national curriculum and also provides authentic and diverse curriculum development study programmes for black children that are generally missing in mainstream schools. This valued task of the Black supplementary school movement is well articulated by Reay and Mirza (1997) who write:

> *'We would suggest that in these four supplementary schools, black children can find 'really useful knowledge' (Johnson, 1979, 1988) which allows them 'to step outside the white hermeneutic* [interpretation] *circle and into the black* [hermeneutic circle]*' (Gates, 1988, p. 258). British state schooling, despite a recent history of multi-cultural initiatives (King & Reiss, 1993; Tomlinson & Craft, 1995), still operates with predominately taken-for-granted assumptions of white-ness as normative.'*
>
> (Reay and Mirza, 1997 p. 17)

It must, nevertheless, be noted that the viewpoint that culture plays an integral part in the work of black supplementary schools should not only be restricted exclusively to the prevalence of the racial stereotypes and negative attitudes that supplementary schools are battling against. These institutions, as we know, do more that just work to subvert the detrimental effects of the racist practices that persist in the education system. Supplementary schools also take on the problem that we sometimes find, where well meaning white liberal teachers in state schools give in to black pupils, allowing blatant misbehaviour and poor standard of work, and relying on endless rounds of meetings with such badly behaving pupils that are totally unproductive. Black supplementary schools have had to counterbalance this unhealthy overcompensation by these misguided teachers by bearing down on pupils showing a lazy attitude to work and demanding from them greater productivity and higher standards of work. Thus, the 'tough love' approach is applied in these schools, drawing on the principle that 'black children can learn, and will learn'.

Conclusion

Finally, this third way that the present authors propose, as discussed earlier on in this chapter is about parents and community ownership of the work of education. The community is blessed with the existence of a well established model of community social capital in the form of the black supplementary school movement. This provides the platform for developing and extending community leadership to the education of its children within the wider education system. The opportunity for this dynamic growth is available through the infrastructure and potential that already exists in the black supplementary school movement. It stands to reason that the development of more of these schools, as a 21st century social capital strategic commitment and drive, will raise the attainment level of black children. The fulfilment of this transformative education vision has a fighting chance for success through collaboration with other important community institutions such as the Black Majority Churches (BMC), mentoring groups, community organisations and black businesses.

The continued existence of black supplementary schools is a statement to the high educational aspirations that reside within the black community and to the fact that the education of its children remains a high priority for them. Nevertheless, honesty to ourselves makes it necessary for it to be acknowledged that regardless of the great work being carried on by the black supplementary school movement, the community's efforts remain fragmented. This condition means that the community's talents and impressive array of educational assets are not delivering the potential impact they are capable of producing. Hence, it might be worthwhile looking at how other ethnic groups, such as the Jewish community, address this issue, that is, how it develops and manages its human resources.

The Jewish community is relatively small in this country, but a highly successful group despite the racism they endured during the 1930s in East London. Although the discrimination they suffered may not be precisely the same as the black community experiences today, lessons can be learnt from their response to racism. The Jewish community placed investment in education at the centre of their resistance to racism. But more profoundly, they systematically coordinate the education of Jewish children in the major Jewish conclaves throughout the British Isles. The Jewish community, like most other ethnic groups, has the usual ideological diversity such as mainstream orthodox Jews, (under the leadership of the Chief Rabbi), purist orthodox Jews and reformed non-orthodox Jews. Nevertheless, they are all united with a common purpose to invest strongly in the education of their children by taking full responsibility for the education provision necessary for that purpose. In terms of national coordination in the Jewish community, this is provided by the Board of Deputies (BOD), which is a non religious national community organisation. This body has been in existence for approximately 250 years. Its main duty is to represent and speak on the behalf of Jewish groups and to explain the Jewish way of life to the British public. Synagogues and Jewish organisations in the country provide deputies to the BOD, and the BOD meets every six weeks nationally to discuss and coordinate issues covering the full spectrum of Jewish life in the British Isles.

Education is central to the life, history and development of the Jewish community. The first Jewish Free School was established in this country in 1732. The purpose of the Jewish education system is to preserve the Jewish community. Jewish parents feel that they are not always fully equipped to provide their children with the knowledge and grounding in the Jewish heritage and values. They believe that Jewish schools will provide the necessary cultural knowledge that can help their children to be successful learners. Currently, there are approximately 39 Jewish maintained schools in the British Isles and a further 100 in the independent sector. These schools are located in major cities such as London, Manchester, Leeds, Liverpool, Glasgow and Birmingham.

The strength and acknowledged cohesiveness of the Jewish community are derived from a raison d'etre that centres on three essential principles, namely: learning; prayer; and social action (charity). Consequently, every local synagogue is in effect an educational centre. From the time a synagogue is set up a school is also established as an intrinsic part of its work and programme for the community it serves. For the Jewish community education is the life blood that preserves its distinctive way of life and the transmission of its heritage to future generations. This is demonstrated by the fact that today 60% of Jewish children of school age attend Jewish schools. Thirty years ago this figure was only 25%. Half of the present enrolment is drawn from the strictly orthodox Jewish community and the other half from what is termed the mainstream Jewish community. Thus, the demand for Jewish schooling has never been stronger and is constantly growing yearly, as is evident by the fact that it has increased by 50% over the last decade (The Commission on Jewish Schools, 2008).

It is not altogether surprising that the Jewish community should display such high levels of coordination and solidarity, given its relatively long history as an ethnic minority group in Britain, and also its well documented experiences of persecution and racial discrimination. Exposure and vulnerability to external threats are important factors that have motivated the much admired cohesiveness that is a key feature of the Jewish community today. In contrast, although black people's presence in Britain can be traced back to pre-Victorian times and earlier, an established and significant black community in Britain is a 20th century phenomenon. Therefore, it follows that its stage of 'spirit de corps' (indomitable group loyalty) will not be at the level and intensity as is now the case for the Jewish community. However, the many social and political actions and struggles by the African Caribbean community during the last 50 years against racism and injustices provide concrete evidence of the capability of the black community to come together in a common cause to protect, build and advance its legitimate interest as stakeholders in a pluralistic and multi-ethnic society. Hence, this overview of the Jewish education system, and how it is coordinated to fulfil the Jewish community's responsibility for the education of its children, can be beneficial to the black community. The aid it can provide is not so much in the details of how their education programme is developed and managed, but more importantly in: (1) the black community endorsing the principle that a community must take full responsibility and ownership for the education of its children, and not just to be engaged in plugging the gaps where the state education system is failing; and (2) building and developing the necessary organisations and strategies for advancing a well coordinated national community education programme, without displacing the legitimate autonomy and power of the many local organisations that have served the black community with dedication and love for many decades.

The real lesson to be drawn from our consideration of the Jewish approach to community education is actually the application of the concept of 'linking social capital' (Woolcock, 2001) from our earlier discourse, under the sub-heading 'Leading writers on social capital'. This form of networking is a reciprocal process, in that all communities have contributed to the ongoing development of our society. No one ethnic group can claim to be the paragon of educational distinction. We learn more together than when we work independently. For the black community now is the time to grasp the nettle and work together to end those elements of fragmentation that have endangered our work to raise the achievement levels of black children. This working together can be achieved by utilising the notion of 'social capital' as an instrumental tool for extending the community's reservoir of education resources to raise the educational performance of black children. Social capital for education can: (1) improve the community's ability to monitor more effectively the performance of the state education system; (2) increase the potential for corporate action for addressing and solving problems affecting the education of black children; and (3) facilitate the dissemination of innovative ideas and the forging of vital links amongst community institutions, groups and organisations.

References

Abdelrazack, M and Kempadoo, M (eds) (1999) *Directory of Supplementary and Mother-tongue Classes 1999-2000,* Resource Unit for Supplementary and Mother-tongue Schools, Department for Educations and Employment, School Inclusion Division.

Burnheim, C. (2004) *Education and Social Capital.* Online.

Coard, B (1971) *How the West Indian child is made educationally subnormal in the British school system: the scandal of the Black child in schools in Britain.* London: New Beacon Books Ltd.

Guardian (1999) *Poverty is the key – not just an excuse.* http://education. Guardian.co.uk/article/05606,3901607 html

Kemp, J (2010) *Cereal academic* Guardian Education, 28 September.

Mirza, H. S. and Reay, D (2000) 'Redefining citizenship: black women Educators and the third space'. In M Arnos and J Dillabough *Challenging Democracy: International perspectives on gender.* London: Routledge Falmer.

Musgrave, P (1968) *Society and Education in England since 1800.* Methuen and Co. Ltd.

Putnam, R. D. (2000) *Bowling alone: the collapse and revival of American community.* New York, Simon & Schuster.

Raffo, C. Dyson, A. Gunter, H. Hall, D. Jones, L and Kalambouka, A (2007) *Education and poverty: A critical review of theory, policy and practice.* University of Manchester: Joseph Rowntree Foundation.

Reay, D. and Mirza, H. S. (1997) 'Uncovering genealogies of the margins: Black supplementary schooling' *British Journal of Sociology,* 18, 4:477- 499.

Simon, D. (2007) *What can teachers do? What can parents do?* In *Tell it like it is: How our schools fail Black children* Edited by Richardson B. London: Bookmarks Publications and Trentham Books.

Smith, M. K. (2000-2009) 'Social capital', *the encyclopaedia of informal education,* [www.infed.org/biblio/social_capital.htm].

The Commission on Jewish Schools (2008) *The Future of Jewish Schools.* London: Jewish Leadership Council.

Woolcock, M (2001) *The place of social capital in understanding social and economic outcomes.* Isuma: Canadian Journal of Policy Research 2:1, p 1-17.

Chapter 3

Parents and schools

'Parents have the primary responsibility for instilling an ethic of hard work and educational achievement in their children' (Barak Obama, 2006)

Introduction

The importance of parents and schools working in partnership cannot be over emphasised. Research in education has highlighted the impact parents have on their children's learning. Therefore, the obligation is placed on parents to take the responsibility to ensure that their children are well prepared for life at school in order for them to achieve their full potential as learners. However, on the other hand parents have the right to expect schools to work with them as lead partners in the educational development of their children.

> *'As parents and educators, we all have important responsibilities to anticipate the very best from each child and young person, so sharing a vision for achieving this,(as well as devising services together that make sense on the ground) and respect home culture and context, is vital.'*
> (National College for Leadership of Schools and Children's Services, 2010, p. 2)

Schools have the academic experts, that is, the teachers, who are the most valuable and expensive resources they possess. These teachers have had the training to impart knowledge to the pupils they teach and the burden should be on them to ensure that the learning which takes place in the classroom environment is effective, so that all pupils make progress. Most parents are not trained educators, but their children learn from them by interacting with them in the home, just like children gain from the teachers they interact with in the classroom milieu. Both parents and teachers are here to serve the children. Children have to be nurtured in such a way that they find learning enjoyable, first of all and secondly, worthwhile. One must not forget that education is a life long process and its purpose is to build life long learners who can make a positive contribution to society.

Parents in 21st century are better informed about education than they were thirty or forty years ago. This is mainly because parents are becoming increasingly more particular about the educational experiences their children are receiving to ensure that their children achieve the knowledge, skills, understanding and gain qualifications that will make them autonomous learners. Children's interests are best served by schools working collaboratively and in partnership with parents. Therefore, it is clear that the relationship between the schools and home has to take on a new type of interaction, where close cooperation and communication are of paramount importance if schools and homes are to work harmoniously first, for the benefit of the children and secondly, for society in general. This partnership with parents and schools is important to support the needs of the children to help them learn and make progress both academically and socially.

Parental influence on their children's education

Being a parent has never been an easy task and it is becoming more challenging even more so in the 21st century, especially as our society is a very competitive one. Davis, Day and Bidmead, (2002) confirm this and assert that:

> '*Being a parent is a demanding role, involving enormous commitment, time, energy, in addition to all other roles undertaken in and outside the family. It is a full-time and permanent post, including life-long concern, if not responsibility, for one's offspring.*'
>
> (Davis, Day and Bidmead, 2002 p. 2)

In addition to this, parenting has not been accorded the recognition it should be given in the society in which we live. Yet, the quality of parenting is of paramount significance if we want to build and develop young people who have high self esteem, self-confidence and self-reliance to interact effectively and become self motivated individuals.

Parents are the single most important influence on their children's education. Therefore, it is the parents' task to make sure that they equip their children adequately for school, by providing their children with good quality experiences for learning both before they start school and while they are at school. The Centre for Social Justice (2011) confirms the importance of the parents' role in education:

> *'A child's education must begin at home; parents should be the primary educators of children. Thus responsibility for a child's education does not rest solely with schools. Marginalised parents should be encouraged to engage with their child's education from the earliest stage possible.'*
>
> (Centre for Social Justice, 2011, page 17)

From the moment children are born, the experiences they encounter and the opportunities that are made available to them help to shape their beliefs, their attitudes, their actions and their behaviour. These influences children receive come from the interaction in the family and the wider community. They have an impact on family life, with all its complexity, which affect every aspect of the children's lives in their development and how they approach their learning (National College for Leadership of Schools and Children's Services, 2010).

Children are being brought up in a world where academic achievement is valued highly and academic qualifications are the passport for them to go on to further and higher education so that they will be competent competitors for employment in the job market. Furthermore, children are the next generation of adult citizens; therefore, they have to be educated to take their rightful place in society.

However, the development of children is not just determined by educational factors. Parents have a very prominent role to play in the holistic development of their children: socially, morally, spiritually, culturally and intellectually. They must take responsibility to ensure that their children have a good understanding about life as they grow up, knowing the different emotions they may have to encounter, how to cope with their physical development and their ability to interact with others, and how to form quality and long lasting relationships with their immediate peers and other people with whom they come into contact. The Centre for Social Justice (2011) highlights the importance the family plays in the development of the children:

> *'Stable, healthy families are at the heart of strong societies. An individual's physical, emotional and psychological development occurs within the family environment. It is from our family that we learn unconditional love, understand right from wrong, and gain empathy, respect and self-regulation. These qualities prepare children for positive engagement at school.'*
>
> (Centre for Social Justice, 2011, page, 13)

Having a sustained commitment in building good and positive relationships between the home and schools so that parents and teachers can work effectively together on an equal basis is not always as straightforward as it may seem, but the results can be of great benefit for the children. Schools need to acknowledge and understand that they cannot meet the needs of their pupils by themselves without genuine engagement and shared understanding which should be developed with parents (National College of School Leadership and Children's Services, 2010).

It is the parents' responsibility to ensure that they communicate with schools regularly so that they know how well their children are working and behaving. Having close contact with the schools will help parents to know about any achievements and concerns regarding their children the schools may have. If the children are achieving well parents should also reward them so that they are aware that their effort and hard work are admired and appreciated. This will help to build the children's confidence as children like to know that their parents are proud of them and their successes are held in high regard. If on the other hand, things are not going so well and schools have concerns regarding the children, the sooner the parents are made aware of the situation the more likely they are to work with the schools to change the situation to a more positive one. This will enable the children to have the necessary support, academically as well as socially, to bring about the desired change, be it the improvement in the quality of work or a more positive attitude such as, their behaviour towards teachers, peers and other staff in the schools' communities. Having this type of communication will improve the relationship between schools and parents who are able to recognise where their children need that extra support and guidance. However, not all parents experience this partnership to ensure their children get the best out of their schooling and education. John (2010) emphasises the overwhelming concerns African Caribbean parents felt (and are still feeling) about their children's mis-education in English schools and as a result they established Saturday and supplementary schools to help to resolve this problem:

> '. . . *African Caribbean parents and community groups established Saturday schools and ran Easter and Summer schools with two principal objectives: one, to provide children with knowledge and guidance about themselves and their background to help build positive identity and counteract the negative attitudes the society displayed towards themselves and people who looked like them, and two, to remedy the poor teaching and low expectations that were leading to educational failure for far too many of them year on year.*'
>
> (John, 2010, p.9)

The damaging effects of IQ tests and poor teacher expectations

Despite all the above, parents need to be aware and conscious that not all children are treated the same and given equal opportunity within the educational system. Children are judged by their social and economic background (working class, middle class), the occupation of their parents, the language they use, their race, their sex and their so called ability, which is measured by Intelligent Quotient (IQ) tests. In addition to this, poor parenting and home background are blamed if the children do not perform well at schools. Father absence homes and dysfunctional families are also other reasons given for the children's underperformance at schools. Notice that none of the blame is attributed to schools whatsoever. However, the most damaging and damning negative categorization of pupils are those experienced by the black children from their teachers. Black parents must be aware that little has changed regarding the perception of the educability of their children, despite the fact that black settlers have been here in England from the Caribbean since the 1940s and are approaching the fourth and fifth generations. The same typification that Coard (1971) referred to still goes on in our schools today. Even though the term 'educationally subnormal' is not thrown at black children today, similar names are used that have direct association with this negative term. Coard claimed that school teachers feel black children are considered to be of low ability and use language that is inappropriate for learning in schools. He, Coard, argued convincingly that African Caribbean and African children have been (and still are) incorrectly judged by their teachers.

A number of issues have placed black children in a disadvantaged position with regards to their achievement in schools. The negative stereotyping of black children is even more acute and serious as the fallacious, erroneous and misleading views given by Eysenck (1971) and Jensen (1969) that black children are genetically inferior to their white counterpart, with respect to their ability. Coard (1971) makes direct reference to Jensen's negative statement:

> '*The notorious Professor Jensen, . . . has added credence to the myth of Black inferiority by openly declaring that Black people are inherently less intelligent than whites, . . .*'
>
> (Coard, 1971, p. 41)

John (2010) lists a number of other proponents of the 'so call' theories of scientific racisms such as Charles Murray and the Bell Curve in the 1990s, Phillipe Rushton, also in the 1990s and James Watson in 2007. He, John (2010), confirms that these theorists' belief had a tremendous influence upon lecturers and academic tutors training teachers, educational psychologists and other people devising the intelligence tests.

What parents must note here is that the sentiment expressed by these so called eminent psychologists, is that no matter what the school did to try and improve the academic performance of black children, there could be no improvement because of their low level of ability. However, Mirza (2007) made it plain that the pseudo-scientific IQ tests of Jensen and Eysenck have been discredited, as they erroneously claimed that black children are racially different and as a result had lower intelligence than other racial groups and in particular, white children. Low teacher expectation is another reason for the negative view formed of black children. From teachers' point of view this, to a certain extent, will affect the level of help, support and encouragement they will be willing to offer black children as the teachers would have already made up their minds about what black children are capable of doing, with regards to their scholastic capability. In relation to the impact on black children, the result of low teacher expectation affects their self esteem and motivation to learn, as they feel a sense of failure, which will eventually damage their performance by lowering the standards they are capable of achieving. This is what helps to alienate black children even further in the English educational system. Mirza (2007) draws attention to the fact that:

> *'The self fulfilling prophecy of low self-esteem leading to low pupil aspirations, which in turn fed into low teacher expectations, was seen as the key mechanism to explain Black underachievement'.*
>
> (Mirza, 2007, p. 109)

Coard (1971) expresses his grave concern about teachers' expectation also:

> *'Most teachers absorb the brainwashing that everybody else in the society has absorbed – that Black people are inferior, are less intelligent, etc, than white people. Therefore the Black child is expected to do less well in school.'*
>
> (Coard, 1971, p. 40)

Are Coard (1971) and Mirza (2007) confirming that it is the teachers who allow black children to fail in the English school system because of the way they are treated by their teachers in the classroom? These two educationalists are writing over thirty years apart and the same attitude observed by Coard still persists today. Teachers need to accept all children and value them equally in the classroom. There will always be some children understanding certain concepts, ideas and learning at a different pace and level, but children will not always remain static with the speed at which they progress in learning. Teachers need to realise and acknowledge that all children have ability, rather than spending time categorizing black children and saying how and why they think they fail in relation to other races.

Practical parental support

The strong negative stereotyping does not change overnight, because it is difficult to change people's attitudes. It will take time. However, the black parents' role and duty are to ensure that they build up the confidence of their children and encourage them to believe that everyone has ability and everyone can achieve if that person has the self belief, good self discipline and a strong yearning to learn. Research in education has shown that parents have a great impact on their children's learning and achievement. Furthermore, it has been recognised that children's attitude to learning and their ultimate attainment are closely linked to good levels of parental engagement. As a result, it is important that parents demonstrate to their children that they value education and create a disciplined home environment that supports school policies and procedures. Parents will need to guarantee that they give their children the right experiences at home to complement their learning. This can be done by parents encouraging their children to review the work they did in lessons at school each day, provide a quiet place for the children to study and to do their homework, support their children with their study and examination preparations, and make an effort to talk with their children about their school work at home, so that the children are able to see the strong commitment their parents have in wanting them to be successful in their school career.

It is not just the schools' responsibility to educate children; parents also have their obligations and have to remember that they are lead partners with schools in educating their children. Parents should resist buying the latest gadgets and dressing their children in designer brand clothes. Instead, this money would be better and more wisely spent on, for example, private tutoring, attendance at supplementary or Saturday schools. They, the parents, should also limit the time their children spend watching television and monitor the type of programmes they view as television makes children passive learners, thus affecting their concentration and reduces their ability to develop higher order learning skills. Parents need to encourage their children to read widely both fiction and non fiction texts. The encouragement of more reading, by parents, will help their children develop their vocabulary, improve their spellings, punctuation, help their writing to be more accurate, have good sentence structure and paragraphing, therefore making them active learners as they are involved in decoding words and making inferences from written text that will develop their understanding, skills and knowledge. Furthermore, parents need to invest in having good quality books in the home that can support their children's learning. Parents should also take their children to the public library so they can borrow books and do research for their projects at school, homework and reading for pleasure. Children who read with their parents every day or at least once each week gained significantly higher scores in their examinations sat at the age of 16 and the Organisation for Economic Cooperation and Development (OECD) found that when parents read books together with their children, they had the greatest effect on the children's performance at school. The Millennium Cohort Study (2000) which has been following the lives of 19,000 British children born at the start of the 21st century also released findings which showed how children's lives look at the age of five years. The survey revealed that by this age, those children who were read to daily by their parents from the age of three years gained a two month advantage over their peers in language, literacy and numeracy. Thus, research after research have shown that parental engagement has a positive effect on improving not just their children's educational attainment, but other aspects of achievement such as attendance and behaviour. Parents themselves should also be engaged in reading so that their children can be encouraged to model that behaviour as children are inclined to copy things that they see their parents do at home. Hatcher (2006) warns that:

> *'Homes where children have few books and seldom see their parents reading or writing tend to generate a different orientation to literacy, a different cultural predisposition, from ones where reading and writing, in particular the sorts of texts which demands language skills similar to those required for school success, are everyday activities.'*
>
> (Hatcher, 2006, p. 213)

In fact, the highest achieving children academically will receive encouragement from their parents well into their teens. All parents can help their children achieve their full potential by spending some good quality time talking and reading with them. Too often, parents are reluctant to offer to help their children with school work because they feel they, the parents, lack some of the skills that would make a difference to their children's success in schools. Parents need not feel uncertain or uncomfortable regarding their capabilities to support their children's learning as any advice, encouragement or guidance will be beneficial to their children no matter how limited they judge their own educational experiences.

In addition to the assistance parents can give to their children regarding their school work, they need to know from the schools what level or grade their children are working at and the target level or grade the children should reach by the end of the academic year. Parents should also be informed by schools what the children need to do in order to ensure that they reach the target levels or grades, so that they can reinforce their children's learning at home. This can all be effectively achieved if parents have good communication with the schools and are urged to work in partnership to enhance their children's education, so that they are able to serve and contribute to society when they reach adulthood. Moreover, the educational standard the children attain when taking public examinations, whether Standard Assessment Tests (SATs), General Certificate in Secondary Education (GCSE) and the General Certificate of Education (GCE), will all become an official record of the children's progress. In particular with SATs, from 2010 the Key Stage 2 results will show whether or not children in every school reached the expected National Curriculum level for their year group. SATs will measure, for the first time, a child's ability in English, maths and science against 600,000 other children, across the UK. The GCSEs are the passport into further education to do 'A' level GCEs and the 'A' level GCEs are the qualifications needed to go on to higher education at degree level.

Furthermore, the evidence is there in the educational literature which shows that where GCSE examinations are tiered for the so called differing abilities, a high percentage of black children are entered for the foundation papers where the highest grade they can achieve is a grade 'C'. Prior to recent examination changes certain papers, such as the mathematics examination had three tiers, which were higher, intermediate and foundation. With this type of examination, the highest grade the pupils could achieve with the foundation paper was a grade 'D', which was of no benefit to the children, because the important grades were A*, A, B and C. Any grade lower than a 'C' would be considered a failure in respect of the recognised five A* – C benchmark and would hinder the children's chances of going on to further and higher education. Many parents and a high percentage of black parents were not fully conversant with the tiered examination papers their children had to sit for the GCSEs. Schools did not go out of their way to inform parents about the level of the paper they were putting their children in for the GCSE examinations or the limitations on the grade that the children could achieve with respect to the tiered paper they are entered for by the schools. This is because teachers were not forthright in explaining to parents about the tiered papers and the consequences for the children's final grades. Subject teachers had made up their minds about the examination paper they felt each pupil should sit, based on the pupils' prior ability and/or the results from the Cognitive Ability Tests (CATs). This assumption is dangerous as it assumes that children's abilities are fixed and no matter what additional learning and level of maturity those children may develop they will be unable to improve their scholastic performance.

Parents must make every effort to be well informed about their children's performance at the schools and even more important, work with them at home and monitor the quality of their work. If they are unsure about any information to do with their children's school work they should contact the schools and ask for an explanation and guidance in order to give their children assistance with the work at home. Schools should provide parents with a list of examination subjects their children will be taking, the tier for which the children are being entered, the examination boards and information regarding the contents of the syllabi. Where the parents are not satisfied, they need to make an appointment with the schools to find out why their children are not being entered for the tier that would give them a grade that will meet the five A* – C benchmark. Parents should also find out what the children need to do to make sufficient progress to be entered for the creditable tier. However, parents who are on the ball will be motivated to guide their children to ensure that they are doing good quality work to enter for the tier that will give them the grade that is recognised as an acceptable pass grade.

A crucial point needs to be made regarding the aspiration of black parents for their children. Black parents keep high on their agenda the goal for their children to have a good education and leave schools with good valuable academic qualifications, which in turn would lead to a secure career path and future for them, that is, their children. Pryce (1979) confirms this view that black parents are keen on their children achieving high academic standards:

> *'The majority of West Indian parents have great academic aspirations for their children. They believe that ultimately education is the most reliable means whereby their group, as a whole, through their children, can achieve recognition and status on equal footing with others in society.'*
>
> (Pryce, 1979, p. 120)

In fact black parents have been criticized for having aspirations that are deemed to be unrealistically too high, as there would appear to be a great disparity between the ambition of black parents and the actual achievement of their children (Taylor, 1981). Black parents view education as vital because this, they feel, is the only channel through which their children will have the opportunity for upward social and economic mobility. They consider that having a good education is necessary so that their children develop life skills and tools to compete successfully in a global, dynamic and changing world.

Despite the determination of black parents for their children to be successful at schools, the schools themselves seem to create a barrier to them, the parents. Many black parents feel uncomfortable, lack confidence or trust in schools because in many cases they found that the apparent good progress reported to them by teachers at parents' evenings later contradicts the children's actual external examination results for the SATs, GCSEs or GCEs. Teachers will say the black children are doing very well, but they omit to state to what extent that very well relates to the grades or levels which would determine success or failure. For example, parents may experience teachers providing glowing generalized reports about how well the children are doing, but later to the surprise of the parents the children's SATs, GCSEs or GCEs results prove to be below the required level 5, GCSE grade C or GCE A level grade C. Black parents need to question teachers to ensure that they are clear about the specific grades or levels their children are achieving when schools report on the 'good progress' that black children are making. In addition to this, schools should also inform parents what the children need to do further to improve their performance for the ultimate goal of gaining good standard educational qualifications. If this information is not forthcoming parents have the right to requested it from the schools which must be able to explain how the children's work need to be developed and improve to attain the necessary acceptable pass grades or levels.

It can clearly be seen from the performance of black children that schools fail to fulfil black parents' high expectation of their children's potential to be successful in their education. Many schools feel, as stated above, that black parents are over ambitious and want their children to achieve beyond what the teachers judge to be realistic for them. The teachers also feel that the black children do not have the learning capacity and the appropriate behaviour to perform at a high academic level. Black parents do not want to hear that their children are not capable of achieving the high educational standards they want them to accomplish. Instead, they want to hear what needs to be done in order for their children to be successful academically. In other words, black parents do not see their children as lacking in ability or being deficient in intelligence to reach the same success as those other children from a different racial groups taught by the same teachers.

As can be observed from the parents' expectations and the schools' perceptions of black children's ability and intelligence, their positions are in direct conflict with each other. Black children are caught between two opposing points of view regarding their ability. On the one hand, parents want their children to achieve high academic qualifications (the A, B and C for GCE A levels, A*, A, B and C grades for GCSEs or level 5, 6 or 7 for SATs) while on the other hand the teachers in the classrooms, who the children spend most of the day with, have the opinion that the black children are only capable of achieving at the most modest examination passes. The black children's belief of themselves tend to be in keeping with the teachers' opinions, as the evidence from educational research shows that black children often live up to the poor and negative stereotypes by their teachers in learning as well as behaviour (Mirza, 2007).

The Every Child Matters from parents' perception

Finally, given that schools have been mandated to deliver the Every Child Matters (ECM) national agenda, it is therefore, important for parents to actively take a lead in ensuring that schools live up to this expectation demanded of them by the government. Thus, parents should monitor the schools to guarantee that the ECM entitlement for their children is being fully provided. In addition, parents can also be active participants in the ECM agenda to give their children the foundation and reinforcement they need to become successful life long learners in the five key areas stated below:

Be Healthy

- Parents should support schools to ensure that their children have knowledge about healthy living: exercise, food choices, drugs awareness, sexual health awareness.
- Provide opportunities within the curriculum and at home to promote healthy lifestyles.
- The school will need to work with parents and external agencies to promote healthy living.

Be Safe

Parents should ensure that:

- Their children feel safe in schools

- Their children are free from bullying – emotional well being
- The children's behaviour is good at schools
- The schools' procedures for promoting safety, managing behaviour and bullying are adequate
- Schools' procedures to protect vulnerable groups of children are effective.

Enjoy and Achieve
Parents have a duty to ensure that their children:
- Attend school regularly and be on time
- Behave appropriately at all times
- Work to the best of their ability – Attainment
- Make good progress year on year
- Improve on their achievement – spiritual, moral, social and cultural development.

Make a Positive Contribution
Parents should encourage their children:
- To take on responsibilities within their schools
- To take on leadership responsibilities within the wider community
- To participate in the decision making process in their schools.

Achieve Economic Well-Being
Parents must work in partnership with the schools so that their children:
- Prepare for the next stage of learning and the world of work – (transition arrangements and careers guidance)
- Have good basic skills (Literacy, Numeracy and ICT)
- Have the opportunities to develop enterprise skills (running projects, handling budgets)
- Have the experience to develop work relate skills – team working, leadership skills, interpersonal skills, presentation skills (Department for Education and Skills, 2003)

Schools

Schools are autonomous institutions; however, this is within the context of being guided by government educational policies and initiatives. As a result, they have to adjust to the copious changes that are 'thrown' at them in the interest, it is claimed, of bringing about improvement in pupils' achievement. Schools are judged on the performance of their pupils in public examinations, with very limited acceptance that the schools being compared have had (and are still having) pupils with different and varying educational exposure and experiences. In other words, schools are being assessed using the same criteria, but some have to cope with a higher proportion of children who are not always well supported and able to benefit from high levels of social capital available to more successful students. The effect of this form of deprivation leads to some schools having a disproportionate number of children with social and learning difficulties/disabilities, and other special educational needs (SEN).

Although schools themselves are now judged by the Office for Standards in Education (Ofsted), they have always made judgment of their pupils from the perception of the class or subject teachers. These judgments made by teachers of their pupils produce a self fulfilling prophecy, which can have a positive or negative effect on pupils' achievement, motivation, self esteem and behaviour. The pupils who have been most affected by negative judgments by teachers are pupils from African and African Caribbean heritages.

Time and time again educational researchers, teachers, psychologists and the media refer to the educational performance of black pupils as the lowest in this country. The examination results are used as a measuring device to label different ethnic groups and black children are expected to under-perform and they do from the prevailing data available. This underachievement, it is said, happens irrespective of their socio economic background.

Less persuasive arguments are offered for this underachievement. It is felt by some that black children do not have the brain power, their language is inferior to the native white pupils, their IQ is low, they are not able to manage academic work to a high standard and so it goes on and on. What is not generally questioned, particular by underperforming schools, is why black children are the most advance academically when they start school and yet they are at the lower end of the educational performance table when they complete their eleven years of compulsory schooling. Gillborn (2008) contends that:

> *'. . . Black children were the highest achieving of all groups in the baseline assessments . . . At age 5 Black children were significantly more likely to reach the required levels: 20 percentage points above the local average. At age 11, however, Black children in the same LEA were performing below the local average. At age 16, the end of compulsory schooling, the inequality was so bad that Black children were the lowest performing of all the principal groups: 21 percentage points below the average.'*
>
> (Gillborn, 2008, p. 99)

Surely, it is clear that something is happening to these children in their school experiences. This 'something' is quite powerful because the black children seem to lose confidence in their ability to achieve well at their school work. So, is it that schools are negatively affecting these children's performances and in particular the teachers they interact with daily in the classroom milieu?

When the volcano eruption struck Montserrat some 20 years ago many families had to leave the island and came to settle in England. The children, when they started schooling in this country, were found to be far more advanced educationally and as a result were performing superior to their white counterparts. For some reason this advantage did not continue and it appears that the Montserratian children fell back in their scholastic achievement and joined the other black children in underperforming in the English school system.

> *'. . . when Montserratian kids were evacuated to the UK after a volcanic eruption in the 1990s ... The news media were full of stories about how these kids from a Caribbean island were ahead of their English classmates . . . But once the kids entered the system all the usual negative stereotypes about Black kids were attached to them. They were treated disgracefully and their attainment fell through the floor.'*
>
> (Gillborn, 2008, p.18)

What makes this underperformance? Is it true that black children lack the intellectual vigour to be just as successful in their school work as the other higher performing groups of children? Surely not! So what causes this underachievement? Is it the home background? Some put the blame squarely and firmly at the home of these children. However, the fault cannot be directed to the children's home alone, certainly other factors must come into it. The home needs to take some of the blame as parents should support their children with their homework and provide other worthwhile learning opportunities to keep the children's mind stimulated. After all, it is the social interactions that take place in the classroom between teachers and pupils, and between pupils themselves that have greater impact on children and their performance. If teachers treat pupils in a way that the pupils feel that they are not capable of achieving as well as their peers, they will achieve very little. Downey and Kelly (1979) contend that:

> *'. . . it is simply not feasible to say that lower working-class or West Indian immigrants perform poorly in school because they come from poor background unless we can confirm that they still perform poorly even when teachers behave towards them in exactly the same way as they behave towards children from higher social classes born of British parents.'*
>
> (Downey and Kelly, 1979 p. 46)

Teachers should treat all children with respect and dignity and remember that it is important to regard them as individuals by having an understanding of their pupils' background and culture. Black children it seems, especially those from African Caribbean backgrounds, lack a sense of identity. The dialect they use and the culture they are brought up in are variants to the majority indigenous culture. When this culture rejects them they do not have anything to turn to like, for example, Chinese and Indian pupils, who have a language and distinctive cultural identities of their own to support their self esteem.

It is also interesting to note, or rather unfortunate to highlight that within the five year period from 1999, when it was reported that black children were the highest achieving at the early years level, to 2004 when the system of assessment on entry to school changed, the performance of black children on these new assessment declined. Gillborn (2008) made some uncomfortable and bold points on this observation. The first is that black children have now become one of the lowest performing groups using the Foundation Stage Profile (FSP) which is based on teachers' judgments. These judgments are established on accumulating observations and the estimation of the teachers' assessment about the whole child at the end of the child's reception year and not when the child first starts school. A second is that the FSP is quite a complex form of assessment where children have to be assessed individually on six areas of learning that are further subdivided into thirteen different scales. Finally, the FSP is a relatively new form of assessment and there is still some uncertainty about its accuracy as teachers have had very limited, inconsistent and varied training for it. This relatively new type of assessment has placed the black children once again in a disadvantaged position, turning their educational success under the former testing regime to an educational failure by a teacher led one. Gillborn (2008) comments that:

> *'In fact, the Education Department was so worried about the quality of the assessment that when the results were first published (in June 2004) the document was entitled 'experimental statistics' and the National Statistics logo was deliberately not used.'*
>
> (Gillborn, (2008, p. 103)

Making judgement of pupils' abilities and their attainment is one of the most important roles teachers have to do in their daily interaction with pupils in the classroom. However, the problem arises when teachers categorise, label their pupils and are insensitive about how their judgments affect pupils' self confidence. These judgments on pupils' abilities, behaviour, attitude and quality of work are expected to be objective; however, there will, to a certain extent, be some element of subjectivity. It is the subjectivity that teachers will have to be carefully about when assessing black children, as there tends to be the opinion that the black children, because of their race are not capable of doing higher order tasks and have flaws in their psychological makeup. This is of grave concern because if teachers expect black children to have difficulty in understanding the lesson tasks and to be disruptive in lessons, there will come a time when the black children will live up to the teachers' expectations by performing poorly and behaving in a manner that is not conducive to learning. Thus, these negative attitudes from the teachers will eventually become a self fulfilling prophecy, just because of the way the teachers treat the black children in the classroom milieu.

Gillborn (2002) draws attention to:

> *'A consistent finding in . . . research on ethnic diversity in education is that Black students are much less likely to be seen as 'able' in comparison with their white peers. However, they are much more likely to be viewed as disruptive, as lacking motivation living in*

> *unsupportive homes. In fact, each of these judgements are stereotypes that are powerfully enacted in the classroom.'*
>
> (Gillborn, 2002, p. 9)

Teachers need to be more aware and conscious about the way in which they interact with their pupils, either verbally, nonverbally or the comments that they write on pupils' work. Every teacher should ensure that they create a classroom environment that is conducive to learning, where they can work with individual pupils in a supportive and effective way in order that the pupils can achieve goals that they have agreed on together. Teachers are powerful due to their position and they can make and develop or break and damaged their pupils' self confidence. The teachers' duty is to acknowledge to their classes that all pupils can and are capable of achieving if they are disciplined and work to their full potential. Their, (the teachers') role is not to make negative judgments on certain pupils, usually black children, by placing them into a category that condemns them to be innately of lower educational potential in comparison with the rest of their peers. Their function is to encourage all children and to have high expectations of them so that they rise to the challenge expected of them. The point being made here is not that all black children can be an Obama, but that, given the right circumstances, they can achieve and do well in their school work. Many people refer to this as 'ability'. Gillborn (2002) asserts that 'ability' is a key factor in shaping pupils' chances of educational success while they are at school. He, Gillborn, goes on to say that:

> *''Ability' is a word that is used frequently but whose precise meaning and significance are rarely discussed in any detail . . . teachers use the word, they tend to exhibit certain assumptions about the nature of ability. Specifically, they tend to assume that ability is a relatively fixed quality, that it is measurable and that it relates to a generalised academic potential.'*
>
> (Gillborn, 2002, p. 3)

Consequently, there is a culture of testing in schools which assumes that ability is fixed from the results of certain tests such as CATs (mentioned earlier). This thinking is damaging as it is perceived that ability cannot change or improve as the children move through their educational career and experience. It is debatable whether or not these tests are culture free or culture fair, especially where the black children are concerned. If teachers take the view that pupils' abilities are fixed, they are doing their pupils a great disservice and injustice by judging them inaccurately. Many black children's education has suffered because of the stance teachers take on how they perform on these tests. These test results are used to predict how pupils will perform in their SATs, GCSE and GCE examinations. What is even more distressing is that teachers use these tests to stifle some children's performance and capability if they perform poorly on them. A further point worth mentioning is that the CATs are taken several years before the children have to prepare and sit their GCSE examinations. At times it is as far back as Year 7, yet these same test results are used to predict the grade the children will be capable of achieving at GCSE four to five years later. There is no consideration that the children may have made progress and therefore exceeded the grade that was predicted from the CATs when they were younger. Teachers rely on these results to set what they consider to be the achievable targets for their pupils. The grade the children are expected to gain seems to be 'cast in stone' and if they gain a higher grade this is seen just as chance or a mere fluke rather than them making improvement, especially if the children happen to be black children.

Tests like the CATs have their benefits for the teachers in giving some guidance and in identifying the area or areas the children might be weak in and need specific and focused intervention. What teachers must not do is to have a preconceived idea that the pupils' abilities are fixed just because the children perform in a particular way at a specific point in time. Teachers are expected to develop and improve their pupils' attainments continuously and not to keep them static or expect them to remain fixed. Educational performance cannot be fixed mainly because learning too, by logical reasoning, cannot itself be fixed. As human beings we learn every day because learning is a continuous process that has no boundaries, just like excellence has no boundary (Davidson, 1998). This can be seen in the way that humankind can create and invent new things to improve our life style, our health, our understanding of the planet on which we live, technology and so forth. Every teacher and every school should bear this in mind. What education needs today are teachers who can inspire and motivate their pupils intellectually.

Conclusion: parental involvement versus parental engagement

Schools now have to make a paradigm shift to engage with parents in a more effective way, so that parents feel competent in playing a positive and direct part in their children's education. The key reason for this is that researchers in education have found that where there is strong evidence of parental engagement in their children's education it has a positive effect in improving their achievement. Harris and Goodall (2007) make a distinction between parental engagement and parental involvement:

> '. . . *what makes a difference to student achievement is not parental involvement in schooling but parental engagement in learning in the home.'*
>
> (Harris and Goodall, 2007, p. 38)

Parental involvement is more about such things as attending Parent Teachers' Meetings, checking and signing homework diaries, serving as a parent governor and being a member of the school's Parent Teacher Association. In other words parental involvement is more about parents' interest in their children's school community and environment. In contrast, parental engagement is about the interaction that takes place in the home where children are given strong support with their school work. This engagement has been shown to have an effective impact on improving educational outcomes for children because these parents impart their knowledge, skills and understanding to help their children succeed with their school learning (Desforges and Abouchaar, 2003).

Despite this however, there are some parents that have had, in their opinion, negative experiences in their own school lives. Other parents feel intimidated by just being in the school environment, because they might feel they do not have the educational experience or the appropriate language to ask the right questions. There are other parents who are not confident because they feel their educational achievements are low and, therefore, lack the skills needed to support their children's learning. These feelings can easily affect how parents interact with their children's schools. Schools should have in place a range of support mechanisms, opportunities and ideas that parents can use to assist with their children's education.

Schools need to think carefully about and find new and more effective ways of engaging parents constructively. To achieve this, schools should concentrate on working with parents in a solid partnership so that the children are given the support they need to develop their learning. The stronger there is parental engagement in children's education the greater will be the impact on the children's performance at schools. Parents, who are not confident or see themselves as not being responsible for having a part in educating their children, must be encouraged to engage more with schools. An example of this is, having Curriculum Showcase Evenings where parents can be shown the type of work and assessment their children do in the various school curriculum subjects. The programme needs to be well managed and organised and should be implemented for all year groups. Parental engagement must be collaborative in order to increase parents' ability to support their children's learning. This can be accomplished by schools creating the right opportunities for parents to develop their skills, understanding and confidence to support their children's learning. For this to be achieved it must be done in a climate of trust with good relationships between parents and schools. However, it must be accepted that if this type of partnership is to be successful it has to be continuous and will require a great deal of tolerance in order to maximise the benefits for the children.

At the beginning of each academic year parents should be provided with a curriculum plan for each subject and the assessment for each unit of work whether it is for half a term, a term or for a specified period of time. In addition to this, schools need to inform parents about the textbooks and other resources that would be used to deliver the curriculum to the pupils.

Parents have a right to be informed about their children's progress during the academic year. Many schools have Academic Review Days for the Autumn and Spring Terms and a formal parent evening/consultation evening in the Summer Term. Targets need to be set for the year and each term. Parents should be informed if their children do not seem to be working well towards achieving those targets set for improvement, so that schools and parents can work together on an appropriate form of intervention strategy to support the children. Schools have to accept that parents should be active participants in their children's learning. Therefore, they must encourage parents to take a strong interest in the children's education, give help and support with homework, other subject projects, assessments and examinations.

This type of communication could extend the relationship and develop a stronger partnership between the home and schools where parents, teachers and pupils have a level of interaction that is vital in contributing to the pupils' educational experiences. Having a three way networking system, will offer the opportunity for schools to have a better understanding of their clientele and their home background and, therefore, dispel any negative biases and judgments that might be perceived by teachers. The main concerns are to concentrate on the children's progress, development (personal, spiritual, moral, social and cultural) and their academic standard.

Schools have an obligation to engage with parents, whatever their race and background. It is also essential that schools work in partnership with parents in an effective way for the benefit of the children they serve. It is important that schools should do more to involve and engage all parents at every single phase of their children's education, so that parents are aware of the educational standards which are expected of their children. Where schools have taken on this function in a genuine dialogue and interaction with parents the majority of children achieve well. Parents are able to see that schools have interest in their children and want them to be confident learners, who will develop into life long learners that can make a positive contribution to the society in which they live. Schools are not just there to show that one group of children is more able than another. They are there to encourage and impart knowledge to all their pupils so that they become well informed and educated young people, with the skills, knowledge and understanding that will equip them with the discipline and confidence to achieve their full potential at the end of their compulsory schooling. More time and effort should be focused on improving learning in the classroom rather than spending unnecessary resources highlighting pupils that are underperforming in the education system. The resources would be better used to provide added funding to schools to improve the quality of education for all their pupils.

Finally, there is no doubt that with all the social and educational research and policies, inequalities continue in the English educational system, especially around those that relate to race, and no lasting solution has been found. This failure of not dealing with the underachievement of the black children has done a tremendous amount of harm and damage to the work of education and has robbed society and prevented talented individuals from making a valuable contribution to the enrichment of their local community, the nation and the wider global community.

Reference

Centre for Social Justice, Breakthrough Britain (2011): *No Excuses: A review of Educational Exclusion, London:* Centre for Social Justice, 2011.

Coard, B. (1971) *How the West Indian Child is Made Educationally Subnormal in the British School System,* London: New Beacon Books.

Davidson, K. (1998) *The Successful Teacher: A concise guide to excellence in the classroom,* London: KAD Publishing.

Davis, Day and Bidmead, (2002) *Working in partnership with parents: the parent adviser model,* London: Harcourt Assessment.

Department for Education and Skills (DfES) 2003 *Every Child Matters,* London: The Stationery Office.

Desforges, C and Abouchaar, A. (2003) *The impact of parental involvement. Parental support and family education on pupil achievement and adjustment: A literature review,* London: Department for Education and Skills.

Downey, M. and Kelly, A.V. (1979) *Theory and Practice of Education: An Introduction 2nd Edition* London: Harper and Row.

Eysenck, H.J. (1971) *Race, Intelligence and Education,* London Temple Smith.

Gillborn, David (2002) *Education and institutional racism: An inaugural professorial lecture,* Institute of Education, University of London.

Gillborn, David (2008) *Racism and Education: Coincidence or Conspiracy?* London: Routledge.

Harris, A. and Goodall, J. (2007) *Engaging parents in raising achievement. Do parents know they matter?* Department for Children, Schools and Families.

Hatcher, R. (2006) *'Social class and Schooling: differentiation or democracy?'* in Mike Cole (ed) *Education, Equality and Human*

Rights: Issues of gender, 'Race', Sexuality, Disability and Social Class 2nd Edition: Oxfordshire: Routledge.

Jensen, A.R. (1969) *How Much Can We Boost I.Q. and Scholastic Achievement?* Harvard Educational Review.

John, G. (2010) *The Case for a Learner's Charter for Schools*: London: New Beacon Book Ltd.

Mirza, H.S. (2007) *'The more things change, the more they stay the same; assessing Black underachievement 35 years on'* in Richardson, B. (ed.) Tell It Like It Is: *How our schools fail Black children,* London: Bookmarks Publications and Trentham Books.

National College for Leadership of Schools and Children's Services (2010) *Leadership for parental engagement*: Nottingham: National College for Leadership of Schools and Children's Services

Obama, Barak (2006) *The Audacity of Hope: Thoughts on Reclaiming the American Dream* London: Canongate.

Pryce, K. (1979) *Endless Pressure. A study of West Indian Life Styles in Bristol*: Harmondsworth: Penguin.

Taylor, M. (1981) *Caught Between: A Review of Research into the Education of Pupils of West Indian Origin Windsor*: The NFER-Nelson Publishing Company Ltd.

Young, L. (2007) *'Accentuating the positive' in Richardson, B. (ed.) Tell It Like It Is: How our schools fail Black children,* London: Bookmarks Publications and Trentham Books.

Chapter 4

The exclusion of black children in the school system

'*Children who are excluded from school tend to become excluded from society*' (Dianne Abbot, 2007)

Introduction

Challenging behaviour is a major obstruction in having an effective classroom environment which is conducive to learning and to raising pupil achievement. Managing behaviour appropriately and in a positive manner can, to a great extent, reduce the stress placed on teaching staff and pupils, consequently making the learning environment enjoyable, safe and secure. Good behaviour is very important for first-rate education as behaviour has a direct influence on learning. Without an orderly atmosphere in the classroom, effective teaching and learning cannot take place. Poor behaviour affects the educational chances of the pupils who are behaving badly and can disrupt the education of the other children. When good behaviour management is emphasized to parents and pupils to be of optimum importance in delivering good lessons, this will encourage positive behaviour responses from pupils and reduce undesirable behaviour that can have a negative impact on teaching and learning. Thus, poor pupil behaviour is identified as a primary factor responsible for causing serious disruptions in classrooms today.

Many teachers find it a strain in schools today to manage behaviour that is challenging, demanding and disruptive as they feel they are unable to control difficult pupil behaviour because children are poorly disciplined. Teaching unions are of the view that physical attacks on teachers are on the increase from the information and complaints they have received from their teacher membership. The government's white paper 'The Importance of Teaching' issued in November, 2010 confirms this and states:

> *'The greatest concern voiced by new teachers and a very common reason experienced teachers cite for leaving the profession is poor pupil behaviour. We know that a minority of pupils can cause serious*

disruption in the classroom. The number of serious physical assaults on teachers has risen. And poorly disciplined children cause misery for other pupils by bullying them and disrupting learning.'

(The Schools White Paper, 2011, p. 9)

Sanctions for misbehaviour

When pupils act inappropriately such as demonstrating challenging, disruptive, difficult, rude and disrespectful behaviour schools have a range of sanctions at their disposal to discipline pupils. Some of the sanctions that schools use are to tell the children to apologise; to reprimand the children; letters sent to the children's parents/carers; inviting the parents/carers into schools to discuss the children's inappropriate behaviour; change the children's class(es) and/or form groups; give the children lines to write (the children have to write over and over again what they should not do); loss of break times or lunchtime privileges; detention (at break time, lunchtime or after school and in some cases on a Saturday morning); internal exclusion (where the children are not educated in the ordinary classrooms for a period of time, but sent to a specific places in schools where they do their work on their own supervised by specified members of staff); exclusion from school for a fixed term; unofficial and illegal exclusions, where parents are told to remove their children voluntarily from schools, or schools just conveniently do not report the exclusions at all; and permanent exclusions for very serious misdemeanours where the children would not be able to return to the schools to continue with their education.

From the information gleaned in the educational literature and research, teacher training programmes do not appear to equip teachers with the necessary skills for the important task of managing behaviour that is inappropriate or challenging in the classroom. This is despite the fact that behaviour is seen in schools as a serious problem as it has a detrimental impact on schools in general and teaching and learning in particular. Furthermore, black pupils as a group have been singled out unfairly for being the most challenging and disruptive in schools. This particular group of children perceived that they are excluded from schools because teachers claim that they have difficulty managing their behaviour than other racial groups. Gillborn and Gipps (1996) confirm this:

> *'black young people are proportionately more likely to be excluded than members of other ethnic groups.'*

and

> *'black over-representation in exclusion is a widespread problem, affecting both primary and secondary schools'*
>
> (Gillborn and Gipps, 1996, p.52)

This over representation of the black children being excluded from school should not be surprising. The image of black children in the eyes of many indigenous English people, and which is still being projected today by the media, is that black children represent troubling (Cole, 1986) and threatening behaviour, and that they need to be firmly controlled (Cole, 2006). They are also often stereotyped as disruptive (Wright, 1992, Connolly, 1995) and violent in behaviour (Gillborn, 1990, Sewell, 1997). These negative perceptions of black children are carried into the classroom by many teachers. Cole and Blair (2006) express their unease about the way that black children are singled out by teachers who have the inclination:

> *'. . . to over-discipline black pupils/students* [which] *has resulted over the years in high percentages of black pupils/students facing exclusion. The long term effects of this can at present only be a matter of speculation. However, it does not require empirical research to conclude that disruption or curtailment of a child's education is likely to have a negative effect on their chances in life.*
>
> (Cole and Blair, 2006, p.78)

Another point worth mentioning is that newly qualified teachers rated their courses 60% good when preparing them to teach children of all abilities, but only 35% felt the courses were good in preparing them to teach black children (Abbott, 2007). This is not a new problem as the issues regarding black children's educational underachievement, the predicament and dilemmas regarding black school children's exclusions were highlighted by Bernard Coard forty years ago. What strikes the authors as disappointing and disrespectful is that teachers, whether experienced or newly qualified, consider that they have to be taught how to teach black children. What teachers need to know is the information regarding black children's culture, custom, traditions and background and be conscious of what they have learned about them when teaching these children. It is not possible to educate young people until one understands the culture of the children that have to be educated. True education embraces people's culture and it is important for teachers to bear this in mind as they interact daily with their pupils in classrooms. Thus, one has to wonder why teachers feel that black children have to be taught in a distinctive way or style compared to other children. Children are children, whether black or white, and should not be made to experience or sense that they are different or treated differently and in a negative way. Children are more astute than we give them credit for in 'picking up' emotionally harmful and disapproving non-verbal communication from their teachers and especially the unjust and unfair treatment the black children receive compared to their peers. This is the experience of black children even today in schools, although educational officials would like to give the impression that racism is unusual in English schools nowadays (DfES, 2006).

Unofficial and illegal exclusions

Schools have become more conscious and aware that information about their exclusion of pupils is being collected and monitored. A number of schools are failing to comply with the legal obligation required for official exclusions. As a result, some headteachers in mainstream education are using unofficial, illegal and unscrupulous practices for excluding children without those exclusions being formally recorded and therefore they would not be reported to the Department of Education (Gillborn and Gipps, 1996, DfES, 2006, Abbott, 2007, Centre for Social Justice, 2011). There are a variety of ways in which schools use unofficial and illegal exclusions. There are repeated fixed term exclusions as an alternative to official permanent exclusions; pupils are excluded on a fixed term basis where their absences are not recorded as official exclusion and as a result does not count against the school's target; pupils may be placed on a part time timetable who schools feel are at risk of exclusion and as an alternative to exclusion the children will spend some of the school week out of schools accessing limited education; sending the children home to 'cool off' rather than using fixed term exclusion as required; transferring pupils to alternative educational provisions without officially excluding them; and dual registration where pupils are registered at both schools and Pupil Referral Units or special schools on a temporary basis, but it could also be extended for an indefinite period of time (Centre for Social Justice, 2011). As a result, the official recorded numbers of exclusions may well be underestimated if parents are persuaded to remove their children from schools voluntarily or some of the ways mention above rather than have the schools exclude the children. Furthermore, parents need to know about these unscrupulous arrangements that schools will use to safeguard against having high official exclusion rates. They must be very careful about what they agree to with the schools in respect of their children's future educational provision if the children can no longer be educated full time in schools.

Using these unofficial and illegal methods of exclusion rob children of their education as they affect the educational provisions that should be provided for them. Often times these pupils' learning is not carefully monitored, adequately structured, tailored to their abilities or aptitudes, and as a result, their educational needs are not met. These practices of unofficial and illegal exclusions bring disengagement from education by the pupils, which in turn causes educational failure. The school system has failed a high number of black children by using some of the illegal approaches mentioned above and also through racism, low teacher expectations, negative stereotyping and lack of challenging school work. Many schools are failing to provide an acceptable quality of pastoral care and education for their pupils. Schools do not seem to understand that changing behaviour which is unacceptable is part of educating the children. John (2011) concurs with this view:

> *'. . . while no child has the right to obstruct the learning of others . . . children do not forfeit their educational entitlement on account of their poor self management and discipline. Moreover, it is as much the purpose of schooling to support them in unlearning inappropriate behaviours and acquiring the values, insight and social skills that make them fit for living in civil society . . .'*
>
> (John, 2011, p. 8)

It appears that the best way schools feel that they can cope with disruptive and difficult pupil behaviour is to exclude the children both officially and unscrupulously to cover up the schools' failure.

The rate of exclusions for black children has caused disquiet over the way that schools manage their behaviour. Schools need to pay attention to positive discipline rather than making themselves unaccountable for their pupils' challenging, disruptive, and disrespectful behaviour toward school staff and the pupils' peers. Not only do schools want to distance themselves from being held accountable for unacceptable behaviour, but it is felt that schools exclude pupils so that their position in the schools' league tables will be viewed in a more favourable position and higher up on the list of pupil achievement ranking. This is achieved, by ensuring that some of the pupils that schools think will not do well in their external examinations in Year 11 are excluded at a particular time. This type of exclusion takes place just after Christmas and therefore these pupils are not listed on the schools' Form 7 returns to the Department of Education. These Form 7s must be completed and sent back in January each year and include the total number of pupils in each year group and the total number on the school's roll overall. The situation is quite disturbing because there is no evidence to show the disparity between the ways that some children are excluded permanently for the same or similar offences while others are given fixed term exclusions or lesser sanctions for poor and inappropriate behaviour. This again does not accord with the Every Child Matters agenda. It is important that schools show consistency in the way they deal with their pupils in respect of behaviour and discipline. However, this is not always the case as some children are treated differently for committing the same offence done by other children. Some are given leniency, while others are punished severely for the same difficult behaviour. Disparity like this does go on in schools and disproportionate amounts of black children have been most affected by this unequal and unfair treatment.

Discrimination and stereotyping

Furthermore, educational research has established that black children are placed in the lower streams at schools not because of low ability, but because of their alleged bad behaviour as the black children tend to be punished far more harshly and praised less than their white peers.

> *'Whilst many teachers . . . believed setting to be based solely on ability, data indicated that African Caribbean pupils were sometimes relegated to lower sets due to their behaviour, rather than their ability.'*
>
> (Tikly et al, in DfES, 2006 p. 22)

The DfES (2006) has the same belief:

> *'This discriminatory behaviour in schools is not said merely to manifest itself at the point of exclusion. Reference is made to a wealth of qualitative evidence which suggest: that Black pupils are disciplined more frequently, more harshly and for less serious misbehaviour than other pupils: that they are less likely to be praised than other pupils; that this differential treatment by school staff can be observed very early on in a child's education; and that such differential approach is likely to be unwitting on the part of teachers.'*
>
> (DfES, 2006, p.11)

This differential treatment by teachers has also been commented on by Gizzard et al., 1988; Mortimore et al. al., 1988; Gill born, 1990; Wright, 1992; Connolly, 1995 and Cole and Blair, 2006. These educationalists feel that the disproportionate amount of unfair reprimands and condemnation used as disciplinary actions against black children have adversely affected these children's educational performance and resulted in the black children having to leave their schools and be educated in alternative educational institutions such as pupil referral and support units for children with educational and behaviour difficulties.

Two key observations need to be drawn out here. Firstly, the low expectations and negative attitude demonstrated toward the black children ultimately lead to the road of expulsion from schools for poor behaviour. School staff and in particular teachers fail to recognize that low expectations and the lack of challenging academic work make the black children frustrated and become vulnerable. The consequence of this harmful stance by the adults in the school will help to make the black children's motivation wane and the best way these children feel they can cope in such an unsupportive climate is to vent their feelings of resentment by exhibiting inappropriate behaviour. Secondly, to make the situation even more worse for the black children, their behaviour is then condemned as undesirable and the blame is placed on them as they are judged to be in a specific special educational needs category. This special educational classification is recognized in the educational sphere as black children having social, emotional and behavioural difficulties (SEBD). Once identified as such the stigma will remain with these black children for the rest of their entire school career. As a result of this, black children and black boys in particular seem to disengage themselves from the school system and develop an anti-academic attitude because of the negative expectations and hostility shown to them by some teachers. However, black children are more ready to accept criticisms of their behaviour. They find it far easier for it to be said that they have behavioural difficulties rather than to be labelled as having, for example, poor literacy skills and/or poor academic performance. In others words they resent the notion that they could be having learning difficulties. The report from the Centre for Social Justice (2011) supports this stance:

> *'Many* [children] *display challenging behaviour to hide the fact that they cannot read, write or keep up . . . They may develop strategies to get out of learning because they are embarrassed that they can't do it. It's not a behaviour problem to start with . . .'*
>
> (Centre for Social Justice, 2011, pp 20 and 21)

From the way black children are treated they become discouraged and disillusioned. This leads to frustration on their part, a feeling of hopelessness with the negative label assigned to them and so they become aggressive, disengaged and develop a street like manner as a way of coping. As a result, these black children think they have gained respect from their teachers and peers. However, in reality it is the fear of these children's attitude and behaviour towards teachers and their peers that will lead them to think incorrectly that they have achieved respect. Eventually, these black children are excluded for their unruly behaviour and in due course this will reinforce the link between school exclusion and social exclusion.

The impact of exclusion for children and parents

Exclusion from school, be it fixed term or permanent, has caused a tremendous amount of ill feelings between parents and schools and most particular black parents. This can be a worrying time for pupils and their families as exclusion denies pupils of the right to learning from an educational point of view. The exclusion of black children have and continues to cause serious concerns as they are three times more likely to be permanently excluded from school than a white pupil. Black children from an African Caribbean heritage are six times more likely to be excluded for inappropriate behaviour than their white counterparts (Gillborn and Gipps, 1996). In addition to this, black children are considered not only to be ill disciplined, but to have some learning deficiencies and to be unteachable. What is frightening is that black children will internalise these negativities and eventually fulfil the negative stereotype by behaving and acting out how they are perceived by staff, both teaching and non-teaching, in schools.

A high number of pupils are excluded each year from schools and the highest it has peaked for permanent exclusion is around 12,300 in 1997/1998. The previous Labour Government's objective was to reduce the number of permanent exclusions. This was achieved as the published figures for 2009/2010 show that there was a decline and the estimated number for permanent exclusion was 5,740. For fixed term exclusions the figure fell to their lowest since 2003/2004, that is, to 331,380 in 2009/2010. The Priority Review on the exclusion of black pupils by the Department for Education and Skills in 2006 found that 1,000 black pupils were permanently excluded from school each year and 30,000 received temporary exclusions. When permanent exclusion is given it is the school confirming that the child will not be educated within its community anymore and that for the child to remain in the school it would have a disadvantageous effect on other pupils as well as the child himself. That is to say, allowing the child to remain in the school would seriously hamper the education and the welfare of the child and other pupils in the school as he has to interact with them daily within the school community and the learning environment of the classroom. The worry that the school has is that other children will measure their behaviour with the misbehaving child's behaviour and judge how far they can go in behaving in a disruptive manner before they are punished. In other words, the other children will tend to use the recalcitrant child's behaviour as a benchmark to establish how far they can go with their misbehaviour before sanctions are applied, either by a temporary exclusion or a permanent one. Children are smart, they know how to 'wind' teachers up and they know the limit they can go to without getting into serious trouble at school. While pupils are accountable for their misbehaviour, it is also reasonable to argue that 'copycat' misbehaviour in the classroom is not purely the result of some pupils leading in this misbehaviour. The behaviour copied could have more to do with the fact that the teacher who is ultimately responsible for behaviour in the classroom may have been negligent in not taking decisive action when the initial disruption occurred. This would have stopped the inappropriate behaviour straightaway before it had time to adversely affect learning in the classroom.

When children are excluded from school, this can affect the children's learning adversely because of the disruption to the children's education due to them being absent from school. If the exclusion is for a few days no damage as such is done, but if it goes on for a long period of time or indefinitely the absence from school will affect the children's education and eventually impede their learning. Attendance at school has a significant impact on children's academic performance. If children's attendance is poor or erratic this will also have a fundamental effect on how well the children achieve. When children are excluded from school they are denied the benefit of having their learning directly from the teachers in the classrooms. Schools are required to provide school work for pupils who have been excluded. The work given should be the same type and quality that the pupils would have received if they were at school albeit that the children would not have their teachers teaching them first hand. However, in reality, some schools rarely put themselves out of the way to provide suitable school work for pupils on suspension. Some of the work given by schools is just to keep the children occupied and not always sufficiently academically challenging for the children's age and ability. It is true, the work that can be provided by schools when the children are on suspension can never be substituted for the work the children would have received in the ordinary classroom as the teachers are not able to teach and explain to the children face to face while they are on exclusion from school. As a result, the work given has to be work that the children can cope with adequately and independently without the guidance and support they would receive when they are in the classroom from the teachers directly. Therefore, the exclusion of pupils, be it fixed term or permanent, should be used very cautiously by schools.

The black children's social class and they being identified as having behavioural problem, associated with special educational needs, are being blamed for the high rate of their exclusions from schools. It is felt that the black children's attitude is inappropriate for learning and they are unable to demonstrate acceptable behaviour in the classroom milieu that is beneficial in enabling them to gain from the good education offered by teachers. Consequently, the black children and not the adults in the school are being made totally culpable for their behaviour and the constant disruption in the learning environment not only for themselves, but also for the other twenty odd pupils in the classroom. Poor behaviour and low academic achievements are considered by schools to go hand in hand thereby bringing about the self-fulfilling prophecy that black children underachieve (and they do). As a result this will affect the schools' ranking in the examination performance league tables published each year by the central government's education department. With respect to the statistical record and evidence gathered by the then Department for Education and Skills on exclusion, it appears that black children are said to be the worse behaved and perceived to be a greater threat and challenge to teachers and schools in general than pupils from other racial groups. This so called defiant posture, by the black children, seems to suggest that the black pupils are vulnerable to influences outside of schools that make them behave in this negative and aggressive manner, which in turn will adversely impede their school work. Nothing is mentioned about the way in which the black children are treated and made to feel by teachers and school support staff within the education community. Whether it is institutional racism or not, the issue of the high rate of black children's exclusion from schools must be addressed as schools will continue to fail generations after generations of black children because they do not want to admit that there are prejudices and racism towards these children of colour whether conscious or unconscious within the school system.

Exclusions will have a detrimental effect on the education of children that have been expelled from school systematically on a fixed term basis or permanently. Very few permanently excluded pupils achieve the necessary 5 A* – C grades and the majority of them fail to achieve any qualifications whatsoever at aged sixteen. As more African Caribbean pupils are excluded from school each year than any other racial group their education is hindered more severely. A disproportionate amount of them are no longer in mainstream school education and as a result unable to access mainstream curriculum work. Many of these excluded pupils feel inadequate because their education has been interrupted for a period, some periods longer than others, and the quality education they then received in alternative provision such as pupil referral units and support units, have had disappointing results for these pupils. From the anecdotal evidence available, the education that excluded pupils receive is substandard and is associated with negative outcomes. This is because being excluded from school affects excluded pupils' life chances as they do not receive the necessary quality education that would suitably prepared them for the conventional examinations at age sixteen years. Moreover, the educational disadvantage suffered by pupils who have been excluded is about the lack of provision offered to them to continue their education while they are excluded from school. They, the excluded pupils, tend to waste time just wondering aimlessly and at times find themselves being enticed into behaviour that will only lead them into criminality (John, 2006).

Not only does exclusion have detrimental consequences on the children and their education, but it also has grave implications for society as a whole. Children, who become disengaged from the education process, tend to become society's outcasts. Although this statement may appear harsh, nonetheless, it is the reality. Research regarding exclusions has shown that there is a strong correlation between pupils who have been excluded from school and youth crime. In other words, a higher percentage of pupils who have been expelled from school end up committing more crimes than those who have remained in mainstream education; in fact they are more than twice likely to commit a crime than pupils who have not been excluded (Gillborn, 2008). In addition to this, excluded young people feel socially ostracised by the mere fact that they cannot be educated in the same environment as their friends albeit that they presented challenging and disruptive behaviour. John (2006) confirms these views:

> *'Labelling and stigmatization follow excluded pupils, black males especially, in much the same way as custodial sentence. In this sense the experience of young black males excluded from school, sits along a spectrum with that of black males offenders seeking to reintegrate within society and access employment. Social exclusion becomes their reality, not least because of the assumptions and stereotypical expectations the society applies to them.'*
>
> (John, 2006, p. 231)

These excluded pupils' feeling of wanting to belong and be accepted is very strong. However, being excluded makes them feel rejected, incompetent and deficient compared with their peers. The unfortunate riots that took place over many of England's inner cities in Summer, 2011 (which was mentioned in another chapter) shows that English society is not fully focused on its young people, whether they are black, white or Asians. However, to blame the riots on black culture, black behaviour, black attitude and black language will be to misinterpret the serious underlining causes for what took place. The point is that society, and schools must take some of the blame, for having done something detrimental to our young people whether they are black or white, to make them feel alienated from mainstream society. There can be no excuse for the intense destruction which unfolded in our towns and cities, but neither can it be divorced from the lack of self-worth of those mainly young people created by the alienation they experienced from society. It is cruel and insensitive to blame one race for such a total collapse in rational behaviour in a civilised society. If these strong and wrong negative feelings are permeated in the mind-set of the educated indigenous English what hope is there for the black children seated at the feet of their teacher or teachers who have very little, if any respect for them firstly as a learner and secondly and most importantly as a human being with feelings and emotions just like any other race of children. With this attitude what chance does the black children have when they are perceived to be of no value or asset to the schools they are attending and where they should be educated. Instead, the black children are being cast out and rejected on the grounds that their behaviour is alien to the school culture which in the first place should have been responsible for their spiritual, moral, social and cultural development. Thus, it is not the black children that are at variance with the schools, but it is the schools that are unwilling to take on their responsibility to educate all their children to a good standard, which includes good behaviour.

Studies regarding the critical position of black pupils' exclusion have been going on for some decades now and show that these pupils' high level of exclusion is a major concern especially in the black community. A significant disquiet is that society unjustly and unfairly treats blacks as a group of underclass people. This unfortunate attitude toward black people being labelled as underclass is racist in its meaning. The concept of underclass clearly suggests that they are unwanted, unwelcome and undesirable. This is not the response that is needed for a problem that is about social and economic injustices. The high level of black pupils' exclusions is indeed a national educational problem, which should not have a place in the education system. Education in its truest sense is about changing behaviour. Therefore, exclusion logically cannot play any effective part or role in positively modifying pupils' behaviour. Exclusion defeats the purpose of what schools are all about which is to shape and build pupils for their role in society. Thus, exclusion cannot do this. Exclusion should not be part of education as it is about taking away education from the children and denying them the opportunities to build their skills, knowledge and understanding in preparation for their adult life. Children, whether black or white, in fact no matter what ethnicity or race they come from, they should not be excluded from school for behaviour except where that behaviour is to do with criminality, danger to life or drugs. Exclusion does not sit comfortably with the concept of education. Schools must not forget that they are there to educate the children they serve and the onus is on them to support all children's learning, together with their social, moral, emotional, ethical, spiritual and cultural development. John (2010) makes it plain that if schools truly profess to be working in the interest of their pupils they would work in a balanced partnership with parents. They would ensure that the pupils are ably supported rather than being in a relationship where the teachers set the agendas for meetings, have the knowledge and insight into the schools' policies and procedures, but where parents do not have such information at their disposal. This is not really a partnership as teachers and parents are not on the same level playing field. Schools need to change their stance and work in a genuine partnership with parents, so that parents have a strong impact on the quality of their children's performance, both academically and socially (John, 2010).

Parents, on the whole, want their children to be well rounded individuals. It is not easy for them to have children whose behaviour is a serious cause for concern. Excluding children from school is very damaging and society will pay the cost at some stage. Schools must take more responsibility and accept that children have the right to be educated in the school environment. To permanently exclude children automatically denies them the right to having a good education.

Proposed changes to appeal against exclusion

Being permanently excluded from school is the most severe sanction available to headteachers when pupils' misbehaviour is judged to become intolerable to the school staff. A permanent exclusion is not a punishment that headteachers would usually (it is hoped) take lightly as they will have specified their reason for making such a harsh decision based on certain evidence that can be proven. For instance, the headteacher would have considered whether, there has been a serious breach of the school's discipline policy by the child, and/or a range of alternative strategies have been tried over a period of time with the child and they have not been successful in bringing about the necessary change in the child's behaviour for the child to remain in the school community. If this is the state of affairs the child would not be allowed to return to the school. The only way that the child could be returned is if the parents/carers appealed and the disciplinary committee of the school's board of governors or an Independent Appeal Panel decided to overturn the headteacher's decision to permanently exclude the child. This would be a very sensitive and controversial decision, which would only take place after carefully reviewing the case and studying the papers presented by the school and the arguments put forward by the child's parents and/or representative.

However, this position has been changed by the Education Act 2011, which has made it more difficult for a permanently excluded child to be reinstated back into school. Therefore, the Independent Appeal Panel will no longer be in existence. Instead, there will be an exclusion review panel, which will re-examine decisions on school exclusions. It will also have the power to recommend that a school should reconsider its decision. This will only happen if the review panel feels that the decision of the governing body was made in error. Should this be the case the review panel can then direct the responsible body to quash the decision of the headteacher and ask the responsible body to reconsider the decision to exclude the pupil (Centre for Social Justice, 2011and Education Act 2011). Therefore, the ultimate power of the headteacher to exclude a child permanently is now strengthened significantly. Thus, the excluded child has less chance of being reinstated under the new Education Act 2011. This has delivered the intention of the government as stated in 'The Importance of Teaching', The Schools White Paper, 2010:

> *'Change the current system of independent appeals panels for exclusions, so that they take less time and headteachers no longer have to worry that a pupil will be reinstated when the young person concerned has committed a serious offence.'*
>
> (Executive Summary, The Schools White Paper, 2011, p.9)

Other alternative arrangements will have to be made by the local authority for children to be educated when they have been permanently excluded. It must be made clear that when children are permanently excluded, it is the local authority's legal responsibility for arranging suitable full time education for those children from the sixth day of their permanent exclusion. Sadly to say that a study conducted by Ofsted found that almost half of the local authorities did not meet this important legal obligation (Centre for Social Justice, 2011).

The coalition government wants to change this arrangement and make schools retain responsibility for their pupils, the quality of their education and the outcomes achieved following permanent exclusion. In addition, schools will also be made responsible for the alternative education provision of the pupils they exclude. Added to this, it is proposed that the excluded children's examination results will appear in the examination league table results of the schools that excluded them in the first place. However, at present, if the excluded children are fortunate they may be able to be transferred to other schools and given a fresh start or take part in what is termed a 'managed move'. This is where the children's schools enter into agreements with each other to exchange amongst themselves poorly behaved pupils. Sometimes a managed move takes place before exclusion, without there being an agreed swap with other pupils, where it is felt by schools that a change would be best for those children rather than go through the traumatic and time consuming route of a permanent exclusion process. The reason for this is that when children are permanently excluded it is far more difficult to arrange a transfer to other maintain schools and this could take many months, if at all. However, a substantial number of excluded pupils find themselves in pupil referral units, where the chances for them to return back to a mainstream school education are very unlikely and rare indeed. In fact, the majority of pupils, especially secondary aged pupils, who have been permanently excluded never return to mainstream education and as a result, it can have a damaging effect on the children's educational progress, prospects and future. This is the key reason why permanent exclusions should only be used as a last resort and for extremely serious misconduct or very dangerous behaviour (Gillborn and Gipps, 1996, DfES, 2006). Furthermore, with respect to permanent exclusion, the schools have actually failed the children. The schools are saying that they are unable to cope or have no solution to help solve those particular children's challenging or disruptive behaviour. However, very few people look at the issue of exclusion in that manner as schools like to blame the homes of the children solely and take no responsibility whatsoever themselves for their pupils' unruly behaviour.

Parental rights and responsibilities

Parents have certain rights and responsibilities. As mentioned above, parents do have the right to appeal against the suspension of their children from schools if they disagree with the exclusion and feel that it is too harsh a punishment for whatever misdemeanour their children may have committed.

They have the right to write to the school governors setting out the reason or reasons why they want to appeal against the exclusion. Parents may appeal if they think that: i) their children were provoked; ii) their children did not do what they have been accused of by the schools; iii) there is no real evidence that their children broke the rules alleged; iv) the breaches their children have been accused of are not serious enough to justify exclusion; and v) their children have been singled out for punishment unfairly. Most times the exclusion period has been served before the appeal has been heard, if it is a fixed term exclusion. This has now changed and appeals have to be heard within a specified time period. However, if the appeal is successful for the parents the papers regarding the suspension should be removed from the pupils' file and the school should ensure that this is done.

What should parents and schools do to avoid exclusion?

Schools and parents can avoid the devastating situation facing black children being excluded, both separately and collectively. It is important for schools to improve the relationship with parents to ensure that they are working in partnership for the benefit of the children. In addition to this, schools need to ensure that practical classroom strategies are in place to tackle low-level disruptions. Teachers must make the effort to create engaging and well structured lessons that cater for all the ability range, improve pupil concentration and motivation thereby limiting poor and unacceptable behaviour.

With regards to the parents, they must instil in their children from a young age, before the children go to school, what is acceptable behaviour and continue to reinforce this as the children go on to schools and move through the school system. Parents need to be up front by recognising their children's challenging and disruptive behaviour; demonstrating to their children the value they place on education; and create a disciplined environment at home that is supportive to the schools' ethos and culture of learning. The Centre for Social Justice (2011) is of the opinion that:

> '*The underlying causes of challenging behaviour and disengagement from education are often rooted in the family environment. There are risk factors that exist in the lives of many pupils which appear to*

> *impact predominantly on their cognitive development, behaviour, emotional and social development, and on their mental health, well-being and educational attainment. It is critically important to look behind their behaviour and focus on their unmet needs.'*
>
> (Centre for Social Justice, 2011, p.10)

Before children are permanently excluded parents should have been informed by the schools about their concerns regarding the children's behaviour. Many parents, including black parents, find it hard to take criticisms of their children's behaviour as they are aware that pupils' behaviour will affect their learning and in particularly reflect badly on the quality of the parents' own parenting skills. Parents usually listen to what their children have to say and will believe the children. This is the case particularly with regards to black children as one must remember that the children's parents experienced the same or similar unfair treatment from their teachers while they too were at school here in England. If parents receive complaints about their children no matter how simple, it would be in their interest not only to listen to the children's views, but make an appointment to see the member of staff who wrote the letter and/or made the complaint as soon as possible. If it is not possible for them to see that member of staff, they should ask to see someone at the school where they can discuss the matter. Parents of secondary aged pupils may ask to see their children's form tutors or year/house head as they have the responsibility for pastoral care in schools. This will signal to schools that parents are interested in their children and want to know about their children's general attitude and behaviour. After the parents have heard the two sides of the story the parents can make up their minds what and who to believe. As parents, they may not agree with the way their children have been treated regarding complaints. However, it is the parents' duty to talk to the children and show them how they should have acted, so that the matter would not have deteriorated to such an extent where their parents had to be informed about those incidents. This would demonstrate to the children how important good behaviour is and that as parents they are not expecting letters from the school that report on their unruly or disrespectful behaviour. Where concerns about behaviour are not followed up straightaway or as early as possible there is the chance that things might become worse and deteriorate further, then the children will be the ones that will be affected and suffer in the long run.

There is also failure on the part of the parents and the community with respect to children who display challenging behaviour. The reason for this statement is that parents and the community have also been unsuccessful, in many cases, in providing black children with the strategy to cope adequately with racism and negative stereotyping in schools particularly, and the media and society in general. As a result, these black children have no confidence in themselves, which is reflected in their behaviour and, therefore, they tend to find themselves being excluded from school. Black children who are able to cope with racism and prejudice are given strong support from their parents and their community. Confident children are less vulnerable to exclusion because they know what acceptable behaviour is and will behave and conduct themselves appropriately in the classroom and around the school.

Finding strategies to limit exclusion

It does not matter whether black children are of primary or secondary school age as the inequality, with respect to exclusions of them, is prevalent from the evidence of qualitative research and statistical information on school exclusions. Various reasons are given for children being excluded from schools. The disobedience could take many forms such as insolent, verbal abusive to a teacher, broken school rules, fighting, playing truant from school, bullying and disrupting learning in classrooms. Schools need to be more proactive in the way they monitor their pupils' behaviour carefully, especially those who have shown challenging behaviour over a period of time, so that appropriate intervention strategies can be in place to bring about a modification of unsuitable behaviour. Schools can and some do provide support services such as a mentoring programme, a role modelling and motivational scheme and, refining and improving discipline methods and techniques within their own extra curriculum programmes. These strategies have to be monitored and evaluated at intervals so that the strengths and weaknesses are known and where necessary adjustments or changes can be made for the benefit of the children. There is a need for schools to use both in school and out of school personnel to ensure that children are given all possible guidance to succeed in changing their undesirable conduct. Having both internal and external support arrangements can be very valuable in offering options, especially from the children's perspectives. Firstly, the internal option would be from the people who interact with the children each day in schools and secondly, the external option would be the provision of objective advice from those professionals or agencies that are not familiar with the children's behaviour. John (2006), however, has questioned the success rate of what he calls 'peripheral provision' as he feels that it:

> '. . . *will not change things for black pupils generally. Those who have been subjected to negative prejudice, destructive stereotyping and low expectations in the past will continue to suffer unless there are fundamental changes in schooling, a refocusing on children's education rights and unless there is halt to the present trend by government to make excluding pupils easier than keeping them in mainstream.'*
>
> (John, 2006, p. 238)

This scepticism is not unfounded according to John (2006) as there is no doubt that schools have produced casualties and are still producing casualties, and have failed to work collaboratively and effectively with parents. It is of paramount importance that schools should engage with parents for the benefit of the children as many pupils may feel alienated and disaffected from what they have experienced in schools. Of course, parents should be involved at an early stage and informed about the support the school will be giving to their children. However, schools are guilty as they put parents in situations where they have limited information. Parents are continually placed at a disadvantage as they are denied the opportunity of gaining an understanding of schools' complex processes and they also have difficulty trying to unravel and make sense of the exclusion and appeal procedures that schools are knowledgeable about. There is no reason for schools to wait until behaviour is serious and completely out of control before parents are invited to work with the schools to bring about the desired behaviour that will allow children to continue with their education in schools. With the schools and the parents working together for the benefit of the children, there will be, in the majority of cases, the necessary positive changes to the undisciplined behaviour of those children for them to remain in the mainstream school community.

John (2006) further elaborates that the restorative justice model being advocated by the Youth Justice Board should not just be used in the work of organisations which support young people in the community, but it should also be used in schools as it is based on:

> ' . . . *the clear assumption that it must be possible to engage young people in looking at their behaviour and aspect of their relationships*

> *which cause offence, allowing for the fact that they, too, might be experiencing the conduct of others around them, and particularly towards them, as equally problematic.'*
>
> (John, 2006, p.233)

The Centre for Social Justice (2011) comments on the effectiveness that the restorative justice approach can have in schools from the findings of the research undertaken by the Youth Justice Board:

> *'Restorative approaches provide an effective means of challenging and changing the behaviour of pupils, resolving conflict and reducing classroom and fixed-term exclusions, as demonstrated by research. Furthermore, young people, staff and parents report high levels of satisfaction with restorative approaches and that young people are thoroughly challenged on their behaviour.'*
>
> (Centre for Social Justice, 2011, p. 18)

It is important that pupils must take ownership for their own behaviour as they are fully aware of what is acceptable and unacceptable behaviour whether in schools or out of schools. Furthermore, it is their responsibility, that is, the pupils, to explain or to share, with the appropriate person or persons, anything that might be affecting them which may bring about unreasonable conduct from them in schools. It could be that the children feel less positive about themselves, because of a situation not necessarily to be found in schools, but could be at home or in the community, which has had a severe impact on them so that they fail to focus on their learning in the classroom. This is also a very important reason why parents should be involved at an early stage before the children's behaviour becomes a cause for grave concern. Black children too can feel that they have been treated unfairly and unjustly when they see that they are punished more severely for the same misbehaviour in contrast to their white counterparts.

Schools should make every effort to encourage parents to take a more active role in their children's education, not just academically, but also socially, culturally, morally, ethically and spiritually. Schooling is a significant stage in young people's lives. This is why it is essential to have schools and parents working in harmony so that the children can gain the very best from their educational experience. For this reason schools need to treat parents as genuine equal partners in their pupils' education. John (2010) supports this view:

> *'. . . schools should . . . be working in the interests of children and in partnership with parents to support children's learning and social, moral, emotional, spiritual and cultural development. Sadly, however, 'partnership' is often interpreted to mean parents working to an agenda set by the school and with methods and arrangements that best suit the school including the timing of meetings with the school. Partnership is seldom the two way process the term implies.'*
>
> (John, 2010, p.22)

Not having this constructive involvement between parents and schools will bring about more failures to be added to the exclusion statistics. As a result, it is imperative that parents and schools foster a good working relationship to support the children, and in particular children whose behaviour need to be changed so that they can benefit from their schooling. After all, changing negative pupil behaviour is an important part of education and schools must accept this and take responsibility for this aspect of children's development also. Just excluding children for poor behaviour can be interpreted as schools saying they do not want anything to do with those children and that they are not committed to the Every Child Matters agenda.

Exclusion and racism

Exclusion for poor behaviour is usually a signal that the children are crying out for help. For schools and some educationalists to claim that it is the 'out of school factors' which schools have no control over, such as street culture, that have a strong bearing on black children's alleged deprived conduct could be construed as racist. Schools forget that children spend most of their time during the course of the week day at school, so schools are in the position to work on pupils whose behaviour are confrontational and difficult to handle. If schools continue to exclude black pupils at a higher rate than they do other races schools could be in breach of their legal duties with respect to the Race Relations Act, 2000 as racial discrimination is unlawful (Abbott, 2007). The argument that intentional racism may be related to the historical and social conditioning that involve having negative impressions of black people as aggressive, threatening and violent are still evident today in schools. This state of mind that encourages school staff to expect black pupils to be the worse behaved and be perceived as difficult is not farfetched. Whiteley (1969) although writing over forty years ago echoes the harmful sentiments, the discouraging feelings and pessimistic attitude of the indigenous population that black people are intellectually inferior and aggressive.

> '. . . *they* (West Indian children) *are generally intellectually slower than their white classmates and . . . So there arises among them that peculiar combination of slow wittedness with the bounce of their high vitality which teachers find hard to cope with. And when thwarted they are said to become sullen or aggressive and will shout the teacher down if he lets them.'* (Whiteley, 1969, p. 87)

What is disturbing is that these same feelings and views are still prevalent and a current perception that is held in our society today. The media must share some of the guilt and blame as it is portrayed by them that black children are greatly influenced by street culture than other races of young people. It is also felt that their aggressive behaviour is a reflection of how people behave in their culture. As a result of this belief, teachers, it is claimed, find the black children's behaviour more difficult and rebellious than other races of children to cope with in classrooms and in the school system.

In addition to this, there is the view that schools need to concentrate on 'in school factors' as there is evidence from qualitative research in education that black pupils are excluded for certain misbehaviour but would not have been excluded if they were carried out by white pupils if they had behaved in exactly the same way (Gillborn and Gipps, 1996 and Majors, 2001). The tolerance extended to the indigenous children regarding recalcitrant behaviour is not experienced by the black children from their teachers. John (2006) is of the opinion that staff development and training are of paramount importance and would need to be undertaken in relation to events that could trigger exclusions if schools are to respond appropriately to the differential treatment metered out to black pupils.

Conclusion: exclusion defeats the principle of education

Ofsted's advice is that exclusions in excess of a few days are counterproductive. Permanent exclusion seems to be used by many schools as a deterrent to other pupils and as a warning about poor behaviour, rather than related to the seriousness of the misdemeanour or offence. Where children are behaving badly schools must ensure that they have the essential resources to cater for the pupils' individual academic and social needs. This is imperative as:

> *'Different individuals or groups of children often require different approaches to meeting their individual educational need in order to deliver their education entitlement as part of integrated maintain schooling.'*
>
> (John, 2006, p. 233)

A warning comes from John (2006) that he is not talking about pupils who have learning and behavioural difficulties as these children he is referring to are not in the category of having special educational needs relating to their learning, nor should these children be labelled and stigmatised. What is needed for the children who have individual educational needs are programmes to help them change or modify that behaviour which will impede their learning or affect the learning of the other children in their classroom and school environment. These children need to be encouraged to examine and scrutinize their own behaviour by consciously engaging them to look at: how they behave; their attitude towards others in the school community; their relationships; and their interpersonal skills. For these programmes to be successful schools must work with parents in a constructive manner for the benefit of these children. At present, black children are not served well by the English education system. In fact, they are let down by the inadequacies of the education service provided to them in the current structure.

Teachers need to give to their pupils more praise and encouragement and work hard at identifying when pupils behaving and working well. It is the teachers' task to give pupils something to reignite their interest in schools and their community by acting positively towards them. Positivity is infectious and it is the teachers' role to promote it, spread it amongst the pupils and make every effort for it to remain within the learning environment of classrooms. In order to achieve this, teachers must develop positive relationships in the classroom amongst the pupils, their classmates and teachers themselves. Teachers need to keep in mind the entitlement of all learning groups as well as the groups' aspirations, to ensure new opportunities are taken and which will work to the pupils' advantage.

Schools should not want to exclude their pupils for inappropriate behaviour; but, instead, they should desire for their pupils to achieve to the best of their ability. If they do not, then they are failing to give their pupils a balanced and worthwhile education and are not managing their pupils effectively for them to become young people who value and respect themselves as well as others. Schools ought to be preparing children to have a meaningful life and contribute in a positive way to the society in which they belong. When children are excluded from schools it is a distressing time not only for the children, but also for the children's entire family. The strain can be enormous especially for the uncertainty that lies ahead. The children come to school to be educated and should expect and be given an all round education that prepares them for adulthood in 21st century. With the schools, parents and the community working together the black children's aspirations, self esteem and discipline can all improve and develop.

It is important that schools need to develop, as a necessity, clear and practical guidelines to help them work more effectively with parents who are experiencing challenging behaviour from their children as it arises especially as they go through their adolescence stage. There are a number of ways that schools can act in partnership with parents to help individual pupils improve on their behaviour and their general conduct. This can be achieved by the strengthening of pupils' relationships with those who they come into daily contact with, especially in schools, so that the communities in which they live and society in general will benefit as a whole. Exclusions are not solving the problem of disruptive, disrespectful and challenging behaviour. Children will misbehave and act in a manner that is rude and inappropriate, but they should not be denied a good education. They should be punished, supported and given training, but exclusion for bad behaviour is simply defeating the essential purpose of education, which is to transform pupils' behaviour and to develop their learning.

References

Abbott, D. (2007) *Parliamentary Debate on Black and Ethnic Minority Pupils and School Exclusions*, London Schools and the Black Child.

Centre for Social Justice, *Breakthrough Britain: No Excuses: A review of Educational Exclusion*, London: Centre for Social Justice, 2011.

Cole, M (1986) '*Teaching and learning about racism: a critique of multicultural education in Britain*', in S. Modgil, G. Verma, K. Mallik and C. Modgil (eds) *Multicultural Education: the Interminable Debate*, Lewes: The Falmer Press.

Cole, M. and Blair, M. (2006) '*Racism and education: from Empire to New Labour*' in Cole, M (ed) (2nd Edition) Education, Equality and Human Rights: Issues of Gender, 'Race', Sexuality, Disability and Social Class, Oxfordshire: Routledge

Connelly, P. (1995) '*Boys will be boys? Racism, sexuality and the construction of masculine identities amongst infant children*', in M. Blair and J. Holland (eds) *Equality and Difference: Debates and Issues in Feminist Research and Pedagogy*, Clevedon: Multilingual Matters.

Department for Education (2010) *The Importance of Teaching*: The Schools White Paper, 2010: The Stationery Office: http: official-documents.gov.uk.

Department for Education and Skills (2006) *Exclusion of Black Pupils: Priority Review. Getting It, Getting It Right*, DfES.

Gillborn, D. (1990) "*Race" Ethnicity and Education, London*: Unwin Hyman.

Gillborn, D. and Gipps, C. (1996) *Recent Research on the Achievement of Ethnic Minority Pupils*, London: HMSO.

John, G. (2006) *Taking a Stand*: The Gus John Partnership Limited: Manchester.

John, G. (2010) *The Case for a Learner's Charter for Schools*: London: New Beacon Books Ltd.

Majors (2001) *Understanding the current educational status of Black children* in Majors (ed.) (2001) *Educating our Black Children: New directions and radical approaches*: Routledge/Falmer.

Mortimore, P., Sammons, P., Stoll, P., Lewis, D., Ecob, R. (1988) *School Matters: the Junior Years*, Wells: Open Books.

Sewell, T., (1997) *Black Masculinity and Schooling*, Stoke-on-Trent: Trentham Books.

Tikly, et al. (2006) *Evaluation of Aiming High: African Caribbean*

Achievement Project, DfES Research in Department for Education and Skills (2006) *Exclusion of Black Pupils: Priority Review. Getting It, Getting It Right*, DfES.

Tizzard, B., Blatchford, P., Burke, J., Farquhar, C. And Plewis, I. (1988) *Young children at School in the Inner City*, Hove: Lawrence Erbaum Associates.

Whiteley, W. M. (1969) *The Uneducated English*, London: Methuen & Co. Ltd.

Wright, C. (1992) *'Early education: multiracial primary school classrooms'*, in D. Gill, B. Mayor and M. Blair *Racism in Education, Structures and Strategies,* London: Sage

Chapter 5

Culture and learning in education

Schooling is about educating 'the person'. This requires that the education process should embrace the student's traditional learning taste. This, metaphorically speaking, is similar to the way in which a chef cooking for a state banquet would prepare a specific menu for the occasion. It would contain all the necessary food balances such as proteins, carbohydrates, fat, vitamins, etc. but served to meet the culinary taste of the guests. For example, a state banquet for Chinese guests would most likely have food types such as noodles to meet Chinese taste or a banquet for an Indian party would feature curry dishes to satisfy Indian traditions.

In a similar way, the literacy, numeracy, scientific, historical and other academic and social skills needed by all learners must likewise be educationally seasoned specifically to meet the learning taste (traditions/culture) of the learner. This illustration in essence is what the issue of culture is to learning and education. Thus, culture brings the school's ethos and classroom pedagogy into harmony with the pupils' background, their knowledge and their identity of who they are.

This chapter will progress one of the key goals of this book, which is the advocacy of an educational renaissance movement and a paradigm shift in the 'how' and 'why' we educate, in answer to the underachievement experiences of many young people in the English education system. The book, so far, has considered the necessity for a revival of parental and community leadership in education. It is imperative for schools to undertake a radical turnaround from the usual view that the pupils must fit into the schools' culture and their way of life, to the contrasting principle that the schools should instead create the ethos around which the learning exercises they offer will find resonance with their pupils' own cultural experiences.

In this examination of the issue of culture and education, the authors challenge one of the prevailing assumptions in education, which is that schools are chiefly responsible for preparing pupils for their future roles in society. The chapter also champions the notion that schools are an embodiment of the cultural ways of the children's community and society. Furthermore, it questions the existing orthodoxy which accepts that it is for parents and children to fit into the way of life of schools, rather than for schools – in every aspect of their work – to purposefully live out the cultural practices and values of the communities they serve.

As a starting point to this discourse, the authors will initially deal with one of the attempts at cultural appreciation and inclusion in education today, namely the annual Black History Month (BHM) event. Its existence is a small – but unwitting – acknowledgement of the principle that education must be culturally based for it to be effective in furthering the learning of all children.

Black History Month – Is this all we can do bring the education process into cultural harmony with its pupils?

For the past 20 years, in the UK, the month of October has been designated BHM. This annual season of celebration came out of the black awareness movement of the 1960s and 1970s. It was also inspired by America's own BHM festival which is traditionally commemorated each February.

According to many who are involved in organising this yearly event, the purpose for BHM is to promote knowledge of black history and its culture. In addition, BHM provides the opportunity to disseminate information on positive black contributions to British society and to build, for the black community, confidence in its heritage and values.

Thus, BHM is now an established event in the education calendar of many schools. However, to the discerning educationalist BHM transcends the perception of being an annual multicultural experience that highlights black achievements. It signals an acknowledgement that culture is an integral part of education and is essential to the success for learning. This is despite the routine and superficial treatment that is generally given to BHM in many schools such as the highlighting of black personalities, food, clothes and music. In addition, the yearly one month fanfare for BHM also misses an important educational principle. This is that deep learning cannot be accomplished without an ongoing engagement by schools and teachers with the beliefs, values and symbols that connect pupils to their own background.

Too often, outside of the annual BHM celebrations, we have seen strong resistance to attempts to engage educators, the media and others into a serious discourse on the need for reform in the way schools teach and educate black children. This is especially needed in a society where (in reality) there is usually an unspoken belief by some from within the majority white population that blacks are an inferior race of people. While this attitude by a significant number of whites is by definition racist, those who hold to its tenets rarely will admit to their true inner feelings on race. They are offended if challenged, particularly when their actions become discriminatory to blacks in the areas of education, employment, housing, health and other services. At the same time blacks who are bold enough to confront racism when it raises its ugly head are criticised and maligned for playing the 'race card'. Nevertheless, despite the reluctance by the perpetrators to face up to the existence of racism in education and other areas, the reality is that it is often expressed in negative attitudes and low expectations in classrooms towards black children. This denial is especially active amongst the teachers' professional bodies when racism, in education, is raised as a legitimate concern. To them this accusation is deeply hurtful as they consider themselves to be on the liberal political wing in society. Thus, they are unwilling to accept that many teachers' lack of cultural awareness and affinity with the cultural background of black children are major impediments to black pupils' learning and educational attainment. Gillborn (2008) captures the nub of this problem most profoundly. He writes:

> *'. . . I was trying to highlight how deeply rooted Whiteness is throughout the education system. . . But there is no conscious plot; there doesn't need to be because White people learn to act and think in ways that have exactly the same outcomes, but they do it almost automatically . . . Black kids don't just happen to be expelled more*

> *than every other ethnic group, they don't just happen to be over-represented in the lowest ranked teaching groups . . . These patterns reflect centuries of White racist domination . . .'*
>
> (Gillborn, 2008, p. 9, 10 & 11)

Thus, in essence, the crux of the problem is the latent but pervasive belief by many whites that they are inherently superior and blacks inferior. This cultural polarisation and the devaluation of blacks are extremely damaging to the education system. Nevertheless, if the critics, who oppose discussion on the role of culture in education, can step back from their defensive posture, it will become apparent that the consideration of the cultural dimension to education is based on sound educational principles.

One of the most eminent educationalists of the 20th and 21st centuries, Jerome S Bruner, a pioneer of the 'cognitive revolution' agreed that he had to re-evaluate his thinking and concluded that the building of a cultural psychology – that takes proper account of the historical and social context of children – is vital to our understanding of how pupils learn. Furthermore, he writes:

> *'How one conceives of education we have finally come to recognize, is a function of how one conceives of the culture and its aims, professed and otherwise . . . culture shapes the mind . . . it provides us with the toolkit by which we construct not only our worlds but our very conception of ourselves and our powers.'*
>
> (Bruner, 1996, p. ix)

Cultural understanding is now becoming an integral part of the educational theory of learning. Culture and race in education should no longer be treated as a 'no go area' when the performance of Black children is being evaluated and debated.

Thus, the focus of BHM on the achievements of black people in both ancient and contemporary life remains a limited response to the challenge of race, culture and education. Nonetheless, it signals the need for a broader understanding of the role that culture plays in shaping children's frame of reference for managing knowledge and for constructing their own personal identity. But to unpack what at times the media wrongly and glibly caricature as a form of black racism, that is, the education of black children and their cultural depravation in the education system, the present authors will now consider the searching question 'why do we educate?'.

Why do we educate?

The trend of ongoing increases in external examination results has been a feature of the education landscape following the reforms of the late 1980s. However, whilst there have been obvious improvements in standards, more recently there has emerged a flattening out of the primary external SATs results. Literacy and numeracy results are now on a plateau at just over 80% of the expected standard for pupils at primary school level. Thus, approximately one in five primary pupils is transferring to secondary schools below the expected national standards.

Even for the secondary GCSE examination results, they too have areas of concerns. There are elements of inflation and distortions to their figures. For example, savvy schools are pushing pupils toward easier subjects. Others schools are entering pupils for vocational qualifications where a single subject can be counted as equivalent to four GCSE higher grades. Notwithstanding this massaging of the GCSE figures, one third of 16 plus year olds are leaving school without attaining the bench mark target of 5 A* – C grades. Furthermore, the introduction of the new English Baccalaureate measure of educational standards in January 2011 – as a further indicator for assessing schools' performances – disappointingly shows that only 16% of all pupils gained 5 GCSE A* – C passes that included English, mathematics, sciences, a language and a humanities subject in 2010. Thus, the aspiration of 'Education for All' remains an illusion.

How do we account for this underperformance of the education system? The answer can be traced back to the 1944 Education Act which reinforced the education divide between children. Three types of schools were created, namely: secondary grammar schools; technical schools; and secondary modern schools. It was also the case that the general expectation by education policy makers was that only 20% of pupils were capable of achieving the then GCE standards, equivalent to today's 5 A* – C GCSE grades. The remaining 80% of secondary pupils would supply the skilled or unskilled labour needed for the economy. Undoubtedly, this was not an education system that was catering for all pupils, since the vast majority of pupils (80%) were supposed to fail, given that success in education was judged by pupils' attaining the GCE national examination qualifications.

Thus, the reforms of the late 1980s and beyond could be said to be synonymous to the well known caution of not attempting to put new wine into old wineskins or bottles. In other words, it will be difficult or near impossible to achieve the goal of 'Education for All', delivered by a system that in the first place accepts failure for the vast majority of children educationally.

The transformation needed to make 'Education for All' a reality necessitates the formulation of a clear education philosophy, expressing the values on which the education system will be founded and the purpose for education. In the prevailing education climate the national government, local authorities and educators in general are caught up mainly with 'how we educate?' and less with 'why we educate?'. But it is the 'why we educate?' that needs to influence the 'how we educate?' aspect of the education system. An evaluation of all the major education reform initiatives since the 1944 Education Act will show that they focused generally on changes to how education is conducted, such as: school structures; curriculum; accountability through school inspections and testing regimes; and teaching and leadership standards. In contrast, the 'why we educate?' has received scant attention from educators and politicians, except for the repetitive cliché that education is to prepare children for society and the world of work or that we must build a world class education system. However, an effective education system must be driven by a big vision – that is, by the 'why we educate?' This vision is missing from our education system today.

In reframing education around the 'why', we need to consider some of the works of influential philosophers in the field of education. The list would include names such as:

- Benjamin Bloom and his taxonomy of learning (Cognitive, Affective and Psychomotor domains);
- B. F. Skinner, the behaviourist scholar who emphasised the effects of reward on learning;

- Carl Rogers and the humanist approach to education, centring on the essential of creating a positive classroom atmosphere;
- Jean Piaget and his four stages to mental growth;
- Howard Gardner's theory of multiple intelligence;
- Abraham Maslow's motivational theory, consisting of the seven hierarchies of human needs.
- John Dewey's approach of balancing knowledge delivery with the interest and experience of the student; and
- Jerome Bruner's theory on the role of culture in learning

Benjamin Bloom (1913 – 1999)

Bloom's taxonomy of learning is the centre piece of his theoretical work in education. This theory identifies three learning domains, that is to say: (1) the cognitive domain; (2) the affective domain; and (3) the psychomotor domain. It also proposes a hierarchy (that is, a graduated level) of learning skills for each domain. The cognitive domain focuses on intellectual capability and the ability to think, and suggests the following progressive learning skills: knowledge acquisition; comprehension; application; analysis; synthesis; and evaluation. The affective domain, in contrast, deals with feelings, emotions, behaviour, attitude and motivation. The hierarchy of skills to be developed in this domain are: receiving ideas; responding to ideas; valuing ideas; organising ideas; and internalising the value systems impacting on the child. Finally, the psychomotor domain relates to manual and physical skills, developed through the following stages: imitate; manipulate; developing precision; articulation; and naturalisation (automatic response). For teaching practitioners, Bloom's work provides a framework for developing learning objectives for planning lessons and for evaluating the influence of teaching on learning.

Burrhus Frederic Skinner (1904 – 1990)

Skinner's theory centres on the principle that learning occurs when there is a change in the behaviour of the pupil, as he responds to teaching stimuli. The response has to be rewarded or reinforced for the behavioural change to take root. However, implementation is better achieved through a process of small step changes initiated by the teacher. In practical terms, reinforcement or reward can be either positive or negative. Positive rewards can include verbal praise, and a good grade in a test will also engender in pupils a feeling of accomplishment and satisfaction. Negative reinforcement, on the other hand, would be designed to discourage unwanted classroom behaviour.

Carl Rogers (1902 – 1987)

Carl Rogers, a psychologist, took a humanistic approach to learning and was a staunch advocate of pupil-centred learning. He believed that the facilitation of learning should be the main purpose of any education system, and that this is really the key function of a classroom teacher. From his research he demonstrated that pupils in the classroom have a preference for a teacher approach that centres on collaboration. Pupils, he found, were happy carrying out their own investigations and would readily share and support each other's learning.

Jean Piaget (1896 – 1980)

Piaget's research study focused on how knowledge is developed and concluded that it takes a progressive path. Children's logic and thinking, he argued, are initially strikingly different from those of adults, and from this premise he advanced his model that described four stages of mental growth. These stages are: (1) the sensory-motor stage, that is, from birth to age two – at this level children concentrate on exploring and interacting with concrete and real objects; (2) the pre-operational stage, from age two to seven – at this stage children learn symbols through language, play and fantasy; (3) the concrete operational stage, from age seven to eleven – at this phase of development children are able to demonstrate classification skills, cultivate relationships, manage numbers and engage in reasoning application; and (4) the formal operational stage, from age 11 plus – at this ultimate stage in the model children begin to develop independent thinking and to comprehend and interpret other people's thought.

Howard Gardner (1943)

Gardner's contribution to philosophical thinking in education is expressed through his 'Theory of Multiple Intelligence'. His theory promoted the view that intelligence cannot be restricted exclusively to cognitive reasoning powers. In so doing he has challenged the notion of intelligence as a single entity that can be measured via IQ tests. In contrast, he identifies seven different types of intelligences that are possessed by learners. These are: Verbal/Linguistic Intelligence; Visual/Spatial Intelligence; Musical

Intelligence; Logical/Mathematical Intelligence; Bodily/Kinaesthetic Intelligence; Interpersonal Intelligence; and Intrapersonal Intelligence. Gardner reasoned that as a result of this diffusion of intelligence amongst learners, effective teachers will incorporate into their teaching these different aspects of intelligence in order to meet the needs of all pupils.

Abraham Maslow (1908 – 1970)

Maslow's hierarchy of needs model consists of the following categories: physiological; safety; belonging; esteem; cognitive; aesthetic; self-actualisation. It is generally represented as a pyramid, with physiological needs forming the base of the pyramid and the self-actualisation being positioned at the top of the pyramid (see illustration below). According to Maslow's theory, each level of need must be adequately satisfied, starting with physiological, before moving through the others and ultimately to self-actualisation. Thus, pupils' learning will be better advanced when these needs are adequately provided for, both at home and at school.

Figure 5.1 – Maslow's Hierarchy of Needs

Self-
Actualisation

Aesthetic

Cognitive

Esteem

Belonging

Safety

Physiological

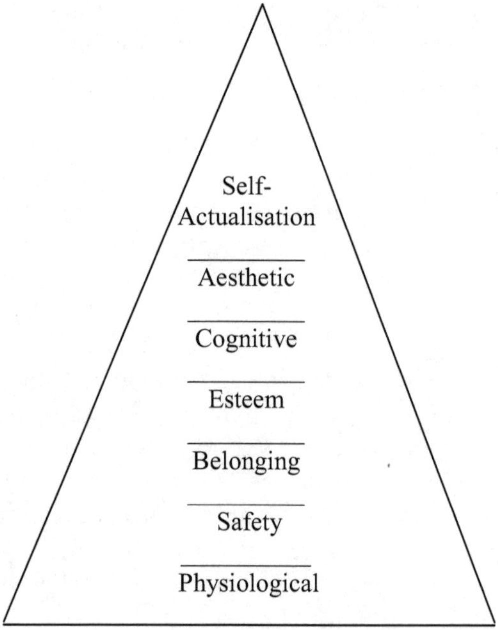

John Dewey (1859 – 1952*)*

John Dewey was an American education philosopher and psychologist, although he wrote on many other topics such as logic, democracy and ethics. On education he argued that education and learning are social and interactive processes. He suggested that students excel more in a learning environment where they are allowed to take part in shaping their own learning experiences by interacting with the curriculum. For him, the purpose of education is for students to fully realise their potentials and to use them for the greater good. Dewey advocated an educational structure that balances knowledge acquisition with developing the interest and experiences of the students.

Jerome Bruner's work on the role of culture in the business of learning is discussed more extensively further on in this chapter.

The model below now provides an analysis of the works and theories of these major educational icons and the extent to which the principles they espouse meet the ideal scenario for developing independent learners committed to high values.

Figure 5.2 – Analysis Model of Educational Philosophers and political ideologies

Educational philosophers and political ideologies: their contribution to high intrinsic values and the development of independent learners

<table>
<tr><td>VALUES
High (H)</td><td>Intrinsic</td><td>H/L</td><td>H/H
Bloom (Holistic Approach)
Maslow (Motivational Approach)
Dewey (Student democracy and education for the purpose of the greater good)</td></tr>
<tr><td></td><td>Extrinsic</td><td>L/L
Capitalism & the free market ideology

Socialist ideology</td><td>L/H
Skinner (Behaviourist Approach)
Rogers (Humanist Approach)
Piaget, Bruner & Gardner (Cognitive Approaches)</td></tr>
<tr><td colspan="3">Dependent Learners</td><td>Independent Learners</td></tr>
<tr><td colspan="4">Low (L) PEDAGOGICAL PRACTICE High (H)</td></tr>
</table>

The model not only deals with the eight philosophers identified above, but incorporates both the capitalist and socialist ideologies into its analysis. The vertical axis is split between intrinsic values, considered to be high and extrinsic (instrumental) values deemed to be low. The horizontal axis is identified by a pedagogical practice that is either low in cultivating dependent learners or high in encouraging independent learners. The capitalist and socialist ideologies are clearly low on values. They consider education to be for the purpose of meeting the needs of industry, the economy, the state and in making the nation either globally competitive or militarily and politically a strong super power. The view that education should primarily be for economic reasons is confirmed by Musgrave (1968) in his analysis of the development of the English education system post 1800. He states:

> '. . . *the weight given to classics in the curriculum becomes less and the demand for science and mathematics rose. The status of these subjects rose and education came to be seen as serving a more instrumental function.*'
>
> (Musgrave, 1968, p. 112)

On the other hand, the analytical model shows that Skinner, Rogers, Piaget, Bruner and Gardner feature high with the pedagogical capacity to develop independent learners. However, in terms of values they concentrate more within the extrinsic dimension of the model. In contrast, Bloom, Maslow and Dewey in their approaches are high on values in that they promote a more holistic approach to learning development and also, as pedagogical instruments, they provide more support for independent learning for pupils.

As the above commentary has shown, the works of the majority of these philosophical thinkers can be seen to be generally centred on instrumental values, but emphasised the development of independent learning. The three exceptions that provide for both intrinsic educational growth and the creation of independent learners are Bloom's taxonomy for learning, Maslow's motivational hierarchy of needs model and Dewey's proposition that education is for developing students' potential for the common good of humanity.

Nonetheless, (with the exception of Dewey) they fall short of offering a cogent answer to the question: 'why do we educate?' They present education still as a process that stops with the individual, centring solely on the holistic development of the person. In contrast, however, what is required is a philosophy of education that will extend educational outcomes beyond intrinsic levels for the person, to education for a higher and nobler cause. This philosophy will move education primarily from the purpose of curiosity and control to one of compassion and love for humanity. The educator Parker J Palmer reinforces this thought by the following questions:

> *'How can the places where we learn to know become places where we also learn to love? How can we educate today so that "the day after" will be a time of compassion rather than combat? . . . When we tap our own resources, we will find a heartening fact: at the frontiers of intellectual life, scholars now regard the concept of community as indispensable in describing the terrain that educators inhabit.'*
>
> (Palmer, 1993, pp. xiii, 9 & 10)

Irrespective of the fact that more investment is being made into education today and the training of teachers is given greater priority, nevertheless many teachers are entering the classroom not understanding the deeper reason for their calling as teachers. It must, however, be acknowledged that there is a committed number of teachers who have a clear sense of the higher calling to teaching. They are guided and motivated by the 'why we educate?' and invariably they are the ones that pupils can always point to as the teachers making a difference to their educational journey through schooling. Nonetheless, the dearth of teachers without the guiding compass of the 'why we educate?' cannot be placed at the doors of these teachers. The way teachers are prepared for teaching today contributes significantly to this situation. One only has to look at the current national professional standards for teachers, published by the Training and Development Agency (TDA), leading to Qualified Teacher Status (QTS). The criteria focused on the following key areas: relationships/expectations; communication; professional development; teaching and learning; assessment and monitoring; subjects and curriculum; literacy, numeracy and information communication technology (ICT); achievement and diversity; and health and well-being.

A teacher undergoing training must demonstrate competence in the above areas (each area having an extended list of specific requirements) in order to be recommended and awarded QTS. However, it is glaringly obvious that the national standards centre exclusively on the 'how you educate?' Sadly, there is a gap in the philosophical preparation for such an important work, that is, the shaping of young minds for future service and leadership in society. The 'why we educate?' is clearly missing, with the 'how we educate?' in high ascendancy. This is not so much a case of the cart being placed before the horse, so to speak. Instead, the reality is that, metaphorically speaking, the education cart is without a horse. Could this be the reason why the education process lacks a dynamic force and constantly has to be pushed by endless initiatives? The answer must be that the system needs a 'why we educate?' philosophy for it to perform effectively for all. And for there to be education for all, all must be valued by those who lead education and practice in the classroom.

As we have seen earlier in this chapter the education system, post the 1944 Education Act, continues to have an outcome that makes a significant group of pupils failures within the external examination system. These pupils do not achieve the current targets for sitting SATs and GCSE examinations, that is, gaining at least Level 2 results for Key Stage 1; Level 4 for Key Stage 2 and 5 A* – C grades for GCSE examinations. We have also seen already that the system was built around the assumption that not all children can succeed academically. High academic performers were considered to be pupils drawn from more privileged background. Schools had lower academic expectations for other categories of children. Ability was simply a function of social class. There was, and still is, a presumed hierarchy to ability level. This means that the nearer you get to the bottom of what is determined to be the social ladder – defined by the employment status of parents, their education and income levels – the more unlikely it would be for the children to be academically successful in the school structure. Children of West Indian parentage in the 1960s and 1970s, more than most, experienced this damaging low expectation of their abilities in the school milieu.

Bernard Coard's telling account of their plight provided an historical account of how many black children were robbed of their intellectual dignity in the notorious schools for children who were educationally sub-normal, referred to as ESN special schools. This is what Coard has to say in resonance with the present authors' earlier point that there existed a hierarchical ability assumption, which placed black children at the bottom of the education ladder:

> *'ESN schools are designed to assist each child in such a school to realise his assumed low capabilities so that he will on leaving school be able to hold down a job . . . A Black child of average or above average intelligence who gets placed in an ESN school can be expected to encounter great difficulties . . . may become upset or even disturbed.'*
>
> (Coard, 1971, p. 7 & 9)

Coard went on to show how the fate of many black children was so cruelly shaped and decided on by the Medical Officer of Health, who had no appropriate qualification in this field or by the headmaster of the school and the educational psychologist, using the notorious IQ tests. But according to Coard, these tests had three unfair aspects, namely: (1) they were culturally biased and did not take account of linguistic differences; (2) in most cases those who administered the test were from a middle class background and believed their interpretation of standard to be right and superior; and (3) they resulted in many children suffering temporary emotional upset, due to culture shock and the hostile environment they were faced with (Coard, 1971).

This situation of casting black children as intellectually inferior continues today. According to Gillborn:

> *'. . . there is growing evidence that white teachers' everyday expectations reflect a view of Black students as generally less able – as more likely to cause trouble than to excel in their studies. Although coded in talk of ability and aptitude, these views have the same effect as the view of intelligence peddled by people such as Authur Jensen . . . Hans Eysenck . . . J.Phillipe Rushton . . . Richard Herrnstein and Charles Murray . . .'*
>
> (Gillborn, 2002, p. 11)

Furthermore, many of these scientists, who are self acclaimed experts on intelligence, still continue to peddle the lie that blacks are less intelligent and that intelligence is a product of genetic inheritance. But this notion must never, ever be accepted by blacks or anyone else. A shortlist of outstanding black leaders and achievers – not forgetting ancient kings of Africa, including Egypt which is a country in Africa – would contain figures such as Martin Luther King (Jnr), Nelson Mandela, Barack Obama, Michael Jackson, Bernie Grant, Diane Abbott, Lord David Pitt, Lord Herman Ouseley, Professor Gus John, great black writers in the field of literature and established black medical figures such as Professor Ben Carson (to name but a few historical and contemporary figures). Thus, are the so-called experts (Jensen, Eysenck and others) saying that the aforementioned list of outstanding black leaders and achievers happened to be freaks, in the sense that they are exceptions? The reverse is the case; they typify and provide proof of what blacks can accomplish when given the chance and, in many cases, when they possess that special ingredient of confidence and commitment to a cause.

In addition to the fact that the education system has developed with an inbuilt acceptance of ability classification and hierarchy, it has also been afflicted too by the divisive and anti-education spirit of competition. For decades educational outcomes revolved around examination results, grades and numbers. Assessment procedures have placed pupils into high and low categories. Education has became a battle ground where pupils compete against each other and schools contend with each other for high ranking places in the education league tables. The inevitable consequence of this is that some pupils and schools have been considered to be failures in the education process. Thus, we have produced an education system that has divided and fragmented learners rather than uniting students into a community of dynamic learners. According to Palmer (1993):

> *'Students are made to compete with one another as a hedge against error, so that only the fittest and the smartest will survive . . .remember that in many classrooms "cooperation" among students goes by the name of "cheating"!'*
>
> (Palmer, 1993 p. 37)

The by-product of this preoccupation with competition in the classroom has resulted in students in later life still carrying into adulthood the disposition to compete in their relationships at work and in their dealings with people in general. Thus, they lack the capacity to contribute to the much needed task of community building and service to others.

The exegesis and dynamic nature of a community of learners

What produces a community of learners is the understanding and acceptance of the principle that each learner enters into the learning process with a cultural identity and that this identity becomes the key or password to the learner's growth and development. Thus, if the education process fails to recognise and utilise the learner's cultural identity code or his cultural toolkit the learner will, therefore, be locked out of the learning process. When this happens it is no longer a learning community but an institution with disaffected and disengaged young people.

So far, it has been argued that education must move beyond just advancing instrumental goals and unto the higher realm of the intrinsic development of the person, for the furtherance of the common good. However, this cannot be accomplished simply by a reliance on the 'how we educate?', but must be refocused on the 'why we educate?' and the jettisoning of the present dependence on an ability and competitive learning culture. Thus, to transform schools into a genuine community of learners, the principle that the school must be the embodiment of the cultural ways of the children's community (as can be seen in Jewish schools today) will only become a reality through the effort it makes in uniting the children's cultural toolkit to all aspects of the school's learning and teaching practices.

This concept of culture and learning that we are talking about must not be confused with the future of multiculturalism that is being debated in general. This has been triggered by reactions to perceived Muslim and other religious fundamentalist movements. In addition, there were comments on the topic by Trevor Phillip, former chairman of the Commission for Racial Equality (CRE) before it was superseded by the Equality and Human Rights Commission (EHRC). He said – in the context of the debate on the future of multiculturalism in Britain – that the country was in danger of 'sleepwalking' its way into segregation and ghettoisation, drawn along lines of race and religion. But, it must be recognised that the multiculturalism agenda of the past two decades has been predicated on the goal of establishing within a growing and diverse society a common centre (culture) that would be identified as multicultural Britain. This has remained an unfulfilled expectation, with some seeing Britishness as a 'community of communities' and others construing it to mean an 'anything goes' multiculturalism. In the opinion of Trevor Phillip the emphasis has been too much on the 'multi' and less on establishing a common British culture (Allen, 2007). However, for the purpose of this discussion on education and culture we must divest our discourse from the corrosive and divisive debate about the future of multiculturalism, which is a concept that lacks consensus on how it should be defined.

Therefore, our exegesis for education as a community of learners advances the proposition that all learners carry a cultural identity code or cultural toolkit into the learning environment. In other words, a child may come to school as a learner from a white British heritage background or as a learner with an Asian tradition or a learner with African Caribbean parentage. However, many times it is claimed that black children have an identity problem. This is not really the case. The so called identity crisis stems from the fact that too often in the school system, black children's cultural identity code or their cultural toolkit is considered to be inferior to other children's cultural codes within the school community. This manifests itself in terms of negative attitudes towards black children, low teacher expectations, unfair treatment with respect to discipline and behaviour and denial of equal access to curriculum opportunities by the overrepresentation of black children in low teaching streams or sets within the learning community. Nevertheless, black children are acutely aware of this devaluation of their cultural identity. This is for no other reason but for the fact that, like all other human beings, they too possess that inner sensor we know as 'feelings'. They strongly feel (emotions) and experience the inferior perception and treatment, and know these to be unjust. However, dissatisfaction sets in leading to the withdrawal of cooperation by the children, and other negative responses will also follow. Eventually, the situation cascades into unwanted confrontations that can lead to their exclusion from schools. Yet, as we have explored in Chapter 1, the emotional and psychological strengths resulting from the confidence building paradigm of parents being first teachers (and supported by the community) can break the vicious downward spiral, described above, for many black children. The evidence, as demonstrated in Chapter 1, shows that – for example – the successful black children in Diane Abbott's awards programme, like other unidentified ones elsewhere, were able to be achievers because of the confidence building investment made in them by their parents and the community (supplementary schools, mentoring groups, churches, etc). They were treated as special (gifted). This affirmed their cultural identity (the identity that says who they are). It has kept their self esteem intact, forming a buttress against the undermining and soul destroying impact of low teacher expectation and negative social stereotyping.

Culture is the toolkit that shapes children's mind and that will influence learning

Schools are required through the curriculum they offer to provide for children's spiritual, moral, social and cultural development, generally referred to as SMSC. The grounds that SMSC cover are not new, and are anchored in the 1944 Education Act. This obligation – to provide for SMSC development – and its implementation by many educators, presupposes that children come to school with an empty mind, and with the belief that they arrive at school capable of using only a limited range of words from their language, and to be filled with information and knowledge by their teachers. It would suggest that children live in a form of educational vacuum chamber, unaffected by the culture they are surrounded by. However, while this has been the prevailing thinking in the education sphere, as we know it, the present authors are challenging readers to re-evaluate this understanding. Children, as learners, bring more knowledge to the learning environment than hitherto appreciated by educators. Children, even at the early age for nursery and reception schooling, are already using the codes and symbols they are surrounded by, as a cultural toolkit, to make sense of their environment and for an understanding of self. Therefore, culture affects the way in which children go about learning at school. The philosophy being advanced is intent on integrating and embracing the total person – mind, body and soul/spirit – with the learning processes and their goals. Thus, engaging the learners through their cultural identity is the key to children's capacity to be confident and successful learners in the learning community.

All mental activities have a cultural link. You cannot understand any mental action unless you take cognisance of its cultural base. Mental operations such as learning, remembering, talking, thinking, imagining are only possible because of the cultural codes, traditions and symbols already gathered by the mind and then applied to the aforementioned mental activities. Therefore, we interpret knowledge within the framework of a cultural reality. Furthermore, when we do understand something, it is really a personal discovery resulting from the learner's own cognitive effort (you can only get it yourself), and the understanding is related to what has been known before. This is why teaching resources for little children will be linked to images they already know and have some experience of. As an example, a teacher may demonstrate that 1 + 1 = 2 by showing pictures of two apples in support of this concept. The child already knows and experienced the fact of the existence of two apples, but that personal knowledge held by the child is then applied to help him grasp the symbolic mathematical concept, that is, 1 + 1 = 2. What was known by the child and used by the teacher has to be culturally based and relevant, in order to move the child from the concrete (the apples) to the abstract (1+1=2). This is supported by the work of Jean Piaget, cited above as one of the influential education philosophers and thinkers of the last century.

The preceding illustration can be linked to the third stage of Piaget's four stages to mental growth. At this stage, that is, the concrete operational stage, the child is able to acquire a degree of proficiency in utilising experiences gained to master classifications, relationships, numbers and ways of abstract reasoning. The fictional child from Mars, not knowing anything about apples – a concrete operational experience – would find it difficult to understand the concept of 1 + 1 being equal to two things. This principle also finds support from Child (1981). Child had this to say:

> *'. . . though the act of concept formation might be in-born, the substance of the concepts is acquired from experience and it is this vital point which is of concern to teachers. Both parents and teachers constitute reference groups for assisting children in abstracting and classifying concepts attributes . . . concepts are dependent upon previous experience . . . background and educational opportunity are possible variables in the formation of concepts.'*
>
> (Child, 1981)

The foregoing statement from Child reinforces the need for the ethos of schools to have an affinity with the cultural experiences of all their pupils. This is crucial if schools are to be truly complementary to parents as reference groups, and in aiding children in abstracting ideas and concepts in the learning process.

More profoundly, it is through children's own narratives (their cultural toolkit) of life that a sense of identity is developed and formed, and this is the cultural identity that teachers who wish to engage learners into the learning community must utilise. Thus, when learners, unfortunately, are made to feel (through the ethos and practices in the learning milieu) that their cultural backgrounds are inferior to other learners their confidence can be destroyed or damaged and become a barrier to learning. Hence, the intention of this chapter of the book is to engage parents, educators and policy makers into giving serious consideration to the pivotal role that culture plays in the process of learning.

Bruner's (1996) influential and profound work on the role of culture in the development of learning brings enormous insight to our reflection on this great issue involving culture and education, and as it relates to the schooling of black children. Attempts to engage a debate on this specific matter, that is, education, culture and black children, elicit a negative response from the media and the education establishment. The view advanced by those who are resisting a debate on the topic, is that schools are neutral places and should not be in the business of pampering to cultural labels and differences. There is a fear that discussing culture in education, as it relates to black children, is tantamount to accusing the education system of racism in its practices. However, the cap of racism only fits where a school perpetuates an ethos or climate that devalues the cultural background of some ethnic groups, while correspondingly it seeks to elevate (overtly or covertly) the European culture as superior. Differentiation and cultural devaluation are reinforced through languages and labels that speak about 'developed and underdeveloped' countries, and 'civilised and uncivilised' societies, while neglecting the truth that Western and European developments can be traced back to early legal, political, religious and scientific systems and developments in Africa, the Middle East and regions of Asia. A holistic and integrated approach to the teaching of history and science is greatly needed today. Thus, Bruner's doctrine on culture and education provides a useful intellectual tool for conducting this debate and to reflect on the relationship between culture and learning.

Generic cultural tenets and their consequences for education

Brunner (1996) argues that education is ultimately the embodiment of culture. In other words, the education philosophy and system of any group, community or nation will invariably be determined by its prevailing culture and values. Thus, he offers nine tenets as a framework for understanding the role of culture and learning. These tenets (augmented with commentary by the authors) are:

The perspectival tenet

Perception plays a part in the process of understanding facts and situations. A person's view becomes his understanding of an event or experience, but such personal interpretation can also reflect rules of evidence, consistency and coherence. Neither will this preclude commonsense and logical reasoning. Interpretations and meaning will always echo not just the history of a group but also its canonical ways that, in themselves, contain expression of the groups' values and virtues. These will also influence the person's own understanding and concept of self. Hence, today in international affairs it is accepted that globally people do have different world views in interpreting and understanding issues and events. And so, as this relates to education, learning can be advanced when the education process is adroit enough in helping children to apply their own cultural perception to a problem, concept or activity in order to establish the particular learning principle being taught. Applying this further to greater issues of life, which is part of the reason for education, one can see that such a process of sharing understanding from a range of perspectives can encourage greater problem solving outcomes. After all, learning is about finding answers to questions and problems in life. This, however, relies on the application of this principle (the perspectival tenet) to whatever are the problem solving activities being used in any given situation.

The constraints tenet

Bruner argues that an understanding of self and also a person's future mental potential and development can be affected by previous mental experiences and activities. These will develop and emerge within the culture of the group as 'common sense' principles, but can also be at variance with other cultural interpretation by other groups. Thus, for many communities there are natural and native predispositions to think and interpret things in their own particular way. This somehow dispels the notion that thinking powers are innately derived, but a person's thinking powers are more likely to be shaped by exposure to a shared communal system and codes. Therefore, in the context of education and learning, and one of the goals of this book, which is the building of pupils' confidence, it is necessary that the teacher and the school should deliver learning instructions within the ambit of the children's cultural toolkit, as part of the process of extending their thinking capacity. This has implications for the training of teachers and the recruitment of teachers to serve in culturally diverse schools (inner city schools). Developing pupils' thinking can only effectively be achieved by connecting to their (the pupils') cultural frame of reference or toolkit to the learning and teaching processes in schools. Children appreciate having teachers who: (1) will have high expectations of their ability; and (2) possess positive attitudes to their cultural background, values and their way of life. However, as a generalisation, black children are at a severe disadvantage in that too many white teachers have low expectations of their potential. In addition, there are insufficient numbers of black teachers – with the understanding of black pupils and their cultural life – in the education system today to inspire black pupils to develop their confidence for learning. The tendency to point to the academic successes of Asian children, as a counter response, ignores the fact that in contrast to black children, Asians children benefit from the high expectations accorded them by teachers. Accordingly, Asian children are able to avoid the low expectations trap that can cruelly undermine the performance of black children in the school system.

The constructivism tenet

The constructivism tenet suggests that the concept of reality, that is, the way things in our world actually exist, is paradoxically shaped by the meaning we give to a situation or a thing. In other words: *'reality is made, not found'* (Bruner, 1996, p. 20). Thus, reality is the product of the mind, but the mind also sees and defines a situation or a phenomenon with reference to the person's cultural toolkit and symbols. The implication of this for education and learning is that teachers' judgment of what might be deemed to be the reality of a situation can be open to challenge, dispute and debate as a result of different perspectives and meanings drawn by pupils or parents on a given situation or sets of facts. In addition, teachers, especially in multi-ethnic school communities, must be receptive to the possibility of pupils offering broader, diverse and what may be deemed to be unconventional interpretations, opinions and conclusions in their responses to learning activities. This is particularly relevant to subject areas such as English, history, Religious Studies, social studies and even with science. Facts and research findings are interpreted through the cultural lenses of the observers. Thus, reality is the function of how the facts, events or the evidence are defined or translated by the mind. This is also well illustrated by the observation that people in different countries and with their individual languages define certain phenomena uniquely in their own way, using the genre and narratives of their literatures. You only need to look at how certain themes such as love, power, justice, freedom are treated in the wide range of international literatures to comprehend the fact that cultures influence strongly the way we see and understand events and situations in life.

The interactional tenet

This focuses on the view that we also learn a great deal about our cultural environment through the interactions we have with others of our community. From them we gain an understanding of our life and who we are. This tenet further implies that humans have a well developed gift of understanding the minds and messages of others through the language, gestures or other means of communication practiced within the community. Thus, a person's culture and membership within that milieu become very powerful and commanding tools for advancing learning. This concept Bruner (1996) terms as '*intersubjectivity*' and goes on to argue that Western pedagogical tradition does not grasp its importance in the business of education and learning. Instead, our system of learning promotes the belief of the all knowing teacher who stands before the class and tells the children something that they did not know. Therefore, one of the reforms needed today in education is that it should discard this impoverished thinking once and for all, as effective learning could never ever take place in such a one-way street approach. The new way of learning must be to create classrooms where pupils learn from each other, respecting and valuing each others' tradition and cultural experiences. The implication of this is that pupils must be provided with a cultural sanctuary where learning will be based on the children's everyday life and experiences. (Reay and Mirza, 1997)

The externalization tenet

All cultural groups produce works of arts, literatures, institutions, by-laws and traditional habits and practices that in many ways form a canonical history of their past and their achievements. These canonical pillars provide valuable and inspirational benefits to present and future generations. They also sustain a group's solidarity and cohesiveness. In many ways, this concept of 'the externalization tenet' provides for any cultural group an essential and tangible record of its people's mental efforts over time. To express this in another way, a people's accumulated knowledge will work its way into the habits and practices that distinguish it as a cultural group. Thus, schools today are given a great opportunity to unreservedly embrace the valuable learning resources residing in the communities from which pupils are drawn to support and develop themselves into inspiring learning communities. Despite the efforts of the annual BHM, which might be in danger of becoming a token gesture, the cultural backgrounds of many black children in the English education system are marginalised. The outcome of this is that they readily feel a sense of being devalued as a cultural group, and in that process they become disaffected and are turned off learning. Thus, as the present authors argue, the community should take more ownership for the education of its children, and, in addition, provide constructive leadership to the wider need for educational reform.

Instrumentalism tenet

Irrespective of the culture in which it is operating, education can never be neutral as its function, ultimately, is to influence change. However, change within any society will still remain anchored to the community's cultural berths and moorings. Essentially, learning is about the person mastering the 'cultural toolkit' he possesses. This 'cultural toolkit' exhibits a range of symbols such as life skills and artistic heritages. Examples of these are: craftsmanship and techniques; values; social habits; traditions; music and literature. Children will be exposed to these skills and cultural practices through family and community interactions. Different cultures distribute these knowledge and skills distinctively and their educational institutions will reinforce them through cultural preferences and the priorities they ultimately give to them. However, more damaging is the truth that educational institutions, at times, can perpetuate negating education practices such as racism. When analysed through the lenses of Critical Race Theory (CRT), these disturbing actions can appear to be so routine, yet so subtle and poisonous in practice that they become less obvious even to the victims and are then accepted as normal behaviour (Gilborn, 2008). The outcome of this is that some children's natural intellectual talents are unfortunately suppressed and stifled. This has been the experience of many black children in the education system, despite the ground breaking work of Coard (1971) some four decades ago. Thus, schools will often reflect the prevailing attitudes and practices of its environment, unless they intentionally challenge issues such as elitism (social class) and racism.

The implication of an 'instrumentalism tenet' is that education will impact on children either positively or negatively. Schools cannot be considered to be 'culturally free standing' since education exists always within culture. Thus, schools and their curriculum programmes are not simply dealing with subjects but are about the schools themselves and the cultural endorsement they provide to all members of their learning communities. However, in the context of the education of black children in the English education system, the past decades have shown that black children, in many urban schools, have remained estranged partners from the learning process in their schools. Thus, given that one of the themes of this book is parental and community renaissance in education, then, it stands to reason that local schools should be strategically owned and managed for the wellbeing of their communities. Some may argue that this is currently the situation, in that schools are generally administered by elected local authorities, and, therefore, in essence are locally controlled. However, the reality is that schools are controlled by local political machines that often are disconnected from the great majority of citizens in their constituencies/wards. Worst still, schools are also governed by national policies that are incapable of addressing decades – yea centuries – of inequalities and social injustices. Thus, now is the time for parents to re-establish their ancient rights to be in charge of their children's education and to realign the education process with the children's cultural toolkit.

The institutional tenet

According to Bruner (1996) the education system in any given culture is an institution along side other institutions in fields such as: religion, medicine, banking and finance, legal, political, and so on. Therefore, institutions are a fundamental part of people's cultural heritage, traditions and history. Institutions, in effect, do a serious job for the cultural groups they serve, that is, they live out the cultural heritage of their members by the contributions they make to the community they are affiliated to. Institutions buttress the values, principles and distinguishing features of the people they serve. Furthermore, they are also in the business of issuing distinctions or credentials to their members, through what is sometimes described as a meritorious system for distributing authority and power in society. But education, as an institution, exercises this power to distribute distinctions in an even more profound and far reaching way, with serious implications for both those who are awarded distinctions and those who are denied distinctions. A cursory glance at the many institutions aforementioned shows a dearth or serious under representation of black professionals in or at the higher echelons of these institutions. Thus, the education system, in its failure to deliver academic 'education for all' is significantly denying many black young people the opportunity to participate equally and at influential levels in many of the important institutions in our society today. Sadly, the educational establishment and system have yet to coherently formulate a solution to the detrimental impact of social exclusion and racism on the attainment of some ethnic groups, particularly black children. This is, despite some fragmented and isolated successes. Given that the black community can ill afford to wait indefinitely for effective reforms to institutions, it has to seriously consider making itself more accountable for its own progress and wellbeing, by the development of parallel institutions within the broader ambit of society and the economy (similar to Jewish and Asian developments in the field of business and education). This could be a complementary approach akin to the concept of 'linking social capital' – discussed earlier in Chapter 2 (Woodcock, 2001). Community institutions have the potential to serve as a constructive response to the problem of under-representation and yet, at the same time, remain non-separatist and non-divisive alternatives for society in general. Linking social capital firstly is about partnership and networking in establishing institutions within one's community for mutual benefits and support. In practical terms these can be community schools or community financial and business institutions that will not only provide greater opportunities for ethnic groups to prepare and develop ethnic professionals and leaders, but will also collaborate within the wider system, thus unleashing positive energy and synergy for the good of all in society.

The failure of education as an institution to deal with contemporary social issues is not exclusive to the UK but is a global phenomenon. Hence, the need to have an earnest root and branch rethink of education is echoed by Bruner, whose work on culture forms the basis for this section of the chapter (Bruner, 1996). He says:

> *'. . . education is too consequential to too many constituencies to leave to professional educators. And I'm sure most thoughtful professionals would agree. Thus, to bring judgement, balance and broader social commitment to the educational scene . . . we need to engage "the best and brightest" as well as the most publicly*

> *committed to the task of formulating alternative policies and practices . . . recognising that education is not a free-standing institution, and not an island, but part of the continent . . . Improving education requires teachers who understand and are committed to the improvements envisioned.'*
>
> (Bruner, 1996, p. 34 and 35)

Professor Gus John, a long standing activist and commentator on the issue of education and race also embraces the thought that education needs to engage more concertedly with social issues. Commenting on the effectiveness or more correctly, the ineffectiveness of government initiatives over the past decade to address the failure of the system in regards to the education of black children, he said:

> *'. . . none of it is being done within an overall policy framework on "race" in schooling and education . . . I argue that a clearly stated Government commitment and a central focus on 'race' is essential . . .'*
>
> (John, 2006, p. 15)

This sentiment that there should to be an educational redesign, expressed so clearly by Bruner, resonates with the call being made in this book for a renaissance movement in education that will restore parents and communities to the frontline of the education process. Such a change will mean that parents and the community will take responsibility and leadership for the strategic direction of the educational needs of their children and also for the education system to deliver the community's education vision. It will mean that the schooling system must be recast to genuinely serve the community, rather than for it to remain a self-serving institution or at best an institution serving a privileged (elitist) group.

<u>The tenet of identity and self-esteem</u>

Education is crucial to the formation of 'self'. We know ourselves from our own inner experiences. However, this phenomenon of self awareness is also crucial in helping us to show respect in the way we treat others, recognising that they too are blessed with their own unique self identity. While children's immediate family background forms and shapes their individual self identity, school life must be recognised as playing a very significant role in determining and moulding children's sense of 'self'. The sequence for the development of 'self', which starts with family background and followed by schools being a sub set of the children's cultural community, raises a challenge to the notion that peer pressure and street wise-ness are primarily responsible for the alienation from the school system experienced by many children, mainly boys and in particular black boys. The issue of the influence of street life on the attitude of some black boys was discussed earlier in Chapter 1. It was acknowledged that parents and the community need to take responsibility for helping young black men to break free from the negative stranglehold of racism and stereotyping which they have experienced in the education system and that has for a long time been snuffing out their motivation and confidence for learning. However, as Bruner (1996) demonstrates – in his description of this tenet of his framework for the understanding of the role that culture plays in children's learning – schools have a profound influence in shaping 'self' and in building the self-esteem of their pupils.

Bruner (1996) argues that there are two aspects to selfhood: 'agency' and 'evaluation'. With respect to 'agency' it can be seen as a type of autobiographical memory, logging a record of past events in a person's life. These form, for the individual, an important body of self history for the future, and especially useful for regulating a person's level of aspiration, confidence and optimism. But it is also important to be aware that while an 'agency' inventory of 'self' has the propensity to govern a person's self-esteem level it is crucially important to be cognisant of the equally powerful role that the institutional aspects of culture plays in moulding, building or suppressing children's personal appreciation of themselves. The cultural environment surrounding children is of course external to them, but nonetheless it carries authority. Thus, in many ways 'self' is governed by obligations to a higher master in our lives.

In religious societies such as Christian, Jewish and Muslim, people deferred to the superior authority of God, while the more secular minded rely on rationality and scientific evidence to guide their thinking and opinions. Therefore, children's identity and self-esteem will not only respond to both early experiences and events in their lives, but also to the pervasive influence of their cultural environment. More profoundly, however, these two factors – records of life events and the cultural environment – in children's development of 'self' will either be reinforced or undermined by the children's experiences at school.

The second element of this tenet on selfhood, that is, 'evaluation' is about how we measure our successes in life, linked to our ambitions. In this context of schooling, it is the mix between the biographical records of children's experiences and their positive valuation of those events that builds the vitally needed self esteem, so essential for children's confidence in learning. Thus, any school system that does not always emphasise high expectations and recognises the achievements and aspirations of black children will inevitably mean that black children will perform below their ability. Again, Bruner has this to say:

> *'. . . school is often rough on children's self-esteem, and we are beginning to know something about their vulnerability in this area. Ideally, of course, school is supposed to provide a setting where our performance has fewer esteem-threatening consequences than in the "real world". . .'*
>
> (Bruner, 1996, p. 37)

Sadly, the above observation is the experience of many black children in the English education system for the last five decades. However, this situation most certainly can change when parents and the community are placed at the frontline of the education process. It will also happen when open discussion on the issue, that is, of education, culture and black children, ceases to be seen as a threat to the education establishment, and rightly be acknowledged as an educational imperative for the vision of 'education for all' to be a reality.

The narrative tenet

This tenet, in essence, illuminates the principle that as children grow they will better understand and learn from the experiences at school, especially when they (the children) can link those encounters to their lives (their cultural toolkit). In any given culture today knowledge is organised and managed in two ways, namely through logical-scientific thinking and narrative thinking. Be that as it may, the tendency in the world of education is to treat the logical-scientific mode of knowledge building as harder or academically superior and the narrative form as softer or less academically strong. The narrative side includes a range of art driven knowledge such as songs, folklore, drama, literature, and so on. But importantly, it is through this narrative aspect of learning that any group of people is able to construct and record their cultural heritages and pass on their traditions and beliefs through story form. It is true to say that we represent our lives to ourselves and to others in the form of narratives. Thus, children should be acquainted with the stories, histories and folklores of their culture(s). Through these they are able to build and nourish their identity. Therefore, any effective education system must foremost be in the business of helping its growing young people to understand their 'cultural toolkit' and find their identity within the wider pluralistic society. The implication of this, as it relates to black children in the English education system is that the recognised identity crisis that many young black children face in schools today can only be addressed properly when, within the education structure, there is a meaningful equilibrium between cultural awareness of self and outstanding learning experiences. But the creation of this equilibrium can only be realised when the community is at the centre leading and managing the education provision for its children.

Figure 5.3 – Cultural & Learning Equilibrium Model

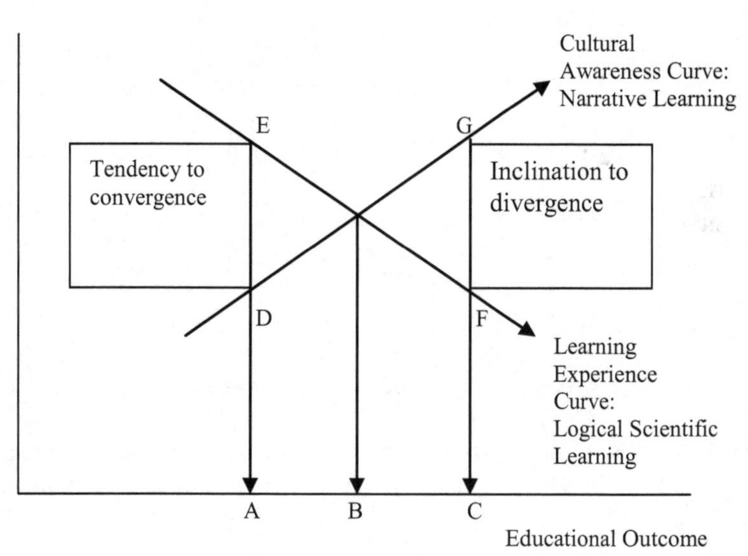

A = Inferiority Complex
B = Equilibrium
C = Disaffection

(A) The danger of inferiority complex

At point A in Figure 5.3 above, the Learning Experience Curve, focusing on the logical-scientific aspects of the curriculum, is at a higher level dominance in contrast to the Cultural Awareness and Narrative Learning curve. The impact of this disequilibrium is represented by the gap DE. Here the children will experience cultural deprivation and be in danger of devaluing their cultural heritage. The risk is that the children could become culturally detached and may develop a sense of inferiority complex. This scenario is likely to occur where children might be enrolled in a private school environment or at a highly selective maintained school that offers the opportunity for academic excellence. However, this could be at the expense of the children's cultural identity grounding, and as a result they may be led to adopt incongruous and dissonance values to their own cultural heritages. Thus, as a consequence this could leave the children emotionally unbalanced as a result of the estrangement from self, leading to the damaging effect of inferiority complex.

(B) A state of equilibrium

At this point of equilibrium (harmony) there is a balance between academic learning and cultural development that emphasises self and identity. Here, the children's cultural knowledge ('cultural toolkit') is utilized in support of the curriculum and the learning experiences provided by schools. There is a balance between the two ways in which we organise and manage knowledge, namely logical-scientific learning and narrative learning. The outworking of this state of equilibrium is the vital development and building of the children's confidence and their engagement with the learning process.

(C) Disaffection from school and learning

At this point in Figure 5.3 the learning experiences provided by schools are insufficient to support the children's cultural and identity developmental needs. For the children, the lack of cultural resonance with the schools' curriculum and ethos results in an initial disaffection from schools and learning, which then ultimately turns into the alluring, but deceptive, comfort of a street culture identity. The gap FG represents the alienation and disaffection from school life that unfortunately has been the outcome for some black children in the English education system. This is most likely to occur for black children in mainly urban maintained schools that are experiencing below standard teaching and high levels of school exclusions for black children.

Barriers to Cultural and Learning Equilibrium

The main barriers to the ideal equilibrium and harmonious state represented by position B in Figure 5.2, and which also contribute to either cultural deprivation as seen at point A or disaffection identified at point C, may be the result of the following factors:

1. the existence of a Euro-centric based curriculum and ethos;
2. low teacher expectations of black pupils' ability and potential;
3. school leadership that does not reflect the black pupils' background and cultural heritage;
4. staffing provision that provides inadequate cultural modelling and affinity for black pupils; and
5. covert and endemic racism in the school system

Likely Solutions

Some likely solutions to the above barriers may be as follows:

1. Creating a learning community that will produce the converse to the five barrier factors identified above.

2. Making the ownership and the operation of schools truly the responsibility of the local community, in contrast to the current reality where many schools are in the hands of a conclave of out of touch local politicians. The rationale for this is that school leadership that reflects the community will more likely be the custodian of the cultural life of the community they are established to serve.

Conclusion

The implication of the message of this chapter, which is that culture is at the very heart of education and learning, is that it challenges our very understanding of what pedagogy is all about. The conventional view is that the learner comes with a blank page and that the teacher is an authority who will fill the children with knowledge, who will occupy themselves with memorising the details. But a cultural approach to learning will centre on helping children to move away from just gathering knowledge and facts about the world they are in and into an understanding that knowledge and facts can only be properly interpreted with reference to the beliefs and values that children hold as learners.

In essence, beliefs are built on our early experiences acquired from the cultural base of family and community. Learning at school really is about developing children's thinking and intellectual capacity to understand more fully and to utilise what they already know and possess. The easiest part of teaching, for the insightful and discerning teacher, is to be able to recognise the opposite to the above convention, which is that children go to school with an array of talents, skills and abilities and not with a blank page. Therefore, it is for the teacher to use the children's gifts to develop and grow that knowledge and understanding. Unfortunately, many children have had their opportunity to mature in knowledge and understanding stunted by teachers who had very low expectations of their (the children's) talents, skills and potential. Commenting on the didactic bias to teaching, Bruner says:

> *'It is blankly one-way: teaching is not a mutual dialogue, but a telling by one to another. In such a regimen, if the child fails to perform adequately, her shortcomings can be explained by her lack of "mental abilities" or her low IQ and the educational establishment goes scot-free.'*
>
> (Bruner, 1996, p. 56)

This is precisely what has been happening to many children, outside of those fortunate enough to have a network of support to build and establish their confidence for learning. This is especially the case for black children in the English education system. The idea that schools can be staffed by teachers displaying at all times, the same measure of high expectations of black pupils that they accord to other groups such a middle class children, Asians and Chinese may be considered a pie in the sky illusion. Similarly, so too is the belief that low expectations of black pupils' and its Siamese twin, chronic racism, can uniquely be eliminated from the education system. This is despite the fact that racism has remained endemic in so many other areas in society, namely employment, the justice system and the service sectors – both public and private. The pragmatic way forward is to adopt what has successfully worked with respect to faith schools.

Faith schools have negated for many children the prejudices, discriminations and cultural destabilisation they would have had to endure in secular minded schools, whose ethos and climate institutionally have devalued black pupils' way of life and heritages. Indeed, faith schools are a culturally based dimension to the overall education system and structure. Today, they form approximately a third of the schools in the maintained sector, as a result of the settlement established for church schools under the historic 1944 Education Act. Therefore, they are a significant part of the education terrain and the parents of children attending these schools contribute fully to the public purse.

The notion that faith schools are selective and secular schools non-selective is a myth and at the worst interpretation, a dishonest suggestion. Every school is selective since, in reality, it is schools in general (in collaboration with local authorities) that will decide who will be enrolled, aided by their admissions policies. Faith schools do not seek to maintain and heighten differences, but rather to map out distinctiveness within what ought to be a pluralistic society that allows all members to be equally valued. Thus, Church of England, Catholic, Methodists and Jewish children are educated from that starting point that they are identified as Anglican, Catholic, Methodists and Jewish heritage learners. These clearly defined faith schools allow pupils to put on, as it were, their cultural dressing gowns. The teachers, in faith schools know the cultural language their pupils speak since they too use the same cultural vocabulary.

This cultural schooling approach works, since they consistently turn out doctors, lawyers, accountants, engineers, teachers, politicians and others leaders in our society. Never can there be an argument that, in terms of actual outcome, faith schools perpetrate segregation and ghettoism, unless we are listening to the intolerant hard core secularists.

Schools, of whatever shade, can never be replicas of the adult world, but are there to teach children to cope confidently with the adult world. Faith schools have been successful in doing this for decades. In contrast, many secular schools have failed to build that self confidence in many children with specific cultural identities, but more so for the black children. The evidence can be seen of the high levels of detachment that secular schools create for black children and black boys in particular. Thus, given that this model of cultural schooling is successful in the education system, it stands to reason that we need more schools that will not only provide for children as Catholic, Anglican, Methodist and Jewish learners, but also culturally for African and African Caribbean heritage learners too. Educationally, this is not only intellectually sound, but operationally necessary to build a strong and cohesive society not only where everyone is deemed to be valued but is actually seen to be valued. Such schools where the children's 'cultural toolkit' is readily utilised for learning will not be fortresses or places of isolation. Rather, cultural schooling will build bridges with others within our pluralistic society on the solid basis of confidence and positive self esteem. In contrast, disaffection – fuelled by prejudice, low expectations and an attitude of superiority to black people as a race – is prevalent in many of today's maintained schools with their very pronounced secular bent. Therefore, the approach of educating pupils nakedly without their cultural dressing gown has been exposed as an education failure. Thus, wisdom demands that a paradigm change be made in education that will more fully embrace the integral relationship that exists between culture and learning.

References

Allen, C (2007) *The death of multiculturalism: blaming and shaming British Muslims.* Online: www.dur.ac.ukantropology.journal/vol14
Bruner, J (1996) *The Culture of Education.* Harvard University Press.
Child, D (1981) *Psychology and the teacher.*_Holt, Rinehart and Winston Ltd
Coard, B (1971) *How the West Indian child is made educationally subnormal* ***in the British school system: the scandal of the Black child in schools in*** *Britain.* London: New Beacon Books Ltd.
Gillborn, D. (2002) *Education and institutional racism.* London: University of London Institute of Education.
Gillborn, D. (2008) *Racism and education: coincidence or conspiracy*: Routledge.
John, G (2006) *Taking a Stand: Gus John Speaks on education, race, social action & civil unrest 1980-2005.* Manchester: The Gus John Partnership Ltd.
Palmer, P. J. (1993) *To Know As We are Known.* New York: Harper Collins Publishers
Reay, D and Mirza, H. S. (1997) *Uncovering genealogies of the margins; black supplementary schooling.* British Journal of Sociology of Education, 18 (4) 477-99
Woolcock, M (2001) *The place of social capital in understanding social and economic outcomes.* Isuma: Canadian Journal of Policy Research 2:1, p 1-17

Chapter 6

A commentary on racism in education

'Education is the key element to all children's development and we all have a right to it.' (Doreen Lawrence OBE, 2007)

Introduction

Research studies on race and education tend to focus heavily on black children and in particular on African Caribbean children and their underachievement (Gillborn, 2008). However, during the 1970s and 1980s there were many discussions within the African Caribbean community about racial disadvantage in education, that went beyond social, economic and language factors that might have been expected to affect the performance of the first generation of black settlers. Nevertheless, the focus in the educational literature on the underachievement of black children avoided dealing with the racist and discriminatory attitude of the English society and its educational institutions, and blamed the disadvantaged position of minority ethnic communities on their own cultural traditions and way of life. Very little notice was taken of the influence of prejudice, discrimination and social class in regard to the educational underachievement of black children.

Early comparative data on the performance of black children presented an exaggerated view of the differences in attainment levels between black children and white children. White children are usually compared from a social class classification basis. For example, working class white children will be compared against middle class white children. The general assumption will be that middle class white children will outperform working class white children as a result of many factors such as access to learning resources and the degree of parental support in the home, which provide significant advantages for the middle class and the success their children have at schools. However, when the attainment of black children is assessed, the comparison invariably is made on racial lines. Thus, black children who are mainly under the working class grouping, based on family income, occupation and the qualifications of their parents, will be compared against mainly higher performing middle class white children's attainment results. The effect is to skew the results and reinforce the myth that the difference in performance is attributable to racial differences. However, the truth is that such difference in attainment levels are the result of class biases, compounded by the added critical element of racial stereotyping.

This negative pervasive view in circulation that black children perform less well than their white indigenous counterparts in examinations has prejudiced the minds of teachers, researchers and other educationists.

> '*It is often commented by teachers that many of the West Indian children are ''dense'' or slow at school work. . . . they are generally intellectually slower than their white classmates and those Asiatics who have mastered the language difficulty.'* (Whiteley, 1969, p.87)

As a result, black children are continually being placed at the lower end of the educational achievement statistics. The black race is perceived as lazy, their families dysfunctional and having low innate intelligence, thus resulting in their educational disability (Eysenck, 1971 and Jensen, 1969). What is strange is that these advocates, such as Eysenck, 1971 and Jensen, 1969, do not consider the content of the curriculum, and also how class and cultural biases are against certain groups of children. Furthermore, assessment procedures, setting and streaming have all been shown to be operating against black and working class pupils. Particular unease has been expressed over the years about the disproportionate numbers of black children who were and still are taken out of mainstream schooling and put in special schools, and in particular educationally subnormal schools, and now into pupil referral units.

As one can see the problem faced by the black children in their educational experience has not changed despite the fact that we are now in the 21st Century. Teachers, educational researchers and other educationalists should have learned valuable lessons regarding the negative labelling and judgments that are made about black pupils and their academic standard and performance. They have not learned and the system is still failing black children and to a lesser extent white working class children.

How the education system blames black children and their family

In Coard's (1971) highly insightful and emotive monograph it is informative to note that he questioned the way that black children are perceived in the educational sphere. He argues that black children are made educationally subnormal in English schools. This adverse judgment on the intellectual position of black children is arrived at because of the inappropriate use of Intelligent Quotient (IQ) test to determine black children's ability. Another view offered by Coard, is that the black children's very exposure and inexperience to the process of the English educational system resulted in those children's entire culture and background being undermined and devalued. In fact, black children became victims of teachers' low expectations, and the stereotyping became a self fulfilling prophecy, which eventually damaged their self image. Baratz and Baratz (1971) contend strongly that black children fail as a result of institutionalised racism in the educational system, an educational system that is still failing to recognise black children's cultural background and experiences. They, Baratz and Baratz (1971), feel that the schools are insensitive to the black children's aspirations, which prevent a positive relationship to be developed between the teachers and the black children. Furthermore, the label of being inferior, attached to black children and, in contrast, the sense of superiority, commandeered by the indigenous white population, are widespread throughout educational institutions, and they alienate black children even more.

The Plowden Report (1967), although it was a response to the underachievement of working class children in the English school system, went on to identify some underlying factors that brought about underachievement in the education system and established that multi-deprivation was the main cause. It found that white working class children achieved lower academically than their white middle class peers because of such issues as, poor housing condition, high unemployment and decaying school buildings. As a result, the Plowden Report recommended the use of 'positive discrimination' to narrow the gap. This was also predicated on the assumption that black children's performances were lower than white working class children even though they were experiencing very similar social and environmental deprivations, and discrimination. In addition, the Plowden Report placed the black children's underachievement on cultural deprivation. It believed that the black family was handicapped due to its lack of familiarity with the English culture and language, and also it blamed the authoritarian home background style of the black children's parents for the problem. It is felt that this type of parental method hinders the democratic approach to education. Thus, it is argued, black children are unable to cope effectively with the democratic style of education, and as a consequence this contributes to their underachievement in the English educational system (Yekwai, 1988).

The schools' responsibility for the underperformance of black children

Not everyone agrees with the proposition that the black children's culture is deficient and is responsible for their poor performance at school. Flude (1976), for example, refers to the quality of social interaction that exists between black parents and their children and points out the danger of placing black children's educational failure in English schools on their family. He, Flude, feels that the responsibility for the educational failure of black children is the schools themselves as they do not provide an educational environment that is supportive to these children and their learning. In fact, the climate prevailing in schools alienates black children as they are exposed to a system that rejects them and makes them feel inferior. Stones (1981) also states that schools should be blamed for the underachievement of black children. She is of the opinion that instead of condemning cultural deprivation – when considering the academic failure of working class and minority group children – researchers and educationalists, including teachers, should not disregard the educational inequalities that are inherent in the English school education system. In Berstein's (1970) critique of compensatory education, he asserts that the term 'compensatory education' draws attention away from the educational organisation of the schools where children from working class background, and especially black children, were not given the opportunity in their school environment to be successful learners. Again, one can see that the focus for pupils' underachievement should be placed squarely at the schools. Therefore, 'positive discrimination' and 'compensatory education' will do nothing to improve the performance of either working class children or black children. With respect to black children, it is even more disturbing as their culture is considered to be a 'deficit culture', a culture that will only guarantee educational failure. Therefore, for black children to learn effectively and achieve in the English educational system they would have to be socialised into the dominant white indigenous culture by rejecting their own culture in order to achieve educational success and upward social mobility (Yekwai, 1988). What a high price black children have to pay to achieve some success! Black children have to reject not only their culture, but also themselves in order to survive and achieve in a society that often rebuffs them because of their racial identity.

Rampton and Swann Reports

After the Plowden Report, came the Rampton Report in 1981, which dealt specifically with black children in the English school system. The report also considered the issue of the over representation of black children in educationally subnormal schools. This over representation was referred to by Coard (1971) as 'social engineering' and as a result black children would find themselves at the bottom of the labour market. The reason for this depressing situation is because the children of colour would be denied the opportunity of gaining good qualifications for employment, due to the educational inequalities they experienced during their schooling. As a consequence, when black children reach employment age they end up becoming unskilled workers in the labour market. This is because they do not have the qualifications or are considered unable to do work that is more intellectually challenging than just basic mundane repetitive tasks.

Black parents have continually expressed their concerns about their children's poor educational performance in the English school system and see the teachers as being responsible for their underachievement.

> *'Certainly it is well known that West Indian parents believe . . . that the performance of their children is very much affected by the expectations which teachers have of them.'*
>
> (Taylor, 1983, p.193 & 194)

The Rampton Report (1981) came about as a response to this concern by black parents, and it confirmed their strong feeling that the racism their children experienced from their teachers was the main cause for their children's poor academic performance (Cole and Blair, 2006). The Report blamed the underachievement of the black children squarely on a school system that, unfortunately, reflects the practices and norms of society in general, part of which is that it holds a negative view of black people. The reason for this, as The Report acknowledged, is that white people, are on the whole, prejudiced against black people, and the prejudice came about from the historical experiences of slavery and colonization, which resulted in lack of respect, abuse and the injustices meted out to black people for centuries. Therefore, the report argued that the curriculum needed to be changed to give a clearer picture of how British imperialism was able to be developed, and the social, historical and economical reasons for the immigration of black people to Britain. However, the Report accepts that these changes cannot take place easily as the people at the chalk face of education and training would have to undergo major transformation in their behaviour and thinking, in addition to bringing about changes in the general attitude of society. The Rampton Report like the Plowden Report also favours 'positive discrimination' where there would be a multicultural approach to education as a way of making positive changes to the school curriculum to give a balanced view of the world and its history.

Rampton became discouraged and frustrated with aspects of the enquiry he was leading. However, his Committee's report to the Thatcher government was swiftly disclaimed by ministers when it was found that the report had identified racism as the problem in education and that anti-racist policies were proposed as a solution to the difficulty faced by West Indian children in the English schooling system (Mahamdallie, 2007). As a result, The Swann Committee took over from the Rampton Interim Report in 1981, and it may be argued that the government hoped that the Swann Committee would dilute the conclusion drawn from its predecessor. The Swann Report published its findings in 1985. The committee continued with the task of addressing the widespread concerns about the poor academic performance of West Indian pupils in English schools. The title of the Swann Report is 'Education For All' and the Report makes it clear that it:

> '. . . *is concerned primarily to change behaviour and attitudes. They need to change throughout Britain, and, while the education system must not be expected to carry the whole burden of that change, schools in particular are uniquely well placed to take a lead role . . . everyone in Britain has a direct interest in ensuring that society and its institutions and the attitudes which inform them, change to take account of the pluralism which is now a marked feature of British life* . . .'
>
> (Swann Report, 1985, p. 767)

The Swann Report went on to state that the performance of schools had long been associated with socio-economic status and social class with respect to all children. It further acknowledged that ethnic minorities are particularly disadvantaged in social and economic terms and the underachievement of these children is as a result of the racial prejudice and discrimination that they experience in society at large and to a certain extent within the educational system. The Report highlighted the observation that society in general faces a 'dual problem'. The first problem is to eliminate the discriminatory attitudes of the white majority, and the second problem is to develop an educational system that ensures that all pupils, irrespective of their race or social economic backgrounds, achieve their full potential in their schooling. However, the Report accepts that the issues are complex and not fully understood; therefore more research was needed if the situation regarding ethnic minority children is to improve in the English educational system and if there is to be equality of opportunities for every child. The committee concluded its report by stating that:

> *'West Indian children as a group are under achieving in our educational system.'* (Swann Report, 1985, p. 63)

All these reports, Plowden, Rampton and Swann, show that schools must take some of the blame, if not most of the blame for the underperformance of ethnic minorities and in particular, black children. This is because institutional racism does exist with the common assumption that black parents, especially African Caribbean parents, have little interest in education or support their children while they are at school, particularly if they are lone parents. This is very far from the truth. Most black parents want their children to excel in their schooling and examinations. It is the aspiration of black parents for their children to become qualified professionals, such as doctors and lawyers, and they see education as a way of gaining respect from the members of their own community and the dominant white culture. Many of these parents consciously withdrew themselves from communicating with the schools where their children attend because of the hostility they themselves experienced when they were at school. Schools must be more sensitive and encouraging to all parents, so that they can feel comfortable and have trust in them (John, 2006) to educate their children and prepare them to make a valuable contribution to society in the 21st Century.

Positive discrimination and compensatory education

The terms such as 'positive discrimination' and 'compensatory education' coined by some of the reports mentioned above are patronising and condescending. How can such patronising and insensitive labels, be of any benefit to black children? In what ways can education be 'compensated' and for what? The idea here is that 'compensatory education' is to try to compensate for and put right the factors that are obstructing the educational performance of the black children. These terms and the programmes would suggest that somehow black children are inadequate in some way and are unable to benefit from being educated, as they are lacking in ability. What is even worse is that these programmes have not really been successful as there is no evidence that they have made improvements in respect of black children's educational performance in English schools. Downey and Kelly (1979) make reference to the:

> *'. . . cultural deficiencies . . . have been hindering the educational success of such pupils. This is an idea that appeared earlier in the USA in answer to the problem of the education of black children.'*
>
> (Downey and Kelly, 1979 p. 264)

The mere fact that the terms 'positive discrimination' and 'compensatory education' are used will negatively work against black children. The terms merely highlight that special arrangements will have to be made for the black children. This is in order for them to cope adequately with the curriculum offered in schools. What is needed is for the black children to be valued and encouraged rather than make these children feel that they have some kind of 'deficit' or 'handicap' that can be remedied in one way or another by such programmes. These programmes have come and gone but the situation is still the same as many black children continue to underachieve in the English educational system.

If early support arrangements such as preschool and nursery education provisions are made for black children these opportunities will benefit these children by greatly reducing various forms of social deprivation, it is claimed that black children suffer from. In addition to this, it was felt by the Plowden

Report (1967) that such programmes will help black children gain substantially from the education being offered in schools when they reach compulsory school age.

No major reviews, reports or study of the educational experiences and achievements of ethnic minority pupils and in particular African Caribbean pupils have taken place since the Swann Report (1985) until the work undertaken by Gillborn and Gipps over a decade later in 1996. The Gillborn and Gipps' review for Ofsted shows that little has changed with regards to the educational performance of black children. The findings reveal that achievements of children from the higher social class were superior to the achievements of lower social class groups, irrespective of ethnic origins. However, the position has not altered for many black children whose performance remained at the bottom of the educational ladder regardless of whether they are working class or middle class. Gillborn and Gipps (1996) confirm this:

> '*. . . a relatively stable picture of African Caribbean pupils achieving less well than their peers of the same sex and social class background.'* (Gillborn and Gipps, 1996, p. 28)

Institutionalised Racism

Yes, it is true that African Caribbean pupils are performing less well than white and Asian pupils, but there is no justifiable reason for this situation except that these children are treated less favourably and as a result less is expected of them in terms of scholastic achievement. The English educational system on the whole is unwilling to accept that institutionalised racism is a factor adversely affecting the education of black children. This form of racism is used to give white people more opportunities and advantages over and above other ethnic minorities (Gillborn, 2008). Yet, there is evidence both blatant (overt) and hidden (covert) that points to institutionalised racism. However, there is no substantive verification in the form of a study or other collective information to provide evidence that the culprit lies in the institutions controlled by white supremacists that has brought about, and is continuing to bring about, this serious situation of the failure of black children in the English education system.

It must be borne in mind that researchers vary on how they categorise ethnic minorities and in particular, black children. This is important as black children can be classified as 'West Indians', 'Black African', 'Black British', 'Black Caribbean', Afro Caribbean and 'African Caribbean'. African Caribbean seems to be the preferred term, but this in the past left out 'Black African' in the black children's category. However, 'Black African' is now being officially used in statistics monitoring ethnic minority pupils' performance. A point that needs to be noted is that the Black Africans tend to achieve higher examination results than the children of African Caribbean heritage (Gillborn and Gipps, 1996). A further point needs to be mentioned here and that is the Asian children used to come under the label of 'black'. However, the then Commission for Racial Equality stopped classifying Asians as blacks (as the Asian themselves objected to this) in the late 1980s and the census in 1991 followed this example (Gillborn and Gipps, 1996).

Whatever grouping or label one may wish to place the black children under, the statistical evidence from examination results is consistent. The black children's performance is a cause for concern. Firstly, black children do not share equally in the increasing rate of educational achievement as their white and Asian counterparts. Secondly, the achievement gap between black children and their peers has remained relatively unchanged irrespective of copious initiatives over the last few decades to narrow the gap. This disappointing observation is even more acute for black male children as they are achieving significantly below their potential, although at present there is growing concern regarding white working class children, and in particular white working class boys who are considered to be grossly underperforming also in their scholastic achievement.

Despite this information, when the statistical evidence on education performance is scrutinized carefully one will find that only working class children on Free School Meals (FSM) perform less well than African Caribbean children. These white working class children on FSM are a small minority and overall it is the black children who are still at the bottom in respect of educational achievement. In spite of the recognition that a small percentage of working class children are failing and lagging behind other ethnic groups, the focus in education and in the media is still on the black children's failure to do better in their scholastic performance. These negative comments that single out, specifically, black children's performance show disrespect for the black community. In addition, continuous comments are made by educational researchers, teachers and the media blaming father absence homes, dysfunctional families, the authoritarian attitude of black parents, and poor and inappropriate behaviour of black children in schools that are not conducive to learning, and which have led to high exclusion rates. No mention or acknowledgement is made about how the English school system has contributed, and is continuing, to fail the black children. The responsibility for the black children's failure surely must lie at the foot of politicians, teachers and other education personnel in the educational system. The reason for this is because they have not been successful in reversing this prolonged and chronic educational failing irrespective of the copious programmes and initiatives that have been put in place to address this so called low level of achievement of the black children.

How did this low level of achievement by the black children come about? Coard (1971) demonstrates this aptly by the way he explains how black children are made to feel inferior each day in the classroom here in the English schools:

> '*He is made to feel inferior in every way . . . he is told by a variety of means that he is intellectually inferior . . . his language is second rate . . . the Black discovers that all the great men of history were white . . he discovers that white horses, white rocks and white unicorn are beautiful and good; but the word 'black' is reversed for describing the pirates, the thieves, the ugly, the witches etc.'* (Coard, 1971, p. 47)

The strong point being made here by Coard (1971) is that if everything associated with the word 'black' is negative, and at times, evil then black children will feel bad about themselves. They, the black children, will become very conscious about themselves and consider themselves of little worth because of their blackness. If one ponders a little longer one can see that these negative word associations are very crippling emotionally for the black children. The negative connotations with the word 'black' are persistent and are repeated time and time again. For example: black death, blackmail, black plague, black list, black magic, black sheep, blackleg, black letter, black look and the inventory continues. This use of the adjective 'black' connected to the nouns mentioned above have a damaging effect that black children would be sensitive to as they experience them daily in the ordinary classroom milieu and society in general. Coard (1971) brings to the readers' attention that these words occur over and over again on the television, on the radio, in the newspapers, magazines and in reading books with disdain and disrespect for black children's feelings. To illustrate this point further, a popular class reader, 'Buddy' by Nigel Hinton, for English lessons usually for Years 8 and 9 classes in some secondary schools refers to racist comments and connotations in a school classroom:

> *'Buddy sat down at his desk near the door and noticed that Julius and Charmian weren't in their places behind him. He hoped that the twins weren't away. He'd never had black friends before – in fact, he'd said some nasty things to some black kids at his Junior School. But he'd been drawn to Julius and Charmian because they were the only other people who didn't fit in with the rest of the class. He'd started off by admiring the cheerful way they ignored all the spiteful jibes that the other pupils, and even some of the teachers, made. They'd become allies and then, gradually, his closet friends.*
>
> *'Mr Normington started calling the register. He looked up when there was no answer from Julius and Charmian. "The Rybeero twins not here? Has anyone seen our coloured cousins?"*
>
> *"I saw them hanging around the fruit shop after school, yesterday," Emma Grove said.*
>
> *'There was a ripple of laugher at this old joke. Fruit shop meant bananas. Bananas meant apes. Apes meant Blacks.*
>
> *'Mr Normington pretended innocence. "Really?" he said. Pause. "I wonder why?*
>
> *'Another ripple of conspiratorial laughter. Everyone was happy.*
>
> *'Buddy could have said something. Something angry about how the twins were worth all the rest of the class put together. At the very least he could have sat stony-faced as his friends were mocked. But he smiled. Mr Normington was looking in his direction and, in an attempt to show that he belonged in 3E, and that he was on the side of*

> *Mr Normington's bastions and standards, Buddy smiled and joined in the general chuckle.*
>
> *'He hated himself for wanting to belong to all that, but it was true – he did. A huge part of him wanted it.'* ('Buddy' by Nigel Hinton, pages 8 and 9)

The extract above speaks volumes for itself as to the type of material black children are exposed to and expected to use as reading text in the classroom. In the extract blacks are seen as '*hanging around . . . fruit shops'* for bananas as apes are considered to like bananas. The main protagonist, a white working class boy, Buddy is friends with the black twins because he and the twins did not fit in with the other white children in the class. What is even more disturbing for the black children reading the novella is the stereotype of blacks and how the teacher acted knowing fully well what the pupil Emma Grove was hinting at about the Rybeero twins. If such a reading text is not handled sensitively and cautiously by the teachers, if they choose to read it with their classes it could give credence to disparaging racial attitude and behaviour by white children and leave the black children feeling embarrassed and uncomfortable. Other damaging and degrading comments are made about Julius and Charmian's parents being '*jungle-bunnies*', Chinese food being referred to as '*Flied Lice and Sweet and Sour Eyeballs'* and Buddy, being told by his teacher; '*Since you speak and look like a dustman, you can do a dustman's job.'* However, the negative impact can be quite destroying for the black children seated in the classroom listening and reading these racist remarks, and also in the way in which Buddy himself was being insulted because of his attire and working class background.

The effect of such an experience for the black children can be devastating. It lowers the black children's self esteem and adversely affects these children's emotions, confidence and intelligence. The black children could become withdrawn and demonstrate aggressive behaviour to cope with the uncomfortable state of affairs they find themselves in, which will in, some way, have serious consequences for their academic achievement. The black children know that they will be judged in a disapproving way just because of the colour of their skin. Coard (1971) again spells out the situation for the black children and how they are made to feel:

> *'The Black child under these influences develops a deep inferiority complex. He soon loses motivation to succeed academically, since at best the learning experience in the classroom is an elaborate irrelevance to his personal life situation, and at worst it is a racially humiliating experience. He discovers in an amazingly short space of time the true role of the Black man in a white-controlled society, and he abandons all intellectual and career goals.'* (Coard, 1971 p.48)

This state of affairs is achieved by not valuing the black children's culture, history, identity and language in the curriculum (Coard, 1971). With all of this negativity surrounding black children is it surprising that they do not do so well in the English educational system? How can children do well in a system that is forever verbally and emotionally abusive to them in a subtle manner by the language used whenever reference is made to those children, their culture, their family and their home background being deficient? Here, one has to stop and ponder that after four to five generations, over forty years ago, black children still lag some way behind their white counterparts in educational achievement (Brown, 2007). Both Bhattacharyya (2007) and the authors concur that the reason why black children are still underperforming and therefore failing in the English educational system is because racism is prevalent and rife in schools. Gillborn (2008) comments that the term racism is considered harsh by some people and as a result they feel uncomfortable and uneasy about mentioning it, and therefore they become defensive to any suggestion that they might in any way have racist tendencies, behaviour or attitude towards the black race.

Racism and the examination system

Another area of concern is the examination system which, in practice, fails the majority of children and in particular the black children. (Reference was made to this matter in chapter 3) The General Certificate of Education (GCE) and the Certificate of Secondary Education (CSE) were both removed from the British examination system in the late 1980s and replaced with the General Certification of Secondary Education (GCSE), which combined both examinations. Parents and mainly black parents were very unhappy with their children taking CSE as only a grade 1 pass at CSE was considered to be a grade C pass at GCE. It was not surprising that a high percentage of entries for the CSE examinations were black children. The GCSE first cohort was in 1988. The top three grades A, B and C were considered good passes. These are the grades that further and higher education institutions value. Grades D to G are also passes, but are deemed to be lower passes and equivalent to the former CSE examination. To make matters even more complicated a tiered entry system came into being with the GCSEs. For most examinations there are the higher tier and the foundation tier, but some examinations such as mathematics originally had three tiers: higher, intermediate and foundation. In other words there were a two tiered model and a three tiered model operating in the same examination system.

A number of years later the grading for the GCSE was altered to award pupils with an A* grade for their outstanding performance in the examinations. The grade of A* is also now given to students who perform exceptionally in their GCE A level examinations, but this was after the grade A* was given to outstanding performance for GCSE candidates for some period of time before it was awarded to A level students. You may ask, what is wrong with this? Nothing whatsoever! What is wrong is with the GCSE examinations tiered grading system. It seems to be the old GCE and CSE disguised and returning through the back door. A serious concern is about the two tiered examination model where a child who does not achieve at least a grade D, sitting the higher tier paper, will end up being ungraded because at the higher tier he can only score a grade between A* to D. In addition to this, the pupil who takes the foundation tier paper knows before he takes an examination that the highest possible grade he could achieve is a grade C and will not have the chance to try for an A*, A or B grade. What will be further disappointing for the pupil is that if he wants to study at A level standard at a further education college, a sixth form college or a sixth form at a school, the chances are very slim if he achieves below a grade C as some colleges and schools will only take pupils with A*, A, B or C grade to study an A level subject. Furthermore, a significant number of these colleges and sixth forms will not accept a student who has a C pass to study a subject at 'A' level. It is these colleges' judgments that a grade C pass is just a pass and not a good enough pass to study a subject at 'A' level standard. The question is: Are teachers preparing their pupils adequately for the GCSEs and GCEs? Not only further education colleges, but also universities are looking to attract the high achievers in respect of examination grades to their courses of study. Universities are expecting their students to have grades A*, A, B and C, but the more prestigious universities would not even consider a C grade even if the C grade is the lowest amongst the candidate's other A level subject grades. One cannot but feel relieved that the tiered grading system has not continued into the 'A' level examinations system.

What was even more distressing with the GCSE examination such as mathematics was that with the three tier model, where a candidate took the foundation tier paper, the student could only attain a grade D, which was the highest grade achievable at that examination level. One can only be thankful that the mathematics GCSE papers are now in two tiers: foundation and higher. The aim was to bring mathematics in line with the other examination subject papers, where a candidate taking the foundation paper stands a chance to achieve a C grade. Furthermore, it is quite obvious that the tiered system was just a cunning way to keep the GCE and CSE divide and to continue with the inequality of the education system in England where black children are overrepresented in the foundation tiers and therefore underrepresented in sitting the higher tier examination papers.

The higher tier is for pupils who the subject teachers consider to be the most able in the class. Gillborn (2007) states that:

> '. . . *the risk of higher tier pupils falling through the grade-floor, and being 'ungraded', prompts many teachers to play safe by entering greater numbers for the lower tier. In this way some teachers are treating the Higher tier in a selective manner so that only those viewed as 'the most able' are permitted entry.'* (Gillborn, 2007, p.93)

The teachers are the ones who decide which tier pupils can enter for in the external examinations. Given what we already know about teachers' expectations regarding black children one should not be surprised that the majority of black pupils will be entered for the foundation tier examination papers and not the higher tier examination papers. Gillborn (2007) alludes to the perception and assumption held by teachers that the subculture of black children is that '. . . *there are some who are afraid to be seen to work hard, that academic effort is uncool.*' This is a strange assertion as the black community does value education highly and there is concrete evidence that black children are more likely to go onto full time further education to accomplish good and higher educational qualifications rather than rush out to work when compared to their white peers (CMPO, 2008).

An additional matter which must be mentioned is the issue regarding vocational courses. These courses have helped schools to massage their examination results so that their percentages look good in the published league tables for GCSE passes A* to C, which now must be five subjects including mathematics and English. Gillborn (2007) confirms this and comments on the false impression these examinations give about the GCSE performance of schools which offer vocational type qualifications. The problem with these vocational courses is that if a child passes in one subject that child will be awarded four GCSE grades. Yes, four GCSE grades for taking one subject!

> *'It has been argued that young people are disadvantaged in the labour market if they do not have higher grade GCSEs in English and maths. There is also a suspicion that some schools made their GCSE results look artificially high by entering kids for vocational qualifications where a single course counted as equivalent of up to four GCSE higher grade in the performance table.'* (Gillborn, 2007, p.102)

The General National Vocational Qualification (GNVQ) is sometimes disparagingly referred to as '**G**oing **N**owhere **V**ery **Q**uickly'. This is because these examinations have a very low currency in the further and higher educational arenas. So much so that the present coalition government intends to have an overhauled or find possible alternatives. What is very sad is that many of the pupils who took these examinations felt that they were of great value until the realisation came to the pupils that further education colleges, higher education colleges and universities do not accept them. It is quite obvious that the children who took these examinations were considered by their teachers as having low ability and a high percentage of them were black children who had been entered for these vocational qualifications. In addition to this, many students have been given false hope with inadequate qualifications which are of no value to them at all.

The reason for this, is because schools had to achieve at least 30% 5 A* – C to satisfy the Labour Government when it was in power to prove that the standard of achievement in schools was at an acceptable level. This has now been increased to 40% in 2012 under the present conservative and liberal democrats' coalition government, and there is talk that this coalition government wants to further increase that percentage to 50% 5 A* – C including maths and English as the minimum school performance level.

Furthermore, the coalition government is of the view that schools should offer their pupils a broad range of academic subjects at GCSE. It feels that a wide range of academic subjects are necessary for Britain to offer quality educational standards and be able to compete with other successful countries internationally. The English Baccalaureate, which is not a new qualification, recognises students' achievements in a core of selected academic subjects for obtaining good passes (A* – C). These must include the following: English, mathematics, a science, a language (which includes Latin, classical Greek or ancient Hebrew) and a humanities subject (geography or history). It has also been suggested that English Literature and Religious Education should be added. Note that no mention is made of vocational qualifications whatsoever. The government is keen for schools to concentrate on valuable traditional academic qualifications which universities and employers want.

The English Baccalaureate would satisfy many universities and employers as it includes valuable academic subjects. However, it is disappointing to note that the national average for the English Baccalaureate in 2009/2010 was a shameful 16% approximately. For the black children, the position is even more daunting. When the English Baccalaureate is broken down by ethnicity the percentage achieved by black children is a mere 7%, which is less than half of the national average. This is extremely devastating to say the least. In fact, on reflection, one should not be that surprised at all as black children are entered for the less academically rigorous examinations. Furthermore, only 22% of the total examination entry for students at age 16 covered all the required components of the English Baccalaureate. When one compares the 5 A* – C, or the equivalent including English and mathematics the league tables give a very disheartening picture indeed. The majority of schools are not providing their pupils with a broad range of academic subjects at age 16 and black children are further disadvantaged as they are not entered for the academically challenging subjects at GCSE, but instead are encouraged to take vocational courses. Even more disturbing is that schools were made to look good in the league tables by entering pupils for these valueless vocational qualifications.

With an examination system that continues to differentiate by using a selection method that discriminates against the black children, there should be no surprise that they underperform so poorly. Mirza (2007) contends that England is:

> '. . . *still plagued by the problem of racial differentiation in educational treatment and outcome for Black Caribbean young people. The question for us three and a half decades on* (after Bernard Coard's seminal pamphlet) *is, why do these racial inequalities still persist . . .*' (Mirza, 2007 pp.108&109)

The reason for this stance is because white society, white educationalists, white racists still want to wrongfully maintain that children of immigrants, especially black settlers, are considered to be culturally and socially deficient because these children come from backgrounds that are judged to be inferior and therefore not as civilised as the white English people, which makes them inherently intellectually lacking in ability (Mirza, 2007). It is this type of belief that has a detrimental effect on black children's performance. The truth is that many black children's confidence has been very badly damaged and destroyed. What needs to be done is to build the confidence of the black children by letting them feel that they are capable and can achieve good educational standards just like any other race.

Black children can become confident learners; they just need to be treated in exactly the same way as their white counterpart, with the same expectations, with the same respect, with the same interpersonal relationship and with the same understanding. It is true from the statistics that examination performance of all children have improved over the last few years because of the government's agenda to improve educational standards in this country in line with the higher educational performance of the more successful European countries such as Finland and Sweden. Despite the improvement, black children still remain in the lowest academic attainment position.

Can schools make a difference?

Many programmes and educational policies have been put in place, it is said, to eradicate black children's poor educational performance, compared to their peers in other racial groups. Black children's performance in regard to their position is that they still linger at the bottom of the educational ranking. There is no evidence, in respect of inspection reports and other educational reports, to suggest that these programmes have been evaluated for the effectiveness of their intervention strategies or how successful these educational policies have been to improve the situation for black children. However, there is the school effectiveness research that confirms the importance of schools in bringing about improved pupil attainment. Reynolds and Creemers (1990) assert that:

> ' . . . *schools matter, that schools do have major effects upon children's development and that, to put it simply, that schools do make a difference.''*
>
> (Reynolds and Creemers, 1990, p. 1)

Blair (2007) concurs with this view and acknowledges where responsibility rests despite the fact that educators, politicians, teachers and some educational researchers still blame and place the responsibility on the black children's race, family and culture for their failure in the English educational system.

> *'Whilst responsibility for the child's education rests with both school and family, research has shown that schools do make a difference. But it is those schools that understand the role of institutions in perpetuating inequality that are able to make a real difference.* (Blair, 2007, p. 214)

The question is how much difference can a school make? It has been well established that schools cannot work in isolation from the home and that a partnership between home and school is essential, as confirmed by Blair (2007) above, for the children to do well academically and socially. However, schools can make a great difference in educating all their pupils well, by giving them the same high quality education irrespective of the pupils' social class, race or socio economic background. Placing pupils into groups where they receive different quality of education according to their perceived ability, black children will invariably find themselves in the lower streams or sets, and this will not improve the situation. Coard (2007) asserts that:

> *'What is needed . . . is a system of quality education for all, and therefore, by definition, one which is not dependent on the parental*

> *wealth, social status and connections; one which does not have schools providing vastly different standards of education, providing differential education for children of different classes, genders and ethnicities.'*
>
> (Coard, 2007, p.184)

As a nation, we owe all our children the very best education. We need to be committed to that by getting our priorities right, using our resources effectively and efficiently, and not looking for false excuses for why one group does not do as well academically as others. In other words, why is it that black children perform poorly when compared with other ethnic groups? What we need to be looking at is how and what makes all children, black, white and others perform and do well in their schooling. If serious changes do not come, the disadvantaged position that black children find themselves in will ruin another black generation and rob society of the many talents and skills that could have been of great benefit to all of us.

Research in education has shown that some schools are making the effort to try and improve the performance of ethnic minority and working class children, and as a result benefit black children also. There are some schools which are more effective than others in achieving improved performances for the black children, but these are in a small minority. These schools in the minority are more prepared to accept, to a certain extent, the serious effect of institutional racism that exists and that the adverse consequences of ignoring racism in schools would be a failure of the organisation to address it openly and competently. However, it is not evident how successful these schools really are and how effectively they are in evaluating their own intervention strategies efficiently to ensure that the blame for lack of performance or poorer educational achievement is not placed directly at ethnic minority pupils, and in particular black children and their families.

Where schools are proactive and reflect on how best to utilise the energies of their students so that they are channelled into their learning, this will help to bring about positive achievement by the students. When success is actually gained teachers should be thinking about sharing this success with other teachers and departments in the school, and even amongst schools themselves so that the majority of their clients, our children, perform to the national expected standards and even better. For this to happen, the education system in this country will need to change and make a paradigm shift to be more critical of itself by finding ways to interrogate and analyse what it does to improve the life chances for individuals and different groups of children, so that inequalities do not persist in England. Some of what is found out will not be easily accepted because people on the whole do not like to take the blame for something that they know is unacceptable.

Schools are learning centres for all members of their community, internal and external. Internally, this includes teachers, support staff, pupils/students, parents/carers and externally, the members of the wider community. However, it is the teachers' attitude and behaviour towards their pupils that have far reaching effect on the performance of pupils and how the schools are perceived by the public as to whether they are effective or not. Where there have been changes so far, these changes have come about gradually with no sense of urgency. Nor have the changes addressed the issues about the black children's low educational performance adequately. Yes, there have been programmes that have been mentioned earlier, which were supposed to tackle the underperformance problem, but they have not been successful. One wonders why such programmes have been referred to as being positive intervention programmes. Positive for whom anyway one may ponder? Is it for the benefit of the teachers to feel that the negative views they have about the black children are corrected? What seems to be missing is an acknowledgement or acceptance that programmes in schools that furnish the curriculum should cater for the diverse society in which we live and not continue to give white pupils a false view of the world, that they are the only race that have contributed to the great achievements that are benefitting humankind. The only time attention is paid to the issue of the black children's poor school achievement is by default, such as when the broader issues to do with social injustices and discrimination confronting the black community result in its tolerance level breaking, exploding and finally erupting into violence. For example, the Notting Hill riot in 1958, the Brixton riot in 1981 and the Tottenham riots in 1985 and 2011 or some such other social unrests which trigger such outbursts. Gillborn (2008) affirms this view:

> *'Often the catalyst for change nationally is a major protest or public injustice, frequently involving bloodshed, even death. These are typically presented, by policymakers and media commentators, as if*

> *they arise randomly, when some fluke occurrence exposes a problem and action is taken to rectify the anomaly; one more step on the steady road of incremental advance towards greater inclusion and social justice.'* (Gillborn, 2008, page 118)

This is when the government decides to act and look into the issue of racism and in particular institutionalised racism, but this tokenism of concern does not seem to last long because there has been no change in the educational system when it comes to the perception of how black children perform, and the government seems to have conveniently forgotten its duty towards the black members of its society. Race equality cannot be treated as something that is a temporary thing (Gillborn, 2008). Institutionalised racism is still rife but subtle in many places.

> *'The fact that institutional racism has been named explicitly as a factor in Britain's police, education and health services is not a solution, it is merely a diagnosis. But in education the diagnosis has been ignored or rejected in most schools while the system rolls along in its familiar racist fashion, treating race inequality as if it were a temporary phenomenon of marginal importance, arising mainly from the minoritized groups themselves, entirely oblivious and/or uncaring about the active role that policy and assessment play in creating and legitimating such injustices.'* (Gillborn, 2008, p.133)

The injustices and negative stereotyping towards the black children is evident still today. In the August 2011riots in the different inner cities of England they have shown that young people from disadvantaged as well as advantaged homes, which include African Caribbean, Asians and whites, seem to have become disengaged from society. David Starkey, the renowned historian, seems to blame the attitude of these riotous young people on them taking on the behaviour and culture of black people. Starkey should be careful with such pronouncements as it could give encouragement to incite racial hatred and intolerance. He said that Enoch Powell predicted the riots many years ago but in a different way in his 'River of Blood' speech. David Starkey went on to elaborate that Enoch Powell envisaged that these riots would involve only black youths as the miscreants. In addition to this, he complained about the Jamaican patois and said that it had intruded into the English language and that black culture militates against education. The mere fact that a public figure can have such a strong and harmful view that echoes Enoch Powell's negative comments regarding black people on a 21st century television programme shows that the mindset of some in the English indigenous society. They have not really changed their perception regarding their negative opinion of black people. No mention of the fact that the riots, which took place over England, were carried out not only by alienated and disaffected blacks, but also by disaffected white and Asians young people. Furthermore, no reference is made about the number of inappropriate television programmes that feed our young people false messages such as having instant success and money without working hard to achieve one's goal in life, for example Reality TV. Destructive and degrading statements about a particular group of people like this will do more damage and reinforce a disparaging stereotype about black people that will in turn affect the way that black children are perceived and treated in schools.

It is depressing to note we are no further advanced when it comes to racial equality, let alone race equality in education. Bell (1980) makes it plain that for blacks to obtain racial equality this will only be achieved when it is beneficial for the interest of the whites. For things to improve social justice must be encouraged and promoted by the government throughout society so that every one can feel respected and valued wherever he lives, works or goes to school. Where skills, talents and knowledge are recognised and used, society on the whole will benefit.

The educational system and more particularly schools are monitored by Ofsted to ensure that good quality education is provided for all our children. However, Ofsted needs to focus more on race equality in schools as at present it is not given the significant attention it should be given by inspections (DfES, 2006). Gillborn (2008) confirms that race equality is given low priority in the inspection scheme by Ofsted and the slow pace of change in education is disheartening. It is disheartening because of the pretence that race inequality does not really exist in education and the underachievement of the black children have nothing to do with what takes place in schools because other children perform adequately, it is said. So the fault must be placed on the black children's race, their family, their background and their innate ability. The authors feel that this view is to make educationalists, and in particular schools and teachers, eliminate any sense of guilt or blame, and further it gives excuses so that the same negative behaviour and attitude can continue without any concerns for the black children's feeling, intelligence and mental growth. What is needed is a strong focus on race equality so that the disadvantages faced by black children will eventually be eradicated and opportunity given, not just for a few or those who are able to benefit from a private education, but to all to experience good quality education, both black and white learners.

On a more positive note, tribute must be paid to Dianne Abbot MP for recognising that there are outstanding young black achievers in the English educational system whose performances are equal to the very best in this country. As the authors have mentioned in chapter 1 every year she hosts a programme to recognise and give credit to black children who have achieved excellent grades at GCSE, A level and degree level. The programme, London Schools and the Black Child (LSBC), has existed for some years now and has been extremely successful. What the programme confirms is that given the right support and encouragement, like any other children, black children can, not only achieve, but achieve very well and is able to compete to a high educational standard showing extraordinary achievement as the black race has gifted and talented children just like any other race. In addition to this, and even more importantly, the programme is inspirational and is a good source of motivation for younger children of colour.

Conclusion

More initiatives like this need to be encouraged, because it focuses on the positive rather than on the negative. However, this takes the blame away from those who should be held accountable such as the government and in particular white educationalists. These positive outcomes for some black children can make the education system feel more comfortable, and instead places the blame for those black children who fail on their race, their family and their community. The time has come, despite the fact that it is long overdue, for radical changes to be made to the English educational system and to challenge the negative attitude of those who teach our children. We are in the 21st Century and humankind has made tremendous progress, the progress is not exclusive to the whites, the Asians or the Chinese, but to black people too who have contributed to this progress. At times, blacks have not been given the credit for what they have achieved. In addition, others have pretended and made claims for things that blacks have invented, and at other times it has been hidden that a black person has achieved such and such because it is convenient for white society to take away or hide the credit that should be given to the black race. It is time for this to stop and the world in 21st Century should be acknowledging the achievements of all people, because all children need to be enthused, inspired and motivated by people who look like them.

Cole and Blair (2006) use the metaphor to highlight the point that racialization has continued '*to deform the educational institutions*' of English society. They, Cole and Blair (2006), further state that the various governments' lack of commitment over the years did not assist in persuading teachers and schools to take on the damaging effect of racism or to challenge the injustices and inequalities experienced in England by ethnic minority people. In concluding on the topic of racism in education, Cole and Blair (2006) comment that there needs to be a challenge to '*the racist nature of British society'* as they '*regret to conclude that British society remains institutionally racist*' and schools are guilty of not dealing with the issue of racism.

Education is of paramount importance to every country and it is crucial to educate all citizens so that they can play their part in building a prosperous, just and fair society. To deny a group, a race, a particular class a chance to have a good education will be detrimental for that society as a whole. Opportunities given to certain sections of society and not to others will see a waste in brain power and also see the less fortunate being treated negatively as an underclass. It can be seen that the English educational system is grossly underperforming when it comes to educating black children because of the inherent racism, be it conscious or unconscious. However, the goal of eradicating racism from society in general and education specifically provides a great prospect for positively changing and transforming our society into one that values all individuals. Thus, education is the key for this to happen.

References

Baratz and Baratz (1971) "*The Social Science Base of Institutionalised Racism*" in 2nd edition of *School and Society*, edited by B. Cosin et.al. 1971

Bell, D. '*Brown v Board of Education and the interest convergence dilemma*', Harvard Law Review, 93, 518-533.

Berstein, B. (1970) '*A critique of the Concept of Compensatory Education*' in Rebenstein, D. and Stoneman, C. (eds) *Education for Democracy*, London: Penguin, 1970

Bhattacharyya, G. (2007) '*It won't make you rich, but it might make you smart*' in Richardson, B. (ed.) *Tell It Like It Is: How our schools fail Black children*, London: Bookmarks Publications and Trentham Books

Blair, M. (2007) '*How schools and local authorities can make the difference to the education of the Black child*' in Richardson, B. (ed.) *Tell It Like It Is: How our schools fail Black children*, London: Bookmarks Publications and Trentham Books

Brown, W. (2007) '*The future before us*' in Richardson, B. (ed.) *Tell It Like It Is: How our schools fail Black children*, London: Bookmarks Publications and Trentham Books

Coard, B. (1971) *How the West Indian Child is Made Educationally Subnormal in the, British School System London*: New Beacon Books

Coard, B. (2007) '*Thirty years on: where do we go from here*?' Richardson, B. (ed.*) Tell It Like It Is: How our schools fail Black children*, London: Bookmarks Publications and Trentham Books

Cole, M. and Blair, M. (2006) '*Racism and education: from Empire to New Labour*' in Mike Cole (ed) *Education, Equality and Human Rights: Issues of gender, 'Race', Sexuality, Disability and Social Class*, 2nd Edition: Oxfordshire: Routledge

CMPO (2008) *White children's educational aspirations lower than those of most ethnic minorities.* Centre for Market and Public Organisation (CMPO) http://www.bristol.ac.uk/cmpo/news/2008/364.html.

Department for Education and Skills (2006) *Exclusion of Black Pupils: Priority Review.Getting It, Getting It Right*, DfES

Downey, M. And Kelly, A.V., (1979) *Theory and Practice of Education: An Introduction* 2nd Edition, London: Harper and Row Publishers.

Eysenck, H. J. (1971) *Race, Intelligence and Education*, London: Temple Smith

Flude, M. (1976) '*Sociological account of Differential Educational Attainment*' in *Education, School and Ideology*, edited by M. Flude et al, 1976

Gillborn, D (2007) '*It takes a nation of millions (and a particular kind of Education system) to hold us back*' Richardson, B. (ed.) *Tell It Like It Is: How our schools fail Black children*, London: Bookmarks Publications and Trentham Books

Gillborn, D. (2008) *Racism and Education: Coincidence or Conspiracy?* London: Routledge

Gillborn, D. and Gipps, C. (1996) *Recent Research on the Achievement of Ethnic Minority Pupils*, London: HMSO

Hinton, N. (1982) *Buddy*, London: New Windmill Series

Jensen, A.R. (1969) '*How much Can We Boost I.Q. and Scholastic Achievement?*' in Harvard Educational Review

John, G. (2006) *Taking a Stand*, Manchester: The Gus John Partnership Ltd.

Lawrence, D (2007) Foreword in Richard, B. (ed.) 2nd Edition in *Tell It Like It Is: How our schools fail Black children*, London: Bookmarks Publications

Mahamdallie, H. (2007) '*Is this as good as it gets?*' in Richardson, B. (ed.) *Tell It Like It Is: How our schools fail Black children*, London: Bookmarks Publications and Trentham Books

Mirza, H. M (2007) '*The more things change, the more they stay the same: Assessing Black underachievement 35 years on*' in Richardson, B. (ed.) *Tell It Like It Is: How our schools fail Black children*, London: Bookmarks Publications and Trentham Books

Plowden Report: *Children and Their Primary Schools*, 1967

Rampton, A. (1981) *West Indian Children in Our Schools*. Cmnd. 8273. London, HMSO

Reynolds, D and Creemers, B (1990) "*School effectiveness and school improvement: a mission statement*" in School Effectiveness and School Improvement Journal 1/1, pp.1-3.

Stone, M. (1981) *The Education of the Black Child in Britain*, London: Fontana.

Swann, Lord (1985) *Education for All: Final Report of the Committee of*

Inquiry into the Education of Children from Ethnic Minority Groups: Cmnd 9453, London: HMSO

Taylor, M. J. (1983) *Caught Between: A Review of Research into the Education of Pupils of West Indian Origin*, Windsor: The NFER-Nelson Publishing Company Ltd.

Whiteley, W. M. (1969) *The Uneducated English, London*: Methuen & Co. Ltd.

Yekwai, D. (1988) *British Racism: Miseducation and The Afrikan Child*, London: Karnak House

Chapter 7

200 years of elitism in education: a new paradigm and renaissance

Introduction

For more than two centuries the true work of education – which is to uplift body, mind and spirit to their full capacity for excellence – has been held back by the rampaging, destructive and selfish force of elitism. Elitism has occupied the education system without much restraint for far too long. Therefore, in order for stakeholders in the education system to comprehend the poisonous nature of this educational tyrant, it is clearly desirable for all involved in the work of education to know how this situation developed historically. Furthermore, understanding how we have arrived at this juncture in the evolution of the education system will also be instructive for constructing a cohesive philosophical framework and a new paradigm for the education system, in order to fulfil the longstanding aspiration of 'education for all'. Table 7.1 illustrates the narrative of an education system that is under performing.

Table 7.1

2011 GCSE Results – 5 A* to C (Including English and Mathematics)

Ethnic Category	**%**
Chinese	78
Indian	73
Mixed White/Asian	67
White	58
White and Black Caribbean	49
Black Caribbean	47
Black African	58
Pakistani	54
Bangladeshi	59

Overall average for all groups = 58%

The 5 A to C GCSE grades (later A* to C), including English and mathematics, have been recognised for over two decades to be the gold standard measure of academic success for children passing yearly through the secondary phase of the education system. The figures in Table 7.1 provide a graphic picture of a system that is still failing 42% of children, who, in all respects, are the future intellectual assets of the nation. However, the story is even grimmer when the new English Baccalaureate measure of school performance is taken into account. The Baccalaureate is designed to provide a more accurate measure of standard by eliminating the inflation of GCSE examination results and its proliferation from the use of equivalent vocational courses, where one vocational subject can provide a candidate with two to four GCSE qualifications. The English Baccalaureate assesses pupils' performances in English, mathematics, sciences, a modern or ancient language and history or geography. In the second year (2011) that this measure of school performance was implemented only 16.5 per cent of pupils achieved the English Baccalaureate standards by gaining five or more GCSE passes at A* to C in the subjects listed above.

Whilst the level of failure – under this dual measure for educational standard – varies between ethnic groups, as seen in Table 7.1, the undeniable message is that no group can be said to have experienced the fulfilment of 'education for all' its children. Thus, 'education for all' remains elusive. This reality is even more worrying, given the increased government investment in education over the past decade. Why is it so difficult to turn this underperformance corner? Is the answer yet again to be more reforms of the education structure like the present coalition government is now implementing under the new Education Act, 2011? In the Foreword of The government's White Paper (2010), prior to the Education Bill that was published in January 2011, the Prime Minister and Deputy Prime Minister described the government's proposals as '*. . . a radical reform of our schools . . . Reforms on this scale are absolutely necessary . . .* ' (Department for Education, 2010). As examples of how the Education Bill, 2011 concentrated on the 'how we educate' dimension of the education process – that is, on structural and operational aspects of children's learning, the Bill dealt with school issues such as: teacher training; bureaucracy; behaviour management; curriculum, assessment and qualifications; school types and institutions; and school workforce.

The present authors do not see that a new round of reconfiguration to the education structure will be an answer to the issue, but instead submit that we need new strategic thinking and reflective insight on this protracted problem of underachievement for so many young people. This means formulating a clear education vision and direction that will transcend the worn out and seesawing changes to the education system and its operational structure ('how we educate') that we have witnessed so often. It should focus our commitment to the task of defining and answering the more profound question: 'why do we educate?' But strategic educational thinking must also be complemented with understanding where we have journeyed from with our current education system. In other words, we must reflect strategically on the history and development of the education system. This approach can be described, in another way, as 'seeing ahead' as well as 'seeing behind' (Davies, 2008, p. 16). Thus, this ultimate chapter of the book in 'seeing behind' not only takes us through an examination of the incremental evolution of the education system over the last two centuries, but also in 'seeing ahead' presents a paradigm shift in our philosophical thinking about 'why we educate?'

'Seeing Behind' – The journey of the education system

Education is no business of the state but is the responsibility of the family

At the start of the 19th century the English education system was very simple and underdeveloped. The lack of incentive for educational development at the time was influenced by a culture in society (economically and politically) that paid homage to the laissez-faire doctrine and made the concepts of individualism and non-interference sacrosanct principles. To reinforce this indifference to educational development, the vast majority of workers in the economy could get by without formal competence in the three Rs by simply learning through observation and practice on the job. The exception to this was the traditional professions such as law, medicine and the clergy. According to Musgrave (1968):

> *'At the start of the century there were only two universities in England, Oxford and Cambridge . . . The two ancient universities were still clerical institutions and were not in general overzealous in their pursuit of learning.'*
>
> (Musgrave, 1968 p. 17)

Learning was virtually nonexistent. It was a rare experience in the life of many individuals and not a priority for government. Therefore, the factory was the only school for children, where skills were acquired on the work bench, yet the vast majority of children and adults at work could not read or write.

The first attempt at state intervention to provide education for children, beyond home education by the well off, was through the enactment of the Health and Morals of Apprentices Act of 1802. This Act made it a requirement for factory owners to provide instructions in the three Rs for the first four years of a child's apprenticeship. However, this duty that was placed on employers proved difficult for the government to enforce. On the other hand, the children of the upper class (the aristocrats) were generally instructed at home by tutors and governesses or at the public schools. They were usually taught to learn languages leading to later studies in the classics and literature. The tutors and governesses would also prepare the children of the aristocratic class with training in social graces to fit them for their future role as members of the ruling class. Character building was accentuated, and in many ways, the emphasis on the development of manliness had currency over the intellectual aspect of schooling. All of these (training in social graces and the classics) were regarded as important tokens of high status. Wardle (1976) had this to say:

> '. . . *children were taught at home by tutors and governesses. This was the customary way for a member of the aristocracy to receive his education, as had always been the case. Such children were taught when young by governesses and later by tutors, who were resident. It was an expensive business to keep a full-time tutor, who would be expected to be a graduate capable of preparing a boy for university.*'
>
> (Wardle, 1976, p. 118)

Thus, the provision of education was exclusively the responsibility and function of the family and applied to all classes. For the upper class (the aristocrats), as we have seen, governesses and tutors taught their children at home, while for the working class – whose children went out to work at age five in factories – the family was the place where children learned the basic skills essential to life throughout that period.

The demise of the family as the central institution for organising and providing education in society accelerated with the expansion of the industrial revolution phenomenon of the period. The result of this was the birth of a new social group in English society – standing between the land gentry (aristocrats) and peasants (working class) – namely, the 'middle class'. The middle class was the growing group of industrialists, entrepreneurs, administrators, managers, clerks, scientists, engineers and technicians that emerged with the advances of the new era of manufacture, that is, the production of goods in large quantity by an industrial process. In other words, to manufacture means to make goods in factories. The revolution in work meant that the manufacturing industries springing up at that time needed a growing army of new kinds of workers, such as those listed above and to whom we refer to as the 'middle class'.

The Impact of the industrial revolution and schools for the middle class

As the industrial revolution gathered momentum, the rising and prosperous middle class demanded the same type of education for their children that upper class children enjoyed. However, they wanted a more utilitarian and wider curriculum than the classical subjects offered by the existing public and local grammar schools. Therefore, the middle class, instead, looked to the local private schools to provide additional subjects such as mathematics and French. These newer types of private schools sprung up to increase both the supply of school places and to offer the more applied curriculum sought after by the growing middle class. These new forms of private schools, nevertheless, modelled themselves on the traditional public schools' ethos. In the main, the significant provider of education for the middle and upper classes was now the mushrooming private schools of the day. They became serious rivals to the established public and grammar schools that had long served the upper class.

However, the elevation of the newer private schools into prominence and academic esteem coincided with the decline in the reputation of the older type public and grammar schools. At that period in time the public schools had a reputation for bad food, inhumane discipline and poor teaching. According to Musgrave (1969):

> *'Early in the nineteenth century the public schools were described with a certain element of truth as "the very seats of and nurseries of vice". Bullying, physical cruelty and sexual malpractices seem to have been common, and little attempt was made by staff to control such abuses.'*
>
> (Musgrave, 1968 p. 13)

Thus, the growing popularity of the developing private schools soon became the catalyst for change for the public and grammar schools. Behind the confidence of the newer type schools was a more fundamental shift in the culture of society. In comparison to the 18th century, which was considered to be a period that tolerated low moral standards in society, the early 19th century was a time of spiritual awakening for the nation. A revival in strong religious values and the striving for social justice were led by men such as William Wilberforce, Lord Shaftesbury, the African writer Olaudah Equiano and other prominent religious figures. Society was challenged to rise to higher moral standards, a reformation in manners and the elimination of unjust and evil practices in society such as slavery. This overt moral leadership by these pioneering men had a profound impact on the growing newer private grammar schools. This was led and driven by the Reverend Thomas Arnold, who became the most influential reforming educationalist of the time.

The Reverend Thomas Arnold's Revolution – the revival of the public schools

Thomas Arnold was the headmaster of Rugby School from 1828 to 1842, during which time he radically changed that school. So pervasive and far reaching was Arnold's transformational work that Rugby became the model for the entire English educational system. His mission was to produce Christian gentlemen and scholars. The school was highly religious in its tone. The key features of his approach were: firstly, Arnold made himself personally responsible for teaching the older boys (6th Formers) and in this way he was their mentor and inspiration; secondly, they in turn, as prefects, were responsible to him for discipline throughout the school, and in this way they exercised a sense of ownership of the learning process (in today's mantra it is called 'student voice'); thirdly, Arnold introduced a very effective and caring pastoral system in the school; and fourthly, he modified the curriculum by adding to the Classics other subjects such as French, mathematics and modern history. Arnold's revolution in education influenced changes in the older type public schools, such as Eton and Winchester and as a result there was a revival in the popularity of public schools. With this, other iconic public schools such as Cheltenham, Marlborough, Wellington, Haileybury, Lancing, City of London School and Liverpool College were established.

The reforms of the public and grammar schools, inspired by Arnold, also cascaded upward to the universities. At the beginning of the 19th century there were only two universities in England, Oxford and Cambridge while there were five in Scotland. However, Oxford and Cambridge did not offer studies in the field of administration, science, medicine or engineering. Thus, there was a dearth of higher academic provision in those fields important to the rapidly growing industries. Both Oxford and Cambridge universities at that time were exclusively clerical institutions. However, in 1858, the newly established London University was provided with a charter to offer its newer degree courses to internal and external students. These courses were in science, medicine and engineering and first introduced in the 1830s before the establishment of the university's charter. This was in response to the educational requirements of the middle class and industrialists. On the other hand, the down side to the innovative and philosophically sound educational approach of the Reverend Thomas Arnold was the fact that this high-quality educational provision catered mainly for the upper class and the elite from the new industrial middle class group. In essence, the mission of the reformed public schools was 'education for leadership' in society and in the British Empire. The children of the working class were, however, left out from this noble enterprise in education. But the climate of change was becoming too strong for the educational needs of the working class to be forever ignored.

The main engine for change at this stage of history was the Chartist movement, set up after the failure of the 1832 Reform Act to give the right to vote to non-property owning citizens. It was the first mass movement by the working class and in 1838 they drew up the famous 'People's Charter' containing the following six demands that: (1) all men should be given the vote; (2) voting should be by secret ballot; (3) parliamentary elections should be held every year; (4) constituencies should be of equal size; (5) members of parliament should be paid; and (6) the practice of using property ownership as the qualification to become a Member of Parliament should cease. Through their mass movement they gathered petitions for political and social change and presented these to the House of Commons on three occasions. However, these demands were rejected by parliament and resulted in violent unrests, but these unrests were put down by the authorities. Nevertheless, despite their failure to achieve quick changes, the sentiments behind their movement could not be suppressed. It motivated the working class into clamouring for education, not necessarily for economic reasons, but for enlightenment and personal development. The masses, at this time, seemed desperate to access reading materials such as newspapers. The ability to read and write was becoming a priority for many ambitious working class people. In addition, the working class was also extending their educational aspirations further by calling for wider social justice. Hence, the agitations of the 1830s for universal male suffrage became the catalyst for later improvements in the education system, when limited educational provision was extended to the working class as part of the growing democratic movement of the period.

Denominational schools for the working class

As the attempt by the Chartist Movement to achieve social change by physical force failed, the emphasis for educational reform for the working class shifted to the use of 'moral force' in the second half of the 19th century, stemming from a belief in the virtues of self-improvement – that is, the development of the person. This was further reinforced by the growth of working class organisations such as trade unions and other political bodies, outside of the existing traditional political parties, namely the Tories and the Liberals. In other words, the political arena became the vehicle to be used for securing educational changes on behalf of the working class. However, it must be recognised that in the early part of the 19th century there existed some degree of education provisions for the working class. These were supplied mainly by religious bodies, such as the established Church of England and the Methodists denominations. They had a clear goal for education, which was to add more believers to the Christian faith. Therefore, in order to assist in achieving this object, children were taught how to read the Bible. To consolidate this strategy – that education would be an important outreach function for religious bodies – they, the denominations, actively spread the view amongst the upper and middle classes that education would be a primary element to the denominations' charitable work. Accordingly, during this period – the early 1800s – there were three types of schools for working class children in the industrial towns, that is to say: (1) Sunday schools provided by the denominations, either free or at a nominal fee; (2) the dame schools, operated generally by women at a small fee, but they did not provide quality education and were mainly, in reality, child-minding services for working mothers; and (3) monitorial schools, that is, schools in which the headmaster would teach the senior pupils (who were called monitors). They, the monitors, in turn would then teach the younger pupils. The monitorial schools, it appears, were modelled or fashioned on the Thomas Arnold approached, discussed above. The Sunday schools were operated by the denominations while the monitorial schools were run by the British and Foreign School Society and the National Society for Promoting the Education of the Poor in the Principles of the Established Church.

The development of education provision for the masses took a further step forward when in 1833 the House of Commons passed a motion that provided £20,000 per annum to religious societies to support their education work. As a result, more denominational schools were established. The spin-offs from this growth in denominational schools, made possible by state funding, were: the appointment of the first national education administrator (Kay Shuttleworth around 1839); the introduction of formal training for teachers; the setting up of Her Majesty's Inspectorate for schools (HMI) in 1840; and the creation of an Education Department in 1856. The newly established HMI grew and numbered 352 inspectors by the end of the century. Its main function then was to monitor the work of the denominational schools that were in receipt of state education grant. Furthermore, because the education grant to schools was given on the basis of how children would perform at each age level of the standard set for subjects, teaching methods and educational materials were directed at getting pupils to pass the required examinations. Thus, teaching to the test was not necessarily a 21st century phenomenon, but had its beginning in the 19th century. In a way, this was a payment-by-result system for the schools. Another parallel to be observed is that, interestingly, in the 1840s the tripartite system of education was already surfacing in some Church of England schools. Education was planned for three grades of middle-class children. Wardle (1976) comments that:

> *'The Woodard schools, Church of England boarding schools established from the 1840s under the aegis of Canon Woodard, were specifically planned for three different grades of middle class children. The three grades were expected to leave schools at different ages – about fourteen, sixteen and eighteen years, and it was*

> *supposed to correspond to the lower-middle, middle-middle and upper-middle classes respectively.'*
>
> (Wardle, 1976, p. 124)

Nevertheless, it must be pointed out that there were also some grammar schools that were founded to provide education for poor children who showed a proclivity to academic work. Thus, we had the birth of the concept of the 'education ladder', which was generally accepted as a principle to work toward and strive for. This was indeed an important turning point in the education journey as it recognised the fact that working class children too are endowed with the potential for intellectual achievement. However, it must still be understood that in the midst of this significant change in thinking, it was nevertheless the prevailing view that those working class children identified with the potential for academic development would represent only a small percentage of working class children. Nonetheless, the door of enlightenment was being opened to the realisation that background does not nullify the innate potential of a child or prohibits intellectual development.

By the 1860s it was still not possible to claim or identify the existence of a national education system, despite the funding provided to the national societies and denominations for operating schools. Eyes were especially on Germany where the development of their industries was supported by a well-structured state education system. The realisation that a national schooling programme was desirable was further reinforced by the reform of the Civil Service, which meant that entry to it was restricted to those who had passed the civil service examinations. Parallel developments took place in other areas, such as medicine, with the establishment of the General Medical Council. There were also similar developments too in the legal profession. Therefore, the professional class was beginning to re-shape its views of education and was now willing to consider the need for greater state involvement in the development of education.

The beginning of the concept of secondary education

The Taunton Commission that sat between 1864 and 1868 recommended a policy for three grades of schools. This was part of its attempt to deal with the deficit gap in the provision of education for the middle class, since private schools existed for the upper class and denominational schools for the poor. Thus, we had the first move towards the establishment of some form of secondary schooling. The Taunton Commission was the first to consider such a proposal of this nature and was influenced by the prevailing social structure. Three types of schools were being considered: (1) schools for the upper and professional classes to study the classics, mathematics, but would include other relevant subjects for the industrial economy, for students up to age 18; (2) schools that would enrol children up to age 16 and designed to serve the mercantile and commercial classes – its curriculum would be focused on practical business skills; and (3) schools for the skilled upper working class – tenant farmers, tradesmen, artisans, etc. They would be taught the three Rs. Aided by the work of the Charity Commission, which was empowered to efficiently use educational endowments to fulfil the Taunton recommendations, the new types of private secondary schools (that is, for category 1 above) increased up until the 1880s. They also had a desire to remain free from state intervention and dissociated themselves from the public and grammar schools. Their growth, during this period, also heralded the founding of the Headmasters' Conference to provide collective support and the protection of their collective interests. On this Musgrave (1969) states:

> *'They were united in two aims, namely the desire to remain free of external control and to dissociate themselves from any attempt by the government to class them with the grammar schools. These two types of schools might be both secondary, but the H.M.C. schools did not see themselves as being in the same system.'*
>
> (Musgrave, 1968 p. 50)

Nevertheless, despite the wish of these new secondary schools to resist being linked with existing grammar schools, once again we find evidence of a structure and culture that fostered elitism in the education system. However, the Disraeli Conservatives in government after 1874 pointedly introduced an amendment to the Public Schools Act 1868 to slow down the growth of these secondary schools. But almost as a neutral act at the same time, it brought in an additional strategy that directed monies away from education provision for the working class and towards the development of new secondary schools for the middle class. From this period, the middle class dominated the state education provision to the detriment of the working class. Under the Liberal government of Prime Minister William Gladstone the first Education Act in 1870 was passed, allowing the religious denominations to continue operating schools and to fill other provision gaps in the education system. However, where they could not eliminate schooling deficiencies the state would step in through local agencies to provide state elementary schools from local rates. This solidified the continuing role of the denominations in the development of the education system. Thus, up to the 1870s education for the working class was being offered mainly by religious denominations. The term 'elementary education', it should be noted, was exclusively associated with the working class, and generally interpreted to mean 'minimal education' in the three Rs for working class children. Thus, the passing of the 1870 Act brought the state into the role of providing education at elementary level. Prior to this development the state's involvement was mainly in supplying education grants to denominations engaged in the running of schools. State education was now both elementary and technical, while secondary education remained outside the boundary of the state. The middle classes (including the upper middle classes) were still buying secondary education from the public and proprietary schools, which had close links with the universities through the examination system.

Denominational schools grew rapidly following the 1870 Act. Between 1870 and 1880 their numbers increased from 8,000 to 14,000. At the same time the development of state elementary schools also accelerated during the said period, so that by 1880 there were over 3,000 such schools. This growth in school numbers was also complemented by the abolition of fees in 1891 for children attending state and voluntary elementary schools. This meant that many more children were being offered places in schools than ever before and this was also helped by the earlier establishment by Parliament of an enactment to make attendance at school compulsory up to age 11. The introduction of specific subjects to elementary schooling such as geography, history, science and mathematics started a significant move to extend a secondary dimension to these elementary schools. This was further expanded by the launch of two other types of schools in the education system, namely: Organised Science Schools and Higher Grade Schools. And so, by the mid 1880s there was a rapid expansion of these secondary forms of schools. This expanse was driven by the Department of Science and Art, as a growing part of its budget was directed towards the development of secondary education to lower and upper working class children. Here began the battle to lengthen the school age for working class children and to offer them a form of secondary education:

> *'What had happened was that the very success of the elementary schools had rendered the existing concept of elementary education obsolete, and this in turn put into question the distinction between elementary and secondary education.'*
>
> (Wardle, 1976, p. 127)

Accordingly, this development also in a way brought to an end the rigid identification of elementary schooling with the working class and secondary as exclusively schooling for the middle class. These new schools were gaining in popularity and became serious competitors to the established public and grammar schools that had links with the older universities. Equally, these new secondary schools were also aspiring to forge similar links, like those of the public and grammar schools, with the newer universities that were emerging within the education structure.

The Drive for Equality of Opportunity in Education

With the founding of the Trades Union Congress (TUC) in 1868 and the Labour Party in 1893 the working class was becoming more politically organised. Support for social justice policies in society was also being articulated by leading middle class intellectuals, such as Bernard Shaw and Sidney and Beatrice Webb. Such political lobbying and demands resulted in the government passing the 1890 Education Act that set up a system of School Boards that were vested with the power to encourage the admittance of children into the growing group of secondary-type schools without having to pay traditional fees. The working class further seized the opportunity available to elect from among themselves representatives to serve on local School Boards. And so the expanding education system now consisted of: (1) children of the upper and upper middle classes being served by public and grammar schools, and boarding schools; (2) middle class children attending the new fee-paying types of secondary schools; and (3) lower middle and working classes using the elementary and post-elementary Organised Science Schools and Higher Grade Schools.

Interestingly, the working class did not challenge the existence of fee-paying schools for the middle class, but they were beginning to think that their children should also have access to some form of secondary schooling.

Hence, with this view attracting support from sections of the middle class, a consensus was developing that all children should have the right to the full range of schooling available, that is, elementary and post-elementary secondary education. The push for extending secondary education to the masses gathered more momentum. In 1897, the TUC officially made the case for secondary education to be provided for all children. It was also the policy of the Fabian Society that secondary education should be afforded to the working class by a gradual extension of free entry to grammar schools. (For clarity, this is not referring to the Organised Science Schools or Higher Grade Schools) Musgrave (1969) echoes this development with the following statement:

> *'. . . the London County Technical Education Board established a system of county scholarships and by 1901 ten scholars were in universities. The route by which students had reached university was from the elementary school and then through the recognized secondary school system. By secondary schools the supporters of this policy meant elitist schools and not some version of the popular post elementary schools which gave education of a secondary nature within the constraints of the Elementary Code.'*
>
> (Musgrave, 1968, p. 62)

The drive for equality in education during this time was also being extended to girls. This was as a result of the rising status of women derived from the emancipation movement. Thus, the education of girls, and in particular middle class girls, became much more important. Also, at this time the family (middle and upper classes) was shedding its function – that had existed for centuries – as the main educative agency in society. As a consequence, more children from the middle and upper classes were being sent to boarding schools. In 1889 the the National Society for the prevention of Cruelty to Children was founded, also in the same year an act called The Children's Charter' was sponsored in parliament. These signalled a change in the historically accepted principle that parents had ultimate authority over their children. The effect of these developments was that parents were no longer viewed as having absolute control over the education and welfare of their children.

The continuing political activities in the closing stages of the 19th century were now leading more people to challenge the class-dominated definition of secondary education, this is, that secondary education was mainly for middle and upper class children. Generally, there was no resentment to those who could afford secondary education, provided by fee-paying schools. In limited response, the Technical Instruction Act of 1889 gave County and Borough Councils responsibility for the provision of rate-aided technical education for working class children and the training of blue collar workers for industry. Instruction by the Organised Science Schools and Higher Grade Schools centred on the principles and practices of science and art, useful to industries. Manual instruction was also given in the use of tools for manufacturing employment. Then, in 1894, a Royal Commission on Secondary Education was set up and recommended that a central body was necessary to coordinate the education system. Therefore, by 1899 the Board of Education was established for the purpose of coordinating the education system.

The most influential administrative figure to emerge at the Board of Education was Robert Morant, as chief civil servant. However, in 1900 Morant got the Board of Education to put a curb on the expansion of the Higher Grade Schools. These were innovative institutions offering working class children the opportunity to develop beyond the elementary provision and to access a form of secondary education. Their development was especially driven by the London County Council Technical Education Board and their (that is, Higher Grade Schools) most interesting feature was the attempt to produce a vocational type of secondary education curriculum. They generally focused on science and technical subjects, but there were equivalent commercial schools in existence. In the 1890s some Higher Grade Schools were also entering their pupils for leaving examinations. According to Wardle (1976):

> *'There were school boards where the educational ladder was extended to reach higher education and it was possible for pupils to pass either directly from higher grade school to the local university college, or to go from higher grade school to a grammar school and then to university. Such pupils were exceptional, but it was not particularly unusual for higher grade pupils to win their way to university. . .'*
>
> (Wardle, 1976, p. 129)

Therefore, the curb placed on the advancement of the work of Higher Grade Schools would appear to have been a regressive act by Morant to protect and sustain the elitist system of education threatened by the innovation of the Higher Grade Schools.

It was Morant's view that the future development of education should be such that the post-elementary education structures should give way to a secondary education system that would emulate the traditional public and grammar schools' model. Morant's influence on the shaping and direction of the education system grew stronger during his tenure. At the beginning of the 20th century, he became a principal figure in the political debate about education and was later knighted (Sir Robert Morant) for his services to education. He greatly influenced the form of the 1902 Education Act which abolished the School Boards and gave responsibility for education to County Councils and County Boroughs and, hence, the arrival of Local Education Authorities (LEAs). Under Morant, the Board of Education developed a more unified system for education through a number of codes and handbooks. The LEAs were to control all secondary education. The regulations for secondary schools in 1904 talked of secondary education going up to and beyond the age of 16. The Bryce Commission of 1895 had earlier taken a broader view of secondary education, suggesting that technical instruction should be part of the secondary education structure. This view was promoted by Michael Sadler who was a member of The Bryce Commission and later head of the Office for Special Inquiries at the Board of Education. However, his view was opposed by Morant who, as we have seen above, wanted secondary education to remain along traditional lines. Thus, there was a clash between these two opposing positions held by Morant and Sadler. The new type secondary grammar schools, under the LEAs, were set up to cater for a middle class elite group, while elementary schooling remained generally for working class children. Thus, under Morant's leadership of the education system the secondary education door was closed to the vast majority of working class children.

The 1902 Education Act retained the three tier system that operated in the latter part of the 19th century. Firstly, there were the fee-paying day and boarding public and grammar schools for the aristocrats, educating students up to age 18. Secondly, there were the new day grammar schools, mainly fee-paying, but were also charged to give 25 per cent of free places to children from elementary schools. As an incentive those grammar schools that gave the free 25 per cent of places to former elementary school pupils attracted a higher education grant from the state. Consequently, this gave rise to the beginning of the 11-plus examination system. Thirdly, there were the free elementary schools that the working class would attend, up to the age of 16. Under the Fisher Act of 1918 the minimum leaving age was raised to age 14, making it easier for working class parents to support their children through secondary education, although Wardle (1976) made this observation on the 1902 Act:

> *'First, it* [the 1902 Act] *reaffirmed the sharp distinction between the elementary and secondary school systems, and completely rejected the notion of a general end-on connection between them* [meaning that children would not pass on automatically to secondary education]. *The distinction was based partly upon social considerations – the bulk of pupils in secondary schools were fee-paying . . . middle class . . . a curriculum which had a literary and non-vocational bias . . . By contrast the new higher elementary schools, which were proposed as a successors to the higher grade schools were forced to restrict their curricula which was given a strong vocational slant.'*
>
> (Wardle, 1976, p. 130)

In other words, these schools assumed that working class children were not academically able. Although the policies of 'Free Places' and 'Special Places' existed in the form of scholarships for working class children to go from elementary schooling to secondary education, many of these places were turned down either because parents could not afford to maintain their children's education post-elementary schooling or because of indifference to secondary grammar school education. However, the honourable intent of the scholarships policy to serve as an 'educational ladder' was being corrupted, as it took on a more elitist modus operandi in the way it extended higher education access to a selected few from the working class. This little grain of appeasement for working class children did not change the prevailing thinking existing within the education establishment that secondary education should primarily be for middle and upper class children only. As Wardle (1976) observed:

> *' . . . there was never a condition of genuine contest mobility, since parents with money could always buy a secondary education for their*

> *children, and, as just been observed, there were barriers in the way of working-class child even if he obtained a free place. These barriers were, in fact, higher than was realized . . . little attention was given to the influence of a child's home environment upon his ability to benefit from a particular form of education . . .'*
>
> (Wardle, 1976, p. 133)

As noted above, the 1902 Act took the development of secondary education a step further with the introduction of the new LEA day schools for middle class children. They became a second form of secondary schools in addition to the earlier private secondary schools developed following the Taunton Commission 30 years earlier. The Act also brought about a shift in the dual education system that existed for many decades. Whereas, prior to the 1902 Act the non-private school system for the masses was operated mainly by the denominations, the 1902 Act changed that position. With the advent of the additional LEA secondary schools and the continuation of elementary education, for the working class, the state had now taken over the lead in the provision and administration of education, but still within the existence of a 'dual system'. There was also the expectation that there would be room within this new education order for both parts of the 'dual system' to experience autonomous development.

The early result of the impact of this legislation, that is, the 1902 Education Act, was not very encouraging. Progress was very slow especially as the new LEAs were struggling to grasp the extent of their functions, but eventually through induction by the Board of Education the LEAs became much more comfortable with their role. From then onwards, after their tentative start, the LEAs' secondary expansion work gathered momentum, galvanised by the Free Place regulation of 1907. This new-found energy was also assisted by the improved economic position of the working class. For this reason between 1914 and 1921 the number of working class children from elementary schools, proceeding on to secondary schools, increased from 56 in every 1,000 to 97 in every 1,000. However, it has to be recognised that this improvement in secondary access for working class children was relative or marginal and was not considered by many progressive educationalists to be a major change.

Meanwhile, during Morant's period at the Board of Education the brakes were also applied to the expansion of the secondary dimension to elementary schools that was also giving working class children extra opportunity for a secondary type of education. But after his departure from the Board in 1910 the post-elementary dimension to the elementary schools again flourished. In addition, a further form of post-elementary school emerged, namely Central schools, where older children would be sent for the latter part of their elementary schooling. These schools became common during the years of the First World War. Post-elementary education continued to be developed with the introduction of the Junior Technical Schools in 1913 to provide extended education for pupils leaving elementary schools, in preparation for artisan and other industrial forms of work. It has to be said that these post-elementary schooling developments were out of line with the broad liberal curriculum favoured by Morant during his tenure at the Board of Education. According to Musgrave (1968):

> *'...these schools became very popular in industrial areas since their pupils often became apprentices or even lower-level technicians, positions that seemed to promise security during the heavy unemployment of the inter-war years.'*
>
> (Musgrave, 1968, p. 83)

In contrast, the secondary grammar schools' curriculum was boosted by the new standardised examination system, resulting in the 'School Certificate' taken at around age 16. This examination served a twin purpose in that it became a 'terminal examination' at age 16, but could also be accepted as a qualification for entry to university. As a result of this, it motivated secondary schools to teach a wider range of subjects such as Latin, English, modern language, history, geography, mathematics and science, thus creating a uniformity of curriculum provision in secondary grammar schools. Hence, a clear dichotomy developed between secondary grammar schools and the technical education offered by the Junior Technical Schools. In many ways, the secondary grammar schools that operated along traditional lines benefited most from the reforms of the 1902 Education Act as it permitted the LEAs to use income from local rates monies for the development of secondary education. At the same time it became accepted that age 11-plus would be the transfer age from elementary schooling to secondary education. Nonetheless, the high expectations of a unitary education system failed after an initial promising start in the early 1900s, when the newly developing secondary grammar schools were given real scope to shape themselves to meet the education needs of all children. This opportunity for a transformation to a fairer education system was undermined by the influences of those at the higher echelon of the education establishment such as HMIs, the administrators of the education system (civil servants) and headmasters who were determined that education should remain a highly differentiated and elitist system.

The 1930s' demand for social justice and the cry for secondary education for all

R H Tawney was a distinguished economic historian and a leading Labour Party educationalist of the early 20th century, who wrote the party's groundbreaking visionary education policy document in 1922 entitled *'Secondary Education for All: A Policy for Labour'*. He considered the relatively low numbers of working class children transferring to secondary schooling through the Free Place selection policy (in some areas no more than two per thousand of the population) as a demonstration that the policy was virtually worthless and, in reality, amounting to no provision at all for working class children. Tawney tellingly observed the negative attitude of mind that prevailed amongst the upper classes and industrialists at the time toward the principle of equality in educational provision. Below he describes their thoughts as the other view to equality:

> *'On the other view . . . equality of educational provision up to sixteen is impossible of attainment . . . Industry needs cannon fodder as well as staff officers, and it is not desirable that the minds of the rank and file, even if capable of development (which the Federation of British Industries doubt), should be unduly developed. When the cream of intelligence has been skimmed off by scholarships, the mass of children must pass at fourteen to the factory . . .'*
>
> (Tawney, 1922, p. 265)

This view was to deliberately deny the working class of their rights to the intellectual development that should be accorded to them as human beings. Tawney, on the other hand, highlighted the position that primary and secondary education should be seen as a single process under which all children should pass, and that the success of this approach would be the building of a stronger human capacity for society. Tawney and his colleagues were now demanding full-time education for all children up to the age of 16.

This argument also found resonance with other progressive educationalists of the time. For example, the Executive Committee of the Incorporated Association of Assistant Masters in Secondary Schools argued that secondary education of the best type should be available to all children and that accident of birth, social position and financial means when set up as barriers to full education (primary and secondary) created social injustice. Tawney asserts in his writing that:

> '*. . . the success of education is proportionate to the degree to which it is related to the facts of natural development.*'
>
> (Tawney, 1922, p. 266)

He further condemns the system in the following words:

> '*. . . the immense mass, not only of average talent . . . but of exceptional talent . . . which is sterilized for lack of educational opportunities.*'
>
> (Tawney, 1922, p. 267)

Another educationalist of the time, Professor Nunn, urged the belief that schemes of education should make it an imperative that their essential curricula and pedagogy should follow the true lines of growth of human nature. In other words human beings all have the capacity for intellectual development (Tawney, 1922). Thus, as a result of the influence of Tawney's persuasive zeal, the aim of a common secondary school system became the Labour Party's policy, especially in the early 20th century era when the Labour movement was growing in strength. Tawney and other intellectuals argued that an egalitarian and socialist society could not be built while the educational system was organised on an elitist basis. Thus, education was to fulfil the function of an instrument for social change. And so, the ambition for the full provision of secondary education to all children was intensifying with more purpose, against the background that the 1902 Education Act had not solved the problem of bringing secondary education to working class children. This theme of educational equality was also picked up by the Consultative Committee in 1926 headed by Sir Henry Hadow, and which reported in 1931. It recommended that children between the ages of 11 and 15, who did not secure places in secondary grammar schools, should, nonetheless, be provided with an equivalent form of secondary education that would include both academic and vocational elements. The thinking by Hadow was that this extension of secondary education to more children from the working class could be delivered in either existing grammar schools or in additional modern schools. The Hadow Report was also responsible for the change in terminology away from elementary to 'primary' education.

Five years later, the Spens Report took the Hadow Report a stage further by recommending that secondary education should be provided free for all children in a tripartite system consisting of Grammar Schools, Technical High Schools and Modern Secondary Schools. These three forms of secondary schools would operate on the basis that there would be 'parity of esteem' for these schools. The assumption made by the Spens Report was that there existed three types of minds and that these three schools being proposed would reflect this belief, that grammar schools would be for the academically minded, technical highs for the vocationally inclined and secondary moderns for those who were not in the first two categories, but who would need to be taught essential literacy, numeracy and other basic life skills (Musgrave, 1968). These recommendations from Spens and Hadow unfortunately signalled a dilution of the vision of secondary education for all children, especially espoused by Tawney and others in the Labour Party, in furtherance of the goal for the establishment of a more egalitarian educational system.

The recommendation of the Spens Report for a tripartite system was the product of the existing of three schools of thought at the time on how secondary education could be developed. These were:

- firstly, a continuation of the elitist tradition, by extending the selective system so that more working class children could be given places at grammar schools;

- secondly, that different types of secondary education could exist alongside each other, catering for the different aptitudes and abilities of the pupils – more a form of segregated secondary schooling; and

- Thirdly, (and what amounts to an egalitarian or comprehensive schooling approach) that all children should be transferred to the same secondary school.

With respect to the third approach, the difference here is that children, irrespective of their so called ability, would be educated in the same school. It was quite clear that the first two schools of thought above were a continuation of the elitist approach. The third would require a radical re-design of the education structure and the dismantling of the barriers that for so long had wrongfully denied many children of the right to full secondary education. Nevertheless, it was the second school of thought that prevailed as demonstrated by the recommendation of the Spens Report, the key precursor to the landmark 1944 Education Act.

The failure of 'parity of esteem' for all secondary schools

The theme of the 1920s and 1930s, articulated by the Labour Party and others, was the call for fairness in educational provision, especially as it related to secondary education. However, at the onset of the 1944 Education Act the original understanding of what was meant by fairness in education began to change. The 1944 Education Act became known as Butler's Act, after R. A. Butler the conservative president of the Board of Education. Butler's aim for the Act was to build a cohesive education system to meet the strains and turmoil emanating from the 1930s debate and demands for a fairer education system. After piloting the education bill through parliament and its eventual enactment, Butler became the first Minister of Education with the abolition of the old Board of Education. The 1944 Act, which became a landmark piece of legislation in the history of the development of education, laid the foundation for the education system that prevails up to the present time. The Act ended the elementary schooling structure that was first introduced by the 1870 Education Act. Instead, the 1944 Education Act instituted a three-stage education system consisting of primary education between the ages of 5 to 11, secondary education from age 11 to a new compulsory age of 15 years and a further post-16 education stage. Secondary education was now provided free to all children. The aim was for every child of secondary age to have equal opportunity to obtain a place in a grammar school, irrespective of family background.

The above aspiration would be achieved by the use of an objective testing regime of pupils' ability. This would be taken at age 11 and commonly referred to as the eleven-plus examination. This 11-plus test involved assessing the candidates' intelligence and abilities in English and arithmetic. However, the aim of the Act that every child should have equal opportunity to enter grammar school was contradicted and immediately undermined by the administrative arrangements for implementing the secondary stage of the education structure. This secondary education stage of the Act established or re-established the tripartite system of education that had existed in the latter part of the 19th century, with the ambition that all three elements would command 'parity of esteem'. This was unrealistic and illogical in its reasoning, since the three schools stipulated by the Act, that the new secondary education structure would deliver, were namely: secondary grammar schools; technical schools; and secondary modern schools. The Act further specified that pupils would be selected for these three types of schools on the basis of ability and aptitude. Grammar schools would mostly be for middle class children and so-called high academic ability pupils, technical schools for pupils deemed to possess vocational and practical aptitudes and secondary modern would provide basic education for the rest of the population. It would always be the case with such a differentiated proposal that the grammar schools would be held in high esteem, and so 'parity of esteem' was a non-starter.

In 1951 the General Certificate of Education (GCE) at Ordinary 'O' and Advanced 'A' levels were introduced to be taken at age 16 ('O' Levels) and age 18 ('A' Levels). But these examinations were designed for the top 20 per cent of children of secondary age. Therefore, the vast majority of pupils were not expected to pass these examinations. It is for these reasons that the authors argue that the claim that the education system would provide equal opportunity for all children of secondary age to enter grammar school was illogical. The basis for this judgment is that the equal opportunity spoken of would never ever be real and true as a result of the preparation (tutoring) the children who were fortunate to be selected for entry received prior to the tests. It is this that enabled them to scale the 20 percent barrier built and be deemed to be a success at the eleven-plus examinations. The notion of the test being fair to all, as it was reasoned to be based on 'merit', is false. This so-called merit for the successful was, in reality, the production of careful preparation for a privileged few. Thus, the 1930s' meaning of fairness in educational opportunity definitely changed in the post-war educational development era. According to Wardle (1976):

> *'On achieving power in 1945 the Labour government allowed the very general requirements of the 1944 Act upon secondary education to be underwritten by the ministry in such a way that the selective system became more firmly entrenched than ever, although the method of selection was made to discriminate rather less against the working-class child when fee-paying places in grammar schools were abolished.'*
>
> (Wardle, 1976, p. 135)

Tawney's dream of the dismantling of all barriers to the best form of secondary education available to all children was unfulfilled under the 1944 Education Act. The 1944 Reform of the education system held to the profoundly wrong assumption that only a minority of children were capable of academic development and achievement. But, more disturbingly it perpetuated an act of discrimination against working class children and maintained an elitist education system for the few, damaging to the nation's interest and its intellectual assets. In addition to the establishment of the three groups of free secondary schools, the raising of the school leaving age to 15 and the creation of the Ministry of Education, the Act also introduced other services such the provision of school meals, free school milk and regular medical examination of pupils. But better welfare provision for children could in no way compensate for the intellectual limit that was placed on working class children.

The development of the comprehensives

As observed above, the post-war election was won by the Labour Party in the 1945 general election and one of its goals was to implement the new secondary school system established by the landmark 1944 Education Act. Nevertheless, there were some members in the Labour Party who were not fully persuaded that the strategy for the continuation of the tripartite structure for secondary education and its reinforcement of the elitist school organisation was the correct path to follow. These dissenting voices remained committed to the building of a more egalitarian education system. They further justified their argument for a fairer education system with the economic reason that to equip more children with the best form of secondary education was necessary in order to provide the skilled manpower needed to achieve national prosperity. In effect, they were advancing an early proposition for the development of a comprehensive school system. And so with the aid of supporters in a few urban Labour-controlled councils, comprehensive schools were built in those local authorities to supply schooling for all secondary pupils in the catchment areas of those schools. From this grass-root initiative other local authorities followed their example, and by the late 1950s there was a rapid rise in the numbers of these comprehensive types of secondary schools. This was despite the reservation of some educators, who argued that the comprehensive school concept would require schools for pupils ranging from between 1,500 and 2,000, with the attending adverse psychological effects on pupils that could ensue from this form of large impersonal school size. Notwithstanding this, the comprehensive option for developing a post-war secondary school system – in the spirit of 1930s' 'secondary education for all' movement of the Labour Party policy – was gaining ground in a concrete and practical way by the work of the early pioneering group of local urban councils. In other words, the dream was being fulfilled in reality by the innovative drive of these trailblazing councils. Furthermore, there were also justifiable grounds to feel that many working class children were losing out academically by the underdevelopment of their potential by the tripartite schooling system. And so, there have been compelling arguments for moving in the direction of a comprehensive schooling system for all children.

Whilst there were never any strong anti-grammar school feelings amongst the general working class, a growing body of opinions were of the view that a less elitist education structure was more desirable than the tripartite system that continued under the 1944 Education Act. Their feelings were also reinforced by the fact that the new secondary moderns had a huge credibility hurdle to overcome. They struggled to secure parity of esteem with the new secondary grammar schools as they (the secondary moderns) mainly recruited pupils from working class background. However, was the denial of parity of esteem to the secondary moderns a consequence of their intakes being intellectually inferior to those of the secondary grammars? No! The lack of parity of esteem had nothing to do with the innate ability of working class children, but was purely the outcome of naked social class stereotyping. The technical schools did not fare any better either. They lost many of their clientele to those grammar schools that extended their curriculum programmes to include some vocational courses, and those ground-breaking secondary modern schools that added science and vocational subjects to their curriculum. The technical schools were squeezed at both ends of the schooling structure. Middle class children looking for a vocational programme would turn to grammar schools that were providing such diversity in their curriculum and working class parents who wanted vocational education for their children would look to those limited numbers of innovative secondary modern schools offering vocational subjects.

In the meantime, the free LEA grammar schools continued to grow in number and size, mainly as a result of the fact that many middle class parents were moving their children from private fee-paying schools to the new free grammar schools. But the middle class was also coming to accept the political inevitability that there needs to be a fairer educational system as more and more working class citizens displayed antipathy towards the tripartite approach to secondary schooling. The election of a new Labour government in 1965 provided a catalyst for driving the comprehensive school movement with the government's publication of Circular 10/65. This circular made it a requirement for LEAs to produce plans for secondary school reorganisation along a comprehensive model. And so the comprehensive school option was now formally being considered as the answer to the demands for greater equality in education. Furthermore, in 1965 the Certificate of Secondary Education (CSE) was introduced. This was aimed at the majority of secondary pupils, that is, the 60 percent of the secondary pupil denizen that were not expected to take the GCE examination at age 16. The comprehensive school system meant that comprehensive schools would integrate the three forms of schooling that existed under the tripartite regime into its structure. Thus, comprehensive schools would cater for children from a range of social backgrounds and would eliminate the social segregation that existed under the tripartite system.

Another significant development in the comprehensive school movement was the 1976 Education Act, which gave the Secretary of State for Education the authority to instruct LEAs to present plans for comprehensive reorganisation. The outcome of this was that by the 1980s approximately 90 per cent of all secondary school children were being educated in comprehensive schools (Chan and East, 2002). Be that as it may, the comprehensive dream did not materialise. The majority of secondary pupils were still not attaining academic success, as measured by the 5 GCE 'O' at A to C passes. In a sense, the comprehensive programme simply replaced the secondary modern schools but not the grammar schools. High quality education was still the preserve of those in grammar schools or those in the higher streams of the comprehensive schools (that is, those selected to sit the GCE 'O' examination). But by the 1970s, there were growing concerns about the performance of the education system and as a result many reviews were undertaken on the national examinations and assessment programmes. In addition, a series of pamphlets called the 'Black Papers' were published in the mid 1970s drawing attention to what they considered to be falling educational standards. At about the same time disquiet was also being raised about the underachievement of children of West Indian origin. Because of these high-profile reports and concerns, education took centre stage in the political arena. This was powerfully illustrated by the Prime Minister James Callaghan's famous speech at Ruskin College, Oxford in October 1976. It triggered the 'Great Debate' on educational standards. This created huge interest and awareness on key educational issues and laid the foundation for the development of the national curriculum in 1988. The period of the 1970s through to the 1990s also saw the publication of a series of other influential education reports that have contributed to the development of the education system and educational thinking over the decades prior to the 1988 Education Reform Act. Some of these reports were: The Plowden Report of 1967 and its re-analysis in 1980; The Bullock Report of 1973; The Warnock Report of 1978; The Rampton Report of 1981 and The Swann Report of 1985; and the report of The Stephen Lawrence Inquiry in 1999.

Influential education reports

The Plowden Report, published in 1967, concentrated its findings on the principle that the child is at the heart of the education process. The report challenged the traditional teacher-directed approach to education and became identified with a progressive child-centred method to teaching and learning. This placed emphasis on 'what the child can do' and not on what the child cannot do and builds on the child's interests. It encouraged the development of independent and child-centred learning activities as part of the classroom experiences for the child. A further re-evaluation of the data in the Plowden Report in 1980 highlighted the influence of economic and family lifestyle factors as determinants to a child's ability to achieve at school. However, there were those who felt that the child-centred approach was contributing to a lowering of educational standards and this concern became part of the education standards debate of the 1970s and 1980s, especially articulated by the Black Papers, referred to above.

The Bullock Report, published in 1975, looked at standards in English, reading, writing and speaking. This report was significant for the fact that for the first time an education report formally recognised Britain as a multicultural society and recommended that school curriculum planning should reflect this reality. As a consequence, it also advanced the proposition that for a child to improve his language skills, the school must firstly give recognition and respect to the child's cultural background and linguistic values.

The Warnock Report, published in 1978, dealt with the issue of special educational needs. The report brought into the open the salient truth that disability was more prevalent in the school population than was acknowledged. The report identified the fact that more than 20 per cent of children of school age had some physical, sensory or mental disability, but that only two per cent had been formally identified in the education system with having a disability. The 1981 Education Act addressed the findings of the Warnock Report. The term 'handicapped' was removed from the education language and replaced with the expression 'special educational needs' (SEN). The Act also made LEAs responsible for identifying the needs of children with leaning difficulties and assessment procedures were also set up for assisting in the process of establishing their specific needs. In addition, statements of special educational needs (generally referred to as statementing) were to be drawn up by the LEAs for pupils, detailing the needs that were identified and how those needs would be met. The provision of the 1981 Education Act was extended with the enactment of the 1993 Education Act, which resulted in the publication of a SEN Code of Practice, offering practical guidance on the assessment of children with SEN and statementing needs.

Also in this period (the 1970s), the performance of the education system, with respect to ethnic minority children was also receiving great attention in the education world and in the media. Firstly, a Committee of Inquiry into the education of children from ethnic minority groups was set up under the chairmanship of Anthony Rampton, with a particular focus on West Indian children. In 1981 it published an interim report, known as the 'Rampton Report'. This report showed that there was a significant attainment gap with only 3 per cent of West Indian children obtaining 5 or more GCE 'O' levels when compared with 18 per cent for Asians and 16 per cent for others. The report named racism, low teacher expectations, language issues and lack of cultural diversity in the school curriculum as prime reasons for the underachievement problem. There were, however, some criticisms of the report in education circles and soon after Rampton resigned as chairperson for the inquiry. He was replaced by Lord Michael Swann. Lord Swann published the final report of the committee in 1985, entitled 'Education for All'. The report's central argument was that there should be a more pluralistic approach to the goal of providing education for all children, in order to avoid the fragmentation of society along ethnic lines. This fragmentation, the report observed, could seriously threaten the stability and cohesion of society. The report further reaffirmed the key findings of the Rampton Interim Report. It stated that the difference in average IQ scores between West Indian and white children was the result of socio-economic factors. The report highlighted the strength of feeling by the West Indian community about prejudice and discrimination in the education service. It concluded that whilst there were no single cause for the underachievement of West Indian children in the education system, there was a need for: greater sensitivity to the education of ethnic minority children; more in-service training for teachers; the collection of data on ethnicity in the provision and performance of the education system; and priority to be given to the learning of English. The report also recognised that racism ultimately should be addressed through legal and political actions and not simply be left to education policy initiatives. In a similar fashion to the Rampton Interim Report, the Swann Report was also criticised for overlooking other factors such as class, gender, age and individual performance.

In as much as the Stephen Lawrence Inquiry, chaired by Sir William Macpherson, was set up to look into the racist murder of the young black man Stephen Lawrence on 22 April 1993, the report published in 1999, highlighted the need to tackle racial discrimination and to eradicate institutionalised racism from public institutions. The report, in some parts of its recommendations, stated that the National Curriculum for schools should add to its programme of study cultural diversity and studies on the prevention of racism in society. In addition, the report also recommended that LEAs and school governors should implement strategies in their schools to address and prevent racism.

Development over the last 30 years

The Conservative government led by Margaret Thatcher came into power in 1979 with a well-thread political narrative on education. The government's line was that the economic woes and the high unemployment rates prevailing at the time were attributable to the education system, which was guilty of failing to equip young people with the necessary skills and knowledge needed for industry. Local authorities and teachers became a target for strong attacks from the government during the early stages of their tenure. In summary, there were four main criticisms levied against the education service by the government, namely that: (1) standards were low; (2) there were wide variations in standards across schools; (3) there were inherent weaknesses in the curriculum planning processes of many schools; and (4) that a more objective system of assessing pupils' attainment was needed. These concerns were later addressed in a government education White Paper entitled 'Better Schools', which provided the platform for a series of education reforms in this closing period of the 20th century.

In 1986 the new General Certificate of Education (GCSE) was introduced, replacing both the CSE and GCE 'O' level examinations. In reality, the new GCSE combined both the CSE and GCE 'O' Level examinations into a single examination to be taken at age 16 and above. Graded on a seven point scale of A to G (now A* to G) it, nevertheless, remains an examination system that can be likened to a railway train, with first and second class attainment compartments. Grades A* to C are akin to the first-class compartment and pupils within this band are considered to be successful with the GCSE examination. These grades provide entry to GCE 'A' level courses, are part of the qualification entries to many universities or professional training courses and are accepted by employers for skilled jobs. Pupils scoring GCSE grades D to G, in contrast, are more like travellers in the economy compartment of our railway train analogy.

Originally, the old GCE 'O' level examinations were designed for the top 20 percent of pupils and the CSE aimed at 60 percent of secondary pupils. However, today – as demonstrated in Table 7.1 – 55 percent of secondary pupils are now gaining 5 A* to C GCSE grades including English and mathematics. As a result of this apparent improvement in attainment for secondary pupils, some self-appointed education standard watchers are of the view that the increase in the numbers of pupils attaining higher GCSE grades is a result of falling examination standards. This judgment by these education cynics seems to be predicated on the continuing assumption that only a minority of children can cope with academic studies at secondary school level. Thus to these critics, when more children are scoring high grades in these public examinations, it has to be a result of falling examination standards. With this mind set, the assumption is that certain children are not capable of improving, since their mental ability is fixed. Some high status secondary schools and universities too are unhappy with the improvements in GCSE and GCE 'A' level results and are uneasy with the pedigree of these examinations. They now look to alternatives such as the International GCSE (iGCSE) and the International Baccalaureate (IB) for determining entry to post GCSE courses or to university studies.

More recently, Michael Gove, the Secretary of State for Education in the Coalition Government that took office in 2010, introduced what is called the English Baccalaureate as a more informative and objective measure of the achievement of secondary pupils at age 16. Instead of basing pupils' performance on the old yardstick of 5 GCSE A* to C grades, including English and mathematics, pupils are now judged on the English Baccalaureate standard, which means achieving 5 GCSE grades at A* to C in English, mathematics, science, a modern or ancient language and history or geography. The rationale behind this new measure of pupils' and schools' performance is the belief that many schools have been recording very high GCSE league table results that are inflated as a result of schools entering a high percentage of pupils for vocational courses. For some of these vocational courses, pupils may only need to study one subject and could be awarded four GCSE equivalent grades, thus, presenting a distorted picture of the performance of schools. The profoundly telling thing to note is that the benefit of this massaging of the examination league table results – by the use of equivalent GCSE vocational courses – works mainly for the schools themselves, who can claim high league table performance rankings. But in truth and in fact, pupils are the losers as these grades are not generally recognised for entry to many further education and university courses. The comparison between these two measures is also very trenchant. In 2010, 55 per cent of pupils achieved 5 GCSE passes at A* to C, including English and mathematics, while in contrast only approximately 16 per cent of pupils gained the English Baccalaureate results. This is the extent of the unmasking of the inflated picture presented by the 5 A* to C measure, including English and mathematics.

The institution of the new GCSE examination in 1986 was the precursor to the enactment of the 1988 Education Reform Act (ERA). This was the most far reaching education legislation since the 1944 Education Act. Its aims were to improve educational standards in response to the growing concerns about the quality of educational provision at that time. It was also intended to provide greater freedom of choice to parents and to encourage the education system to be more responsive to market forces. The 1988 ERA also established, for the first time, a national curriculum for all schools, requiring LEAs, governors and headteachers to ensure that its demands are met. Despite at least two revisions since its inception, such as Lord Dearing's review of 1994 and the introduction of the National Literacy Strategy and the National Numeracy Strategy of 2000, the basic structure of the National Curriculum has endured. Firstly, the National Curriculum design consists of a programme of study – establishing the knowledge, understanding and skills to be developed by pupils covering the four statutory stages, namely Key Stages 1 and 2 for primary education and Key Stages 3 and 4 for secondary schooling. Secondly, it also identifies attainment targets, defining the standards pupils are expected to achieve at the end of each key stage. In addition to this, national tests for Key Stages 1 to 3 were established and generally refer to as Standard Attainment Tests (SATs). These are linked to the national attainment targets, consisting of eight levels (1-8). Thus, for example: at the end of Key Stage 1 pupils are expected to achieve Level 2 in their SATs tests (taken at the end of year 2 of primary schooling); at Key Stage 2 they are to attain Level 4 (taken at the end their primary schooling) and at Key Stage 3 they are to advance to Level 5/6 (determined by assessment at the end of year 9 of secondary schooling). The national test for Key Stage 4 at the end of secondary schooling remains, as before, the national GCSE examinations.

Running in parallel to this policy of national testing, the government also launched the national publication of SATs and GCSE examination results, referred to as the league table. The purpose of which was to reinforce its goal of injecting more competition and choice into the education system. This was built on the assumption that in order for parents to exercise real choice, they would need to have vital information on school standards and pupils' performance. Armed with this information, parents would then be in a better position to exercise effective preference when deciding on the schools they deemed suitable for their children to attend. Nevertheless, many educationalists and parents consider the league table strategy to be flawed, in that scores of hard-working schools would be given a low ranking without taking into consideration important contextual factors, such as the socio-economic background of pupils attending schools in socially deprived areas.

For this reason an additional measure of standards called 'value added' was adjoined to the league table system. This quantifies the extent that a school is able to assist pupils to extend their attainment beyond what is expected from a normal year group progression. Therefore, for example, should a secondary school be able to progress a group of children from Level 2 (where they would be below the expected Level 4 standard for entry in Year 7) to Level 4 at the end of Key Stage 3, that in itself would be clear evidence of the school's success in adding value to the children's attainment, since they would have taken the children beyond their expected Level 3 progression at the end of Key Stage 3. Thus, with a value-added measure, our hypothetical school would not just be graded on the basis of the crude examination results, which would naturally be a low position in the league table, but its results would also be adjusted for their value-added impact. This would place the school at a relatively higher position in the league table. The school would be rewarded for its effort in raising its pupils' attainment beyond their presumed level instead of simply being judged on just the raw examination results.

The 1988 ERA also introduced the concept of local management of schools. This, in essence, meant the decentralisation of financial management of schools away from local authorities to the schools themselves. It gave headteachers more power and control to determine how resources would be deployed in their schools. Another major aspect of the 1988 ERA was the introduction of Grant Maintained (GM) Schools. These in effect were schools that opted out of local authority control and received direct funding from central government. As with the government's rationale for its policy, in relation to local management schools, it was also argued that GM schools would be free to determine their own destiny, and avoid the hindrance endured under the bureaucratic control exercised by local authorities. For opting out of local authority control, these schools received large financial grants as an incentive. However, many commentators saw that development as an attempt to privatise the education system. But despite the huge financial carrot dangled to entice schools into GM status, only about 18 per cent of schools took advantage of the opportunity to move out of local control. Eventually, in 1997 – when the new Labour Government under Tony Blair took office – the GM school programme was dissolved, as it was considered to have been divisive and provided unfair financial advantages to some schools, at the expense of others. Another structural development emanating from the 1988 ERA was the addition of City Technology Colleges (CTCs), which were set up to offer more vocational education for pupils aged 11 to 18 years. In these vocational institutions (CTCs) pupils were enrolled on the principle of commitment, orientation and motivation and not on ability (Chan and East, 2002). However, congruous to what happened to the technical schools, following the 1944 Act, the CTCs did not grow in number and credibility. The reason could be that their narrow focus on vocational education was unappealing to many parents who held aspirations for their children to attain academic qualifications. The anecdotal evidence would suggest that most parents will always vigorously resist attempts by schools to deny their children entry to academic GCSE examinations, such as English, mathematics, science and modern foreign language. Thus, vocational qualifications are pragmatically interpreted by parents to be inferior qualifications when compared with GCSE qualifications. Parents do not take kindly to attempts to persuade them that their children are academically incapable, which to them means 'having no brains'.

The public snubbing of the CTCs was also corroborated by the 2004 recommendation of Sir Mike Tomlinson – former HMI Chief Inspector of Schools – that GCE 'A' Levels and GCSE examinations should be abolished and replaced by a baccalaureate-type overarching diploma qualification system (Working Group on 14 – 19 Reform, 2004). The Tomlinson Report consisted of two main elements: (1) a core learning component for the development of essential literacy, mathematics, and information and communication technology (ICT) skills; and (2) a main learning component chosen by the learner to develop knowledge, skills and understanding in academic and vocational subjects that would provide a basis for future training, higher education and ultimately employment. The intent of Tomlinson, it seemed, was to once and for all remove the differentiated qualification structure that existed, whereby academic qualifications were given higher currency and vocational ones were of lesser value. This has contributed to a divided education system and wasted human potentials and assets.

Nevertheless, despite the welcomed support that the Tomlinson report received from teachers and their professional bodies, leaders in industry and also universities were not in favour of the recommendations. They concertedly argued for the retention of the existing examination system. As a result of this strong opposition voiced against the Tomlinson proposals, the government in 2008 offered an alternative 14 to 19 qualification programme, consisting of a three-dimensional qualification pathway, namely: (1) the continuation of the existing GCE and GCSE qualifications; (2) Diplomas at foundation and higher levels; and (3) Apprenticeship programmes, that is, industry-specific learning programmes linked to vocational programmes and extended work experience. We can see clearly how 'the three minds' for learning ideology and the tripartite system have continued to linger, albeit not so much in the school structure, but in the qualifications regime. Thus, the GCE and GCSE academic examinations would remain the gold standard qualification for 14 – 19 education; and it does not require any great comprehension to understand that the other two pathways offer a lower status qualification (Department for Children, Schools and Families, 2008). The present Coalition Government's intention is to reform vocational education so that it supports progression to higher education and employment; and for vocational qualifications to be at least at the same standard with others globally (Department for Education, 2010).

The Labour government, led by Tony Blair, dismantled the GM structure – which was a form of independent maintained schools. But within a short period of the government's tenure it introduced the Academies as another model of schooling to the education system. They were to be directly funded by central government, but would have to receive up to 20 percent of the capital funding required from their sponsor(s) who would have majority representation on the Academies' governing bodies. Today there are basically three types of Academies: (1) those high-performing schools converting to Academy status that have demonstrated a 3-year trajectory of improving academic results; (2) new Academies set up to increase school provision capacity – sponsored by businesses, universities, charities and faith groups; and (3) Academies established to replace failing schools. In reality, Academies are publicly funded independent schools, in similar fashion to former GM schools. The incentives for pursuing the Academy route are:

freedom from local authority control; the flexibility to set their own pay and conditions of service structure for staff; latitude to implement the national curriculum in a flexible manner; and the scope to be innovative in the design of school terms and the school day. Notwithstanding the aforementioned advantages, the main criticism of the Academies is that a great number of their sponsors and promoters are rich business persons committed in many cases to their own brand of educational ideology that they are able to support financially. As such, it gives them an unhealthy influence over the education system. An opposing position to this argument is that political parties, the middle and upper classes, the historical public schools and the denominations (faith schools) together exercise an oligarchy of influence on the education system. Thus, it is not necessarily a bad thing for this influential control to be diluted by the injection of other ideas about the way education can be developed.

Finally, the most recent government initiative in the drive for raising educational standards and offering parents more choice has been the introduction of a the Free Schools programme as a further option for providing new school places. As with all the other educational initiatives and developments over the past 30 years, the Free Schools programme is designed – it is said – to raise education standards, provide greater choice and to extend the range of school providers in state education. New school providers are being urged to come forward from existing school leaders, teachers and parents themselves, to set up their own schools, especially where they are unhappy with the existing state provision. In comparison with the Academy programme, the financial and capital start-up commitment bar for the Free Schools option is set much lower. Thus, potential new providers from school leaders, teachers and parents are expected to demonstrate a convincing education vision and plan, evidence of demand for the proposed school(s), organisational capacity and competence, access to suitable premises, and initial funding and financial viability (Department for Education, 2011).

The continuation of the dual system of education

To complete the 'seeing behind' journey of the education system, covering more than two centuries, the authors ultimately considers the position of the dual system that has been a basic component of the education system over time. In the midst of all the changes brought on by the 1944 Education Act and other reforms that have followed since, the dual or parallel role of the church and the state sharing the responsibility for the provision of education has remained intact. This demonstrates the integral position of denominational schools (faith schools) to the education system, irrespective of the vast array of legislative changes and developments resulting from the watershed education acts of 1870, 1902, 1944 and 1988. Paradoxically, although the period following the First World War saw a decline in the link between the family and the church, this did not adversely affect the continuation of the dual educational system between state and church. In fact the early 20th century saw a huge growth in the numbers of Roman Catholic schools. The 1936 Act provided the denominations with further financial support for the establishment of secondary schools. However, some of the smaller denominations decided that the best way to secure their influence would be by spreading their religious values throughout the state education system, rather than by the operation of schools themselves. But the dual system remains an important part of the education structure as is evident by the fact that R. A. Butler, President of the Board of Education (who historically has been linked to the 1944 Act), ensured the continuation of the long established role of the denominations in the provision of education. This, it could be argued, was justified as approximately half of the schools at that time were still church schools. Another significant change that came out of the 1944 Act was that it made religious instructions compulsory in all LEA schools. In a way, it confirmed the need for the spiritual and moral development of pupils to be a necessary element of the education process.

Post the 1944 reforms, the 1959 Act further strengthened the position of the denominational schools, as it eased their financial positions and made it easier for them to add more school places to the overall national provision. This is despite the opposition to their existence by anti-religious groups such as the humanists and the secular societies. Nevertheless, in spite of the decline in church attendance, denominational schools have remained popular with parents who have appreciated the leadership they offer with respect to moral instructions, the development of values and the academic attainment of pupils. Today, denominational schools account for approximately 35 per cent of primary schools and 17 per cent of secondary schools. Thus, they continue to be a significant segment of the education system. The right to operate denominational schools (termed faith schools today) has now been expanded beyond the traditional denominations such as the Church of England, the

Catholic faith and Methodists, and now embraces other faith groups like the Seventh-day Adventist Church, the Greek Orthodox Church, the Jewish faith, the Muslim faith and Sikh religious groups (Chan and East, 2002).

'Seeing Ahead' – Framing a new vision for education (A renaissance paradigm)

The 'Seeing Behind' section of this closing chapter systematically took us through a series of educational developments from the beginning of the 19th century to the present day. This has been a concise tour of the history of the English education system and is meant to inform this ultimate section of this chapter, that is, 'Seeing Ahead' in shaping an education system for the 21st century. Thus, in so doing the sub-sections below will draw out the key lessons to be learnt from the process of 'Seeing Behind'.

<u>Key lessons to be drawn from the retrospective 'Seeing Behind' chronicle of the development of the education system</u>

Firstly, children of the upper class (aristocrats) at the beginning of the 19th century were educated at home. In this early system of home education children were taught by governesses and tutors. Instructions centred mainly on character development, social graces and the classics (taught by the tutors), especially for those intended to go on to university. Thus, children's education was entirely the responsibility of their parents. And whilst today's middle and upper classes do not have full-time governesses and tutors educating their children at home, the general principle of parents leading in the education of their children continues and can be seen in the way middle class and upper class parents manage the educational development of their children, such as by hiring private tutors to support the education of their children. Furthermore, the on-going education of many middle and upper class children through the independent school sector testifies to this principle of parents taking full responsibility for their children's education. In other words, these parents have the resources to consciously decide on who will be responsible for the education of their sons and daughters. However, it is important to note that while middle and upper class parents have the good fortune of being in possession of the financial resources to take full responsibility for their children's education, the important lesson to be learnt is the fundamental doctrine that parental responsibility for the education of the child is a vital role in life for all parents, irrespective their financial status. This role should not be exclusively about providing private school education for the children, but the role can be fulfilled within the contemporary education milieu, as for example, the supplementary schools movement that exists especially in the African Caribbean community today.

Secondly, the 'Seeing Behind' chronological history and development of the education system is a story of how the virus of elitism continues to reside within the body of the English educational system. A dispassionate evaluation of the findings of our education journey cannot but acknowledge that like in the early years of the 19th century, the best-quality education is still provided by the public schools and other secondary schools that operate along the public school principles and ethos. Money will still secure the best education today, as it did 200 years ago. Excellent educational provision is still the preserve of those who can afford it or those parents who make the daunting financial sacrifice to invest in their children's educational development. Nevertheless, it is not the qualities and ethos of the public schools that are virulent, and need to be cured. Far from it, they (the qualities of the public schools) remain the standard to be emulated by those in the business of operating schools (the private sector, social enterprise groups, faith groups or the state). What is virulent and corrupting is the elitism that is associated with the very best of education, in that it deliberately offers its most excellent provision to a minority of citizens it considers to be capable, simply on the only basis of their social standing. This bias works against the moral principles of equality and fairness.

Thirdly, the transformational reforms of education led by the Reverend Thomas Arnold and his pioneering work at Rugby public school have to be seen and evaluated in the context of the climate of moral revival that existed at that time. It placed a high premium on values, justice and citizenship promoted by Christian leaders such as Wilberforce, Equiano and others. Thus, the purpose of education, for Arnold, was to produce Christian gentlemen and scholars, through the spiritual, physical and intellectual development of students. This philosophy he implemented in the education practice under his leadership at Rugby. The lesson from Thomas Arnold's approach to education is that excellent (holistic) educational standards cannot be cultivated in isolation, away from the moral code of the wider society, but ultimately has to be rooted in the nurturing soil of an ethical community framework. Thus, excellence in education and a society, under-girded by moral values, are mutually inclusive imperatives.

Fourthly, during the two centuries of educational development, covered by our 'Seeing Behind' evaluation, there has been a polarisation on the question of who should be educated. On the one hand, there are those who believe academic education should be the preserve of the elite, and the authors have argued that this position still dominates the educational landscape. On the other hand, it is also true to say that the belief that academic education should be available to all classes has existed as far back as to the early 1840s when the Church of England established some schools for the purpose of providing grammar school education for poor scholars who could eventually go on to university (Wardle, 1976). The Science and Higher Grade schools of the late 19th century also extended the education ladder to working class children by making it possible for pupils to either go from Higher Grade or Science schools to university or from those schools on to grammar schools and then to university. Furthermore, in the 1920s and 1930s R H Tawney and other progressive educators challenged the elitist provision of education to be morally and socially unjust and persistently campaigned for social, economic and political equality; and for secondary education to be available to all children. The Swann Report of 1985 reaffirmed the call for the provision of education for all children, despite ethnicity. Thus, the spirit and the urge for academic education for all children, irrespective of background, have not been extinguished or faded even with the debilitating virus of elitism, which continues to inhabit the body of the English educational system.

Fifthly, historically the real purpose of education – under both the home schooling and the reformed public grammar school regimes – was established on the principle that it should develop the person. By implication, that would mean that good schools would develop leadership in students and community and nation building, and not be havens for elitism and exclusivity. The mid 19th century agitations by the working class for education were not because of a desire to participate in the growing economy as a consequence of the industrial revolution, but purely for self-developmental reasons. The denominations' investment in education again was not motivated by economic factors, but for the purpose of developing good Christian citizens. The 1920s to 1930s movement for a just education system was also driven by a desire to stop the waste of intellectual and human potential amongst the working class.

The final lesson to be drawn from reviewing the development of the education system is that the provision of education for the working class in the early period of the 19th century, by the denominations, was in reality community centred education. As we have seen in the earlier section of this chapter, the three types of schools for working class children were generally located in the industrial towns. These were namely: denominational Sunday schools; the Dame schools, operated generally by women – mainly as child-minding services for working mothers; and the monitorial schools, where the pupils practiced as both learners and teachers. Therefore, drawing on this important heritage from the past, placing the community and its culture at the heart of the education process will further pedagogy by helping children to connect the abstract principles of knowledge and learning fundamentally to their cultural anchors and experiences. Thus, this docking of their learning to their cultural harbour aids their comprehension and understanding of concepts and principles. But more profoundly, education in every respect then becomes the life and centre of the community and no longer a servant to the economy, but the master for shaping the purpose and direction of our lives.

A new paradigm for improving the education system

From the 'Seeing Behind' chronological history and development of the education system discussed above it is reasonable to conclude that the main purposes of the education system are: (a) to determine or to select the ruling class, who will establish society's political, legal, social and economic directions; and (b) to supply the human resources (labour) and skills required by the economy. But the purpose or the reason for doing anything in a particular fashion will always generally be from a philosophical basis (overtly or covertly), that is, based on a system of beliefs, values or tenets. Thus, it is the authors' view that the basic philosophy that has underpinned the education system's dual functions of dispensing power and supplying labour for the economy is the belief that society is divided into three social groups, namely the working class (lower), the middle class and the upper class, but with the evident differentiation in status, as the three categories would obviously suggest. To put it crudely, it is a philosophy that divides and devalues some groups in our society, resulting in privileges and unfairness as consequential realities in society today.

Therefore, it stands to reason that if this is the prevailing belief system (philosophy) the beneficiaries from it will attempt to maintain their control of it by seeking to offer some form of rational justification for this form of social inequality. Thus, the social stratification categories are argued dubiously on the grounds of merit, evidenced by the higher intelligence quotient of the ruling classes, that is, the middle and upper classes. Thus, if society is made up of higher- and lower-ability citizens – so goes the reasoning – the education system logically must accommodate such differences. But this highlights the naked abuse of science, under which intelligence testing stands as a discipline. Intelligence is defined as the capacity for understanding or the ability to perceive and comprehend meaning.

However, this definition has been wrongly interpreted to mean that intelligence is an innate phenomenon, or related to genetic factors and age development. The abuse also descends to the macabre when some immoral scientists try to link the levels of intelligence scores to a person's racial background. The science on intelligence does not accord with this interpretation and practice. The authors' argument is not so much against intelligence testing as a tool for assessing cognitive skills, but more so about: (a) the assumption that intelligence is biologically determined; and (b) the methodology used to design and administer intelligence testing – many of which are not culture free or fair. The truth is that intelligence testing is really about assessing the cognitive or mental skills that the person has learnt and developed over time. Thus, intelligence is a function of the quality of the learning experiences that the person has been exposed to and not anything to do with the person's race, social class or genetic make-up. Intelligence is the result of a process of intellectual development, but everyone is gifted with innate and latent intellectual potential or ability (naturally supplied). The brain is a learning system that in a way is analogous to a computer. The computer hardware has the capability to perform, but it is the software that gives the computer its kudos or practical applications (skills). Similarly, the human brain has innate and unlimited intellectual powers. However, it is the learning experiences, formal and informal, that will develop the person's intellectual capability, leading on to the acquisition of mental skills such as understanding, comprehension and analysis. Thus, intelligence is the product of the experiences and the quality of the child's intellectual development and not a consequence of biology or genes. (See the works of education philosophers such as Benjamin Bloom, Jean Piaget and Howard Gardner.) Do we reason that the hands, feet or lungs of an upper class person are better than those of a working class person? Of course not! It would be laughable to do so. Therefore, why should it be assumed that the brain of an upper class person is far superior to that of a working class – considering that it is just another very important part of the human body? Such a proposition is itself not intelligent thinking. Thus, it stands to reason, that if it was the case that middle and upper class children are biologically superior to other children, there would be no need for the extraordinary levels of intellectual investment and the support that middle and upper class parents give their children to help them to succeed at school and ultimately throughout their life. They (the middle and upper class children) would just sit their examinations, not needing instructions or tutoring from teachers, and still pass with flying colours, since it was all to do with their superior biological make up. But Musgrave (1968) observes this about selection testing:

> *'Part of the continued interest in psychology stemmed from the work done on scientific selection by the armed services, who had relied on such methods for choosing their officers. After the war some of the results of this work . . . were applied to selection of primary pupils for secondary grammar schools. This* [it was wrongly assumed] *. . . met the political demands for fairness . . . but in the majority of junior schools much effort was expended in achieving the maximum possible number of eleven plus successes. This was done by giving pupils in the final year extensive practice in intelligence tests . . . Such training could hardly be called educative . . . '* (Musgrave, 1968, pp. 110 – 111)

And so, the first new paradigm that is required is for the education system to stand on the philosophical foundation that fully accepts the principle of biological equality, with respect to a person's spiritual, intellectual and physical capability, barring where there are obvious physical disabilities. Humans are generically the same in terms of our biological trademarks, except for specific gene characteristics. We do not inherit our parents' behaviour or intellect (intelligence). Thus, elitism and the culture of privileges for a minority (the ruling class) that have dominated the education system and society in general, would – with this new paradigm – give way instead to social recognition and acclaim, based solely on: (a) the individual's personal investment in the development of his capability, (b) the service and leadership he gives to community advancement and (c) professional or career distinctions and achievements, based on the principle of meritocracy.

Closely aligned to a new paradigm that accepts the vision and principle of access for all children to an education process that will develop their innate intellectual potential (capability) is another much needed complementary change of philosophy, which is, that the 'why we educate?' should be about intrinsic value as opposed to the widespread instrumental purpose it has been given for centuries. The prevalent and accepted view by many in education and society in general is that education is for economic and extrinsic reasons. On the micro level, education gets you a job in the employment market, and on the macro level, it provides industry with a highly qualified workforce, and keeps the economy competitive in the global market. However, an education system that focuses mainly on extrinsic values and on instrumental outcomes will, invariably, produce intellectual underachievers, unfulfilled citizens and wasted human potential and resources. The call that the authors are making is for parents, educators and political leaders to rise to the vision of creating an education system that will truly develop the individual (spiritually, intellectually and socially). Although the spiritual, intellectual and physical development of children is enshrined in the 1944 Education Act, confusion will remain in the education system if we continue to give lip service to the goal of an holistic education experience for pupils when the 'how we educate' continues today within an elitist ethos that separates children into categories of academically gifted, average ability, vocationally suited or simply those just in need of basic life skills. This is incompatible with a philosophy that supports the proposition that all children are in possession of intellectual capability, based on biological equality. Furthermore, the elitist values and beliefs of the education system undermine the vision of 'education for all' that governments of all shades have given lip service to for the past few decades. Thus, intellectually there is a dissonance (or lack of harmony) between our education vision and values. This will only change when our vision is fully aligned to a value system that truly believes that all children are intellectually capable.

A further paradigm in the visioning for a more inclusive education system is the exigency to eject the convenient notion of making poverty an excuse for the underachievement existing in the education system. It is a widely held view (supported by research evidence) that children from disadvantaged backgrounds are less likely to succeed at school. A recent study by a group of researchers based at the School of Education, University of Manchester and supported by the well-known Joseph Rowntree Foundation, sought to develop a framework for examining the links between poverty and educational outcomes in the UK. In this study the researchers reviewed the literature on poverty and education and concluded that there are two conceptual tools that can explain the reasons for the relationship between poverty and education. The first they described as 'Functionalist', which assumes that education plays an important part in the functioning of society. Thus, the functionalist approach sees the underperformance of students in the education system as the result of dysfunctions at the level of the individual. Students underachieve because of negative family issues, such as broken homes, one-parent upbringing and other social-related problems. Controversially, other functionalists point to inherited capabilities, although this has been discredited methodologically, theoretically and morally. In effect, they make the individual the focus and reason for the problem. The second conceptual perspective identified by the study is termed 'Socially Critical'. This assumes that education is potentially beneficial and can make a contribution to the economic and social development of the nation. However, it argued that education in its current form reflects an unequal distribution of power and resources in society today. Thus, this school of thought implicates the education system for reproducing and sustaining inequality.

The present authors take issue with the former proposition that underachievement is caused by poverty and the effects of dysfunctional families. This is a myth. While it is true that there is a correlation between pupil underachievement and poverty; nonetheless, a correlation in itself does not provide an explanation or a reason for the underachievement of children from disadvantaged backgrounds. Rather, the correlation, it can be argued, gives some evidence to the prejudice and discrimination that exist against children from poorer families, manifested in such ways as low expectations, stereotyping – leading to a self-fulfilling prophecy and the denying of those children of a place on the academic ladder. It is not poverty that de-motivates the children, but rather it is the negative perception about the children, the absence of belief in the children's capabilities and the withdrawal of esteem from the children that will affect performance at school. On the other hand, it is positive motivation at school that can give the children the confidence and the determination to scale barriers like the social and economic disadvantages that they may be confronted with. When the removal of prejudice and discrimination are in tandem with the renaissance of parental leadership the children's capabilities will be realised. Some observations from Gladwell (2008) can help us to understand the pivotal role of parents in children's success. He writes:

> *'There were only two parenting "philosophies" and they divide almost perfectly along class lines. The wealthier parents raised their kids one way, and the poorer parents raised their kids another way. . . the middle-class children learn a sense of "entitlement". . . middle-class children . . . shift interactions to suit their preference . . . They knew the rules . . . acting on their own to gain advantages . . . By contrast, the working-class and poor children were characterized by "an emerging sense of distance, distrust, and constraint" . . . They didn't know how . . . to "customize" . . . whatever environment they were in, for their best purpose . . . It is important to understand where the particular mastery of that moment comes from. It's not genetic . . . Nor is it racial: . . . "It's the culture you find yourself in that determines that." . . . In the end, only one thing mattered: Family background...You're simply seeing the difference between those schooled by their families to present their best face to the world, and those denied that experience . . . Not something expensive . . . not something encoded in DNA . . .* [but] *. . . a community around them that prepared them properly for the world.*
>
> (Gladwell, 2008, pp. 102 – 113)

Indeed, centring the work and the ethos of a school in the midst of the community's life, practices and heritages (its strengths) is another paradigm that is needed. The transformation of the public grammar schools in the earlier part of the 19th century from dens of vices to institutions of excellence came about under a culture of moral reform and a vision for uprightness in all aspects of society. It provides a powerful example of community leadership. The denominational schools of the early 19th century that initiated the provision of education for the working class demonstrated this principle of community leadership, in as much as they were an integral part of a wider mission and vision of the denominations playing a central role in community life. Work, despite the exploitation of labour at the time, provided the basic needs for living, but the purpose for living resided in the broader aspects of communal living. Working alongside community building and leadership is the value of compassion. A genuine community cannot exist without compassion, care, selflessness, neighbourliness and love. These values are the essence of a community, and ultimately it is the education system that must drive the cultivation and nurturing of these virtues in society. The school is the embodiment of the community. Palmer (1993) states:

> *'But a knowledge that springs from love will implicate us in the web of life; it will wrap the knower and the known in compassion, in a bond of awesome responsibility as well as transforming joy; it will call us to involvement, mutuality, accountability . . . How can the places where we learn to know become places where we also learn to love? How can we educate today so that "the day after" will be a time of compassion rather than combat?'*
>
> (Palmer, 1993, pp. 9-10)

We are in dire need of a renaissance movement in education today that places parents at the frontline of the education process as first teachers and the building of more social capital in communities to support the education of all children. We call for a renaissance in education that will move schools to accept that it is parental engagement that is desirable above parental involvement. Parental involvement places parents on the periphery of the education process, by: offering parents a limited role in the decision making process of the school through minority status on the governing body; giving parents restricted influence through the PTA; and supplying parents with information through school reports and parents' meetings. However, parental engagement challenges schools to become less defensive about demanding parents. Indeed, having demanding parents make the work of a school lighter, since such parents will 'move mountains' to see their children succeed, which in the end will provide credit to the school. Parental engagement means parental leadership in setting values and arranging a network of support for the children's holistic development. A renaissance is required that will resurrect the aspiration of pioneers such as Tawney and others who worked for the cause of genuine education for all children, by educators and politicians today leading in the elimination of the virus of racism and social class injustices from the education system. The unfortunate, but latent belief that the white race is superior to the black race is also destroying the intellectual capability of many black children in our schools today. However, what is not understood by those who harbour this evil belief is that it is destined to destroy them, since that is the result of evil (that is, it is a cul de sac that takes you literally to a dead end). However, the paradox is that while the perpetrators of evil will ultimately perish, in contrast the victims of evil can overcome and eventually gain the prize of hope and a force for good. The renaissance spark should also ignite the pedagogical truism that culture affects the way children go about learning at school. A paradigm change is needed in the education system that will allow it to embrace the undeniable relationship that exists between culture and learning. The attempt to educate children without their cultural dressing gown has turned out to be a failure for many ethnic children and in particular African Caribbean pupils. Reforms are needed in teacher training, staffing, school leadership and in national policies to address this issue. But equally, creative and innovative strategies around community schooling by institutions in the black community such as faith groups (churches), social enterprise groups and supplementary schools – using avenues such as the new 'Free School' programme and other maintained school routes – should be seriously responded to by the government. Wisdom and foresight demand that the intellectual resources of sound educational principles and well established pedagogical practices be now applied to a problem that has remained unsolved for decades.

Finally, when we limit the education of the majority of our children to economic reasons the danger is that should the economy fail, the individual with a narrow education will be left helpless and hopeless. However, when we educate to uplift and develop the person spiritually, intellectually, socially and physically, in an economic downturn the educated person (with the intellectual horse power), as opposed to workers who were simply trained for specific jobs in the labour market, that person will be a much more resourceful individual, who will be able to survive economic hard times. Furthermore, such resourcefulness will also lessen the severity of an economic dip. Therefore, having a paradigm and renaissance movement in education that moves the emphasis away from the 'how we educate' to the 'why do we educate?' will remove the constant upheaval experienced by the education system as governments constantly experiment with a variety of structural reforms (models) in the search for a solution to the underachievement problem. However, a vision of education centring on the person will be underpinned by high values and principles. A renaissance that can recapture the Thomas Arnold mission and model of schooling, built on moral values and scholarship, can inspire the education system toward a transformation to excellence for the 21st century. In conclusion, this book challenges readers, that is, pupils, parents, educators, education agencies, the media and politicians to rise to this 'Seeing Ahead' new paradigm and renaissance in education aspiration. Without this vision we are in danger of allowing the true work of education to perish under moral decay and decline. This can be avoided if we can grasp the renaissance model offered in this book.

References

Chan, S and East, P (2002) *Primary and Secondary Education in England and Wales: From 1944 to the Present.* http://learning.unl.ac.uk/education/EducationHandbook2002.html

Department for Children, Schools and Families (2008) *Promoting achievement, valuing success: a strategy for 14 – 19 qualifications.* The Stationery Office

Department for Education (2010) *The Importance of Teaching – The Schools White Paper 2010*: The Stationery Office. http:official-documents.gov.uk

Department for Education (2011) *Free Schools in 2012 How to Apply.* Crown Copyright 2011

Davies, B (2008) *Leading the Strategically Focused School – Success & Sustainability*. London: SAGE Publications Ltd

Gladwell, M (2008) *Outliers (The Story of Success).* Penguin Books

Musgrave, P (1968) *Society and Education in England since 1800.* Methuen and Co. Ltd

Palmer, P. J. (1993) *To Know As We are Known.* New York: Harper Collins Publishers

Raffo, C; Dyson, A; Gunter, H; Hall, D; Jones, L; and Kalambouka, A (2007) *Education and Poverty* Joseph Rowntree Foundation

Tawney, R (1922) *Secondary Education for All: A Policy for Labour* In *Education, the child and society: a documentary history, 1900-1973* (Eds.) Willem van der Eyken, 1973. London: Penguin Education

Wardle, D (1976) *English popular education, 1780-1970:* London: Cambridge University Press

Working Group on 14 – 19 Reform (2004) *14 – 19 Curriculum and Qualifications Reform: Final Report of the Working Group on 14 – 19 Reform.* Crown Copyright 2004

Name Index

Subject Index